THE
COMMUNITY
TABLE

THE COMMUNITY TABLE

RECIPES & STORIES

· from the ·

Jewish Community Center

IN MANHATTAN & BEYOND

Katja Goldman, Judy Bernstein Bunzl, and Lisa Rotmil

FOOD PHOTOGRAPHY BY JOHN TAVARES

GRAND CENTRAL
Life & Style
NEW YORK · BOSTON

Grand Central Life & Style
Hachette Book Group
1290 Avenue of the Americas
New York, NY 10104

www.GrandCentralLifeandStyle.com

Printed in the United States of America

Design by Laura Palese

Q-MA

First Edition: March 2015

10 9 8 7 6 5 4 3 2 1

Grand Central Life & Style is an imprint of Grand Central Publishing.

The Grand Central Life & Style name and logo are trademarks of Hachette Book Group, Inc.

The Hachette Speakers Bureau provides a wide range of authors for speaking events. To find out more, go to www.HachetteSpeakersBureau.com or call (866) 376-6591.

The publisher is not responsible for websites (or their content) that are not owned by the publisher.

Library of Congress Cataloging-in-Publication Data

The community table : recipes and stories from the Jewish Community Center in Manhattan and beyond / JCC Manhattan ; with Katja Goldman, Judy Bernstein Bunzl, and Lisa Rotmil. Food photographs by John Tavares — First edition.

 pages cm

Includes index.

ISBN 978-1-4555-5435-5 (hardcover) — ISBN 978-1-4555-5434-8 (pbk.) — ISBN 978-1-4555-5436-2 (ebook) 1. Jewish cooking. 2. JCC Manhattan. I. Goldman, Katja. II. Bunzl, Judy Bernstein. III. Rotmil, Lisa Anne.

TX724.C5494 2015

641.5'676—dc23

                2014025089

This book is dedicated to our families, Nick, Alexandra, and Natasha; Michael, Joya, Forest, Isaac, and Sophia; Shai, Lydia, and Julia. They enthusiastically encouraged us, supported us, and showed endless patience and adventurous appetites. They were well fed during this project.

Contents

Foreword

WHY DO WE COOK? How many of us have asked this question as we rush home on Friday afternoon, or for that matter any afternoon, having ambitiously planned a feast and not left enough time to cook it? Despite the fact that there are take-out options in abundance and a restaurant on every corner where I live, I spend the week poring over recipes, planning menus, and shopping for food. And all in all, it's a pretty joyous experience.

The desire to nurture our family and friends is at the heart of why we cook. A special dinner at a restaurant or lunch out with friends can be lovely (I personally have a secret love for department store cafés), but when we sit down at the table at home, time slows down. Gratitude bubbles up around me—for the people I love, for the food we too often take for granted, for the conversation (however mundane), and especially for the time to appreciate it all.

In Jewish tradition, we say a blessing before we eat, giving thanks for the bread that comes from the earth. But bread doesn't actually come from the earth. There are a multitude of steps that take place before bread appears on our table. The soil has to be prepared, the wheat planted, and then watered by the rain, warmed by the sun, harvested, and brought to the mill to make flour. When we combine the ingredients, knead the dough, let it rise, and shape it into bread, we become a part of the blessing.

We begin with a single ingredient when we cook, but that ingredient quickly becomes transformed. Is there anything as wonderful as a crisp Macoun apple on a chilly autumn day? Try combining that apple with other apples of different varieties and add some sugar, oatmeal, flour, and butter and bake it for an hour or so. The sum really can be greater than its parts. Cooking is an opportunity to create, to take raw material and shape it into something more, something wonderful and even magical.

This idea, this power to transform, is what animates JCC Manhattan and indeed JCCs throughout North America and beyond. Every day, we remember the central Jewish teaching that every person is unique, bringing something important to the world. Every day, we are witness to what happens when one person is joined with others in community. We become different; we often become better. There is strength when we build good communities and we are reminded that, as special as we are as individuals, when we come together we can be more, do more, and expect more.

The Community Table is the result of these two big ideas—the values inherent in cooking and the value of community—coming together. Like most projects, it started with a few people who later became the architects, chefs, and authors of this cookbook. Our three authors have each been intrinsically connected to JCC Manhattan over many years.

It was Judy Bernstein Bunzl's idea to do a JCC cookbook, celebrating the ten years JCC Manhattan has been a catalyst for community building on 76th Street and Amsterdam Avenue. A major foodie and terrific cook, Judy has spent the last several years tending her magnificent organic garden in the backyard of her Riverdale home. Judy's garden not only feeds her friends and family with beautiful produce, but also feeds her soul.

Katja Goldman is the professional and published chef of the group. An invitation to Katja's Shabbat table is prized for its culinary treats and for the stimulating conversation that occurs there every week. She is one of the leaders and primary teachers of the New York home challah baking trend: For Katja, challah making is an act of meditation and giving challah is a gift of compassion.

Lisa Rotmil is also a foodie who has previously edited a community cookbook and cooks every night for her family. For Lisa, cooking is a way of slowing down the hectic pace of a busy Manhattan family and provides her with a strong bond to her grandfather, who as a master craftsman taught her the importance of paying attention to detail and artistic expression.

Each of these women is a force of nature in her own right and together they have collaborated to create a work of art for all of us to savor. They share a love of food and a love of JCC Manhattan and the many ways we create powerful community every day. They have brought the best of themselves to the project, sharing recipes and memories as they diced, braised, and roasted. When they disagreed about a recipe, they simply made the dish each way and sampled them. Would that all our conflicts could be settled by tasting chocolate cookies three ways!

For Judy, Katja, and Lisa—and for us at the JCC—sharing food is an important way we nurture one another, whether we are on the Upper West Side of Manhattan or in places like San Francisco, Detroit, Atlanta, Pittsburgh, Washington, or Houston. We are grateful to our fellow JCCs in those cities for sharing their stories with us, which you will find throughout the book. When you walk into a JCC, you may see a gym and a pool, a nursery school or day camp—but there is so much more at play. We hope through these stories you will come to know the JCCs as they really are— places that bring people together, that support, nourish, and value the mind, body, and spirit of everyone who walks through our doors.

We invite you to make these recipes your own and to build your own community table. The food you make will delight; the community you create will inspire.

From our community table to yours,

Joy

RABBI JOY LEVITT,
EXECUTIVE DIRECTOR,
JCC MANHATTAN

Introduction

When you invite someone to sit at your table, and you want to cook for them, you are inviting a person into your life.

—MAYA ANGELOU

WELCOME TO OUR COMMUNITY TABLE—a celebration of the remarkable community built at JCC Manhattan. We are the lucky three authors who embraced the challenge to create a cookbook celebrating the JCC. It is a cookbook that reflects how we cook today: conscientiously, healthily, creatively, locally, and internationally inspired. We are three New York women, all mothers, wives, and committed cooks: one art historian, one professional chef, one organic vegetable gardener; one traditional, one Conservative, one Reform Jew. We come from different backgrounds, yet share many passions and priorities, most important our love of food. As one of our daughters said, "You are always in your kitchen, or in each others' kitchens talking, cooking, or tasting food."

How true, and how fortunate we are. Whether we are poring over seed catalogues, discussing farmers' markets in New York City or elsewhere, or helping with homework, we are most often found in the kitchen—the center of our homes. Each of us has always enjoyed cooking on her own, but cooking together for the last few years has been addictive. While we have always built mini-communities around our individual dining tables, together the three of us formed a micro-community. We started with different cooking styles and different palates, and emerged with those preferences intact, but with an added ability to compromise, and an eagerness to share.

Better yet, this food journey has turned us into the fastest of friends. For us, food is a way to nurture and build relationships. Our process of spending days, weeks, months together in the kitchen has made us tightly bonded. We've had a delicious time.

How did we choose the recipes to include in our book? We first looked at our community of JCC Manhattan. What are they cooking? If the wealth of languages one hears in the lobby—English, Hebrew, Korean, Spanish, and any number of others—is any indicator, the home kitchens of our members are extraordinarily diverse. We have relished all the culinary influences this community has shared with us. Beyond that, Jewish communities of both the present and the past have inspired us. Throughout Jewish history, Jewish cooks have adapted recipes and styles of cooking from their adopted homelands. As such, we have included classic recipes and our own updated versions of those dishes from Italy, Spain, France, Hungary, Morocco, the Middle East, India, and more. We did not set out to write a survey or a comprehensive chronicle of Jewish cooking. Rather, we wrote a book that reflects the great joy and diversity in cooking today—when exciting changes are happening in our food sources at the local level and every influence and ingredient is available to the chef on the web or around the corner.

Why this book now? Living in New York City, or really anywhere, life is fast-paced and can shift in a heartbeat. As home cooks, we passionately protect those precious times preparing meals for family and friends and the gatherings that ensue. Sure, the food is delicious, but the time spent together, creating our own "islands in time"—these are the moments that make us feel connected, engaged, alive, and thankful.

Food, family, and community have always been at the center of our lives. We hope this book will add to the bounty of your table and the richness of your lives. May your copy be filled with splatters and crumbs, and may you enjoy many new wonderful gatherings drawing inspiration from our book.

—Lisa, Katja, and Judy

The shared meal elevates eating from a mechanical process of fueling the body to a ritual of family and community...

—MICHAEL POLLAN

How to Use This Book

OUR FOOD AND COOKING PHILOSOPHY is fairly simple and straightforward, but in this section we're including some basic guidelines for how we prefer to shop and how to adapt these recipes for your home.

The recipes in this book were written for all home cooks, including traditionally kosher ones. But we respect the diversity in the homes of our community members, so adapt these recipes to fit your kitchen. We've included comprehensive charts at the back of this book, designating each recipe as dairy, meat, or pareve, including a complete list of recipes that are kosher for Passover.

The Market

PRODUCE

In an effort to avoid sounding pedantic, we have not specified "organic" before every ingredient in our recipes. However, we believe in buying organic as often as possible. Organic farming reduces the synthetic chemicals and poisons put into our water sources and soil, which would otherwise be harmfully consumed by humans and all living things. Check out the Environmental Working Group's *Shopper's Guide to Pesticides in Produce* (including the "Dirty Dozen" and the "Clean Fifteen") at EWG.org /foodnews/ for starting guidelines.

But we also suggest using organic eggs, grains, sugar, dairy products, meat, poultry, and nuts. One of our particular obsessions is to use organic lemons, limes, and oranges as we frequently use the zest with the juice (and we highly recommend squeezing your own citrus juices).

We also feel strongly about cooking with ingredients that are in season and locally grown, when available. Food tastes better when it's eaten close to its harvesting and from a nearby source.

Obviously, where you live plays a big factor in how you shop, and we are aware of the challenges that you might face. Still, we urge you to shop conscientiously. Above all, we encourage you to shop for what is fresh in your markets and use those ingredients to inspire your cooking.

FISH, MEAT, AND POULTRY

The environmental impact of our food systems should not be ignored. Unfortunately, the information out there is very confusing. We wouldn't dare suggest that we have all the answers, but we would encourage you to do a little research on the products you buy. Take a look at Seafoodwatch.org to learn which types of fish to buy and which types should be avoided. Or simply ask your local fishmonger—he or she should be able to answer any questions about sustainability.

Regarding meat—the same applies. Your butcher can be a great source of information. One easy way to be conscientious about your protein consumption is to simply buy and eat less of it.

Please note that our recipes were made and tasted with kosher meat. Because kosher meat is salted, we really mean it when we say "salt to taste."

EGGS

When a recipe calls for eggs we always use extra-large organic eggs. In truth, the size differential becomes important only when you are using five or more eggs at a time. But for simplicity's sake we used extra-large while we were testing recipes. Whenever possible, buy eggs straight from a farmer. You will be amazed at the difference in taste, color, texture, and freshness.

MILK AND MILK SUBSTITUTES

While we've taken a health-conscious approach to cooking, avoiding the heavy creams of classic French and Italian cuisine, we do use low-fat milk in many of our recipes. However, if you are dairy-free, there are now many alternatives on the market: almond milk, rice milk, coconut milk, and many other alternatives can be substituted for regular milk. But be aware that these milks have distinct flavors and the end result will be different.

BUTTER AND MARGARINE

Unless otherwise noted, when a recipe calls for butter, we mean unsalted and organic. Current health findings have led us away from partially hydrogenated vegetable oil and trans fats, and steered us back toward butter. Nothing is better than butter, really. And many of our recipes call for it. But if you'd like to make something pareve or dairy-free, margarine, non-hydrogenated vegetable shortening, or grapeseed oil can be substituted in several of our dessert recipes. However, when using a butter substitute, we usually add a dash of vanilla or nut extract, a pinch of cinnamon, or lemon zest to fill in the flavor profile. For baking, you can also experiment with solid oils such as coconut oil.

The Pantry

OILS

Olive Oils: We always recommend using a high-quality extra-virgin olive oil, though on occasion you will see us specify a lighter variety. Be careful in choosing your olive oils—not everything claiming to be extra virgin really is. We recommend referring to the website truthinoliveoil.com. In addition, we are specifically sensitive to the expiration date on olive oils. It's best to buy an olive oil with a harvest date so you know exactly how fresh it is. We use our best olive oils for finishing dishes and to dress salads. We tend to cook with less expensive versions, but ones that are still high in quality. Olive oils have distinct flavor profiles depending on where they are produced. So taste a variety of oils to determine what you like best.

Seed Oils: For cooking, try other oils such as grapeseed, safflower, and sunflower. Many times we select an oil based on its smoking point or neutral flavor. Grapeseed and peanut oils have the highest smoking points so you can really crank up the heat without worrying about burnt flavor and a smoky kitchen. Grapeseed oil is also good for baking. We tend to buy organic oils in the hopes of avoiding GMO products.

Nut Oils: Nut oils should always be stored in the refrigerator as they go rancid rather quickly. For this reason we suggest you buy small bottles to avoid waste.

SALT, SUGAR, AND FLOUR

In our recipes, we always use kosher salt, which we prefer for its texture. We also like sea salt for its mineral benefits and intense flavor. Flaked sea salt can garnish sweets, and fine sea salt is wonderful sprinkled over a salad. When we say "salt to taste" we truly mean you should take into account what salt you are using and how salty you prefer your food. Flavored salts are increasingly popular. Use them for an extra burst of flavor to finish a dish.

In keeping with our overall philosophy, we use organic sugar. Due to its coarse granulation, we suggest pulsing it in a food processor fitted with a metal blade for 10 to 15 seconds when preparing delicate baked goods.

At times we suggest experimenting with whole-grain organic flours instead of all-purpose flour. Please note that when using whole-grain flour you will need to increase the amount of salt.

SPICES

We recommend seeking out the harder-to-find spices that are used in some of our recipes. Specialty markets are wonderful for finding treasure troves of aromas and flavors, so we always recommend starting there, but you can also find many ingredients online if necessary. Keep in mind, while there are no expiration dates on spices, the fresher your spices are the more flavorful they will be. It's a good idea to cull your spice cabinet periodically. You can prolong the shelf life of spices by storing them in your freezer.

HERBS

Unless otherwise noted, all our recipes call for fresh herbs.

PASTAS

Recently, there has been an explosion in the range and quality of pastas available in your local grocery store. Once upon a time, whole-wheat pasta tasted like cardboard. Today, there are many superior whole-grain options to choose from. You can even find pasta being made from ancient grains, such as farro, barley, and spelt, which have a slightly nutty flavor and firmer texture. We also love their whole-grain health benefits.

BEANS, LENTILS, AND GRAINS

Again, we suggest using organic whenever possible. Choose what works best in your kitchen and with your schedule, as long as you add these nutrient powerhouses into your repertoire in some form. A great time-saver is to cook extra beans and grains and store them in the freezer for future use.

STOCK

Stocks are an essential part of well-flavored cooking. We keep our Vegetable Consommé (page 98) and chicken stock (strained Chicken Soup, page 106) in our freezers to always have on hand. You can also buy stocks from your butcher, in boxes, or even organic bouillon cubes. We prefer homemade (no surprise) because you can control the flavor and the sodium content.

Equipment

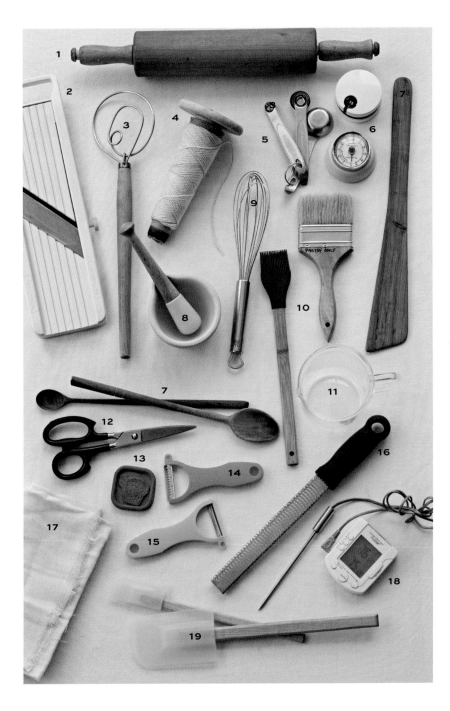

Assuming you already have well-sharpened knives, assorted pots and pans, mixing bowls, and mixers, below is a list of our favorite and most-used kitchen tools. None of them are fancy or expensive, but they are all great investments for a well-rounded kitchen.

Bamboo steamer
Brown sugar saver (13)
Cast-iron grill pan
Cast-iron skillets
Cheesecloth (preferably unbleached) (17)
Dough whisk (3)
Dumpling press
Heat-resistant rubber spatulas (19)
Instant-read thermometer (18)
Julienne peeler (14)
Kitchen scale
Kitchen timers (6)
Liquid measuring cup (11)
Mandolin (2)
Measuring cups
Measuring spoons (5)
Metal tongs (assorted sizes)
Microplane zester (16)
Mortar and pestle (8)
Parchment paper
Pastry brushes (10)
Rolling pin (1)
Shears (12)
Small ceramic paring knives
Spaetzle maker
Undyed kitchen twine (4)
Vegetable peeler (15)
Whisk (9)
Wooden chopsticks
Wooden spoons (7)

BREADS

Weekly Challah

Preparing the Shabbat loaves is a wonderful way to wind down at the end of a busy week. For us, challah isn't just bread. It's home, family, and tradition. When you're preparing to make challah for the first time, take a deep breath and relax. It's not as hard as it may seem. The dough is very forgiving and with practice we know you'll ease into it and own the process, creating your own family traditions.

NOTE: *To prepare challah the night before, place the dough in an oiled resealable plastic bag and refrigerate it overnight. The next morning, open the bag and, with the dough still inside it, punch the dough down by pushing on it 3 or 4 times with the heels of your palms. The dough will need to come to room temperature before you shape it, about 2 hours. To speed up the process, remove the dough from the bag, flatten it out on a parchment-lined baking sheet, and place it in a warm, draft-free space. It will be at room temperature in about 30 minutes. Shape the dough into braided loaves and proceed according to the recipe below.*

MAKES 2 LARGE LOAVES

To make the bread, place the warm water in a large bowl and sprinkle the yeast and 2 teaspoons of sugar over the water. Let stand until foamy, about 10 minutes (this is called proofing or activating the yeast).

Add the honey, eggs, 2 cups of all-purpose flour, and the remaining sugar to the yeast. Beat hard with a bread whisk or stir vigorously with a wooden spoon until smooth.

Add the salt and oil and continue to whisk or stir until the oil is incorporated. Stir in white whole-wheat and bread flour. Gradually add remaining all-purpose flour, starting one cup at a time. When you can no longer stir in the bowl, transfer to a lightly floured surface and continue to gradually add flour, kneading gently until dough is smooth, elastic, and no longer sticky. (The flour amount may vary depending on the age of the flour, the humidity, and the size of your eggs.) Form the dough into a ball.

Oil a large bowl and add the dough, turning it once to coat it. Cover the bowl with a damp cloth and place it in a warm, draft-free spot, such as in an oven that's turned off. Allow the dough to double in bulk, 1 to 2 hours. (To slow the rising process, refrigerate it at this point and let it rise for as long as 8 hours or overnight, see the headnote.)

Poke the dough with 2 fingers; if the indentations remain, the dough has adequately risen; if the indentations fill in, cover the dough and allow it to rise 15 to 30 minutes more.

When the dough has doubled, transfer it to a lightly floured work surface and deflate the dough by pushing down on it with the heels of your palms 3 or 4 times (called punching down the dough). If the dough feels sticky or seems

Bread

2 cups warm water (105°F)

2 packages dry yeast (4½ teaspoons)

2 teaspoons plus ⅓ cup sugar

¼ cup honey

4 extra-large eggs

6 to 7 cups unbleached all-purpose flour, as needed, plus more for dusting

4 teaspoons kosher salt

1 cup grapeseed or safflower oil, plus more for oiling the bowl

1 cup white whole-wheat flour

1 cup bread flour

3 tablespoons of one or a combination of sesame seeds, poppy seeds, and za'atar (optional)

Glaze

1 extra-large egg

2 tablespoons water

2 teaspoons honey (optional)

recipe continues

too soft, knead in more flour. Divide the dough into two portions and braid them according to one of the sets of braiding instructions below.

Transfer each loaf to a parchment-covered baking sheet. Allow the shaped dough to rise in a warm place until an indention remains when the dough is poked lightly with a finger, 30 to 40 minutes.

Meanwhile, preheat the oven to 350°F.

To make the glaze, beat the egg in a small bowl with the water and honey, if using.

Bake the challot until they sound hollow when tapped (or to an internal temperature of 195 to 199°F; you can use an instant-read thermometer to test the temperature), 45 to 60 minutes. Just before the they are done (at 190 to 193°F), remove them from the oven and brush with the glaze. Return the breads to the oven and bake until golden brown, 5 to 10 minutes. Brush again with the glaze, sprinkle with the seeds, if using, and return them to the oven until they look shiny and the glaze looks cooked, about 2 minutes. Remove from oven and cool on racks.

Braiding Instructions

NOTE: *We have given directions below for making two large challot. However, the recipe can easily be divided into four portions to make four medium-size challot. If making four challot, roll the strands (for braiding) 1 to 2 inches shorter than indicated below.*

THREE-STRAND BRAID

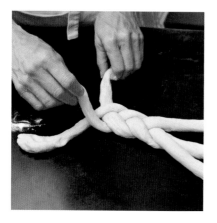

1   For each challah, divide one dough portion into three equal pieces. Roll out each piece into a long uniform strand (about 16-inches). Place the three strands side by side lengthwise.

2   The strands will be braided from the center down and the center up. Starting at the center, take the strand on the outer right, cross it over the middle strand, and bring it into the middle.

3   Take the strand on the outer left, cross it over the middle strand and let it rest in the middle.

4   Repeat this procedure, alternately bringing the one on the outer right to the middle, and then bringing the one on the outer left to the middle, to the bottom.

5   Reverse the loaf so the free ends point downward and finish braiding in the same manner.

6   At each end, pinch the individual strand ends together and tuck them under the braid to finish.

FOUR-STRAND BRAID

1 Divide one dough portion into four equal pieces. Roll out each piece into a long uniform strand (about 14-inches). Place strands side by side and pinch together the ends at the top.

2 Beginning from the left and working to the right, take the outside strand and weave it over the next strand, under the next, and over the last on the right.

3 To continue, from the left take the outside strand and weave it over the next strand, and under the next and over the last on the right.

4 Proceed as above weaving each strand over and under the other strands until the ends of the strands are reached. Pinch the ends together and tuck them under the loaf to finish.

DOUBLE BRAID

Follow the steps for a three-strand braid with slight modifications: Divide one dough portion into four equal pieces and roll out three of the pieces into long uniform strands (about 14 inches long each). Follow braiding directions for a three-strand loaf. Divide the fourth piece into three equal pieces and roll them into strands the same length as the already formed braid. These pieces will be much thinner. Make a long thin braid out of these strands. Place on top of the three-strand loaf and stretch it so you can tuck the ends under the loaf. Pinch the ends and pinch along the top (every inch or so) to attach the top braid to the challah.

ROUND CHALLAH

1 Using one portion of dough, roll it out into a long strand approximately 18 inches long by 3 inches wide. The strand should be tapered with one end thinner than the other.

2 Hold the thicker end in your hand and coil the dough around your fingers to form a spiral. Gently and slowly remove your hand. Tuck the tapered end under the challah.

ROUND CHALLAH WITH HONEY BOWL

1 Using one portion of dough, divide the dough into four equal pieces. Roll one piece into a very long, thick strand. Working on a parchment-lined baking sheet, wrap the strand around a 3-inch ovenproof glass bowl. Pinch to close.

2 Roll the remaining dough into 3 equal strands and make a braid following the three-strand directions.

3 Wrap the braid around the dough that surrounds the bowl. Tuck the ends under the challah so the braid appears continuous. Bake with the bowl empty. Fill the bowl with honey before serving.

recipe continues

VARIATIONS

For earthier-tasting bread: Substitute 1 to 2 cups of whole-wheat flour for the equivalent amount of white whole-wheat flour. You can experiment with different white, whole-wheat, and bread flours to get the texture and flavor you like. NOTE: *When using more whole grain or bread flour you will want to increase the salt by ¼ to ½ teaspoon.*

For dairy bread: Substitute melted butter for all or part of the oil.

For Rosh Hashanah bread: Before you begin making the dough, place ½ cup raisins in a small bowl with ¼ cup hot water. Let the raisins plump for at least 30 minutes. Add the plumped raisins to the dough before the first rise and shape the dough to make a round loaf. Add 2 teaspoons honey to the glaze for a sweet New Year.

Round Challah

Round Challah with Honey Bowl

BREAKING BREAD

Any dedicated baker will tell you that there's a particular kind of joy in making bread and sharing it with others. Bread is worth every bit of the effort that goes into making it. We can't have a celebratory meal without it, really, or a meal of any kind. The Jewish blessing over the bread is the umbrella blessing for the entire meal.

Of all the breads though, it's challah that holds a special place in our hearts and our tradition. So it's no surprise that challah also plays a pivotal role at JCCs around the country. At the Jewish Community Center of Greater Pittsburgh, Shabbat is celebrated by the entire community, with young children leading the charge, sharing challah with everyone.

Every Friday, two hundred preschoolers and their teachers set up a Shabbat table in the light-filled community-gathering hall, complete with candles, a kiddush cup, and a huge plate of challah. They lead a song and dance fest that draws everyone in—parents, teens, seniors, and staff—whoever happens to be walking by at the time. Everyone stops, recites the blessings together, and then challah is passed around.

The children welcome the guests and serve the seniors first, embodying the values of honoring your elders, respect, and hospitality. For these young students—children of all Jewish denominations and non-Jews as well—challah means Shabbat, a celebration to look forward to every week. For the seniors, challah provides an opportunity to connect with the younger generation, witnessing the continuity of Jewish life.

Within Jewish communities, homemade challot are baked to celebrate life-cycle events such as births, b'nei mitzvah, graduations, and more, and also to provide comfort in times of loss and pain. Beyond the making and giving of challah, breaking bread and sharing it is the key to nurturing communities large and small. Challah (or any bread for that matter) is the ingredient that is the foundation of our community table.

Queen Esther's Crown Purim Bread

Rabbinic commentators suggest that while Queen Esther (the Jewish heroine of the Book of Esther) lived in the palace of King Ahasuerus in Persia, she ate only seeds, nuts, fruits, and vegetables in an attempt to keep kosher. As a result, many Jews eat seeds and fruits on the holiday of Purim; hence the poppy or fruit-filled hamantaschen tradition at Purim. Another tradition is to make a twisted bread in the shape of a crown. We use our Weekly Challah and fill it with poppy seeds and onions. This recipe is one of our most requested and unusual holiday culinary treats.

MAKES 1 LARGE RING

½ recipe Weekly Challah (page 23)

Filling

1½ cups very finely chopped yellow onion

6 tablespoons olive oil

½ cup poppy seeds, plus more for sprinkling

½ teaspoon kosher salt

Glaze

1 extra-large egg beaten with 2 tablespoons water

It is a Purim custom to exchange food baskets (*mishloach manot*) filled with sweets, fruits, and delicious treats. The dough in this recipe can be easily halved so you can make two smaller loaves, the perfect size for *mishloach manot* packages.

Prepare the challah dough through its first rise of 1 to 2 hours (see page 23). (**NOTE**: *Do not punch down the dough or knead further.*)

Combine the onion, olive oil, seeds, and salt in a small bowl.

Divide the dough portion into two pieces. Using your hands, roll one piece into a 26-inch-long strand. Then, using a rolling pin or your hands, flatten the strand into a 30 x 4-inch rectangle. (If the dough is too elastic to hold the rolled out shape, let it rest for 10 to 15 minutes on the counter and roll it again.)

Spoon half the onion-poppy mixture lengthwise down the center of the dough. Fold one long edge of the dough to just cover the filling. Take the second side of the dough and fold it so that it overlaps the first side by ½ inch. Pinch firmly to seal. Pinch the short ends closed.

Repeat with the second piece of dough.

Arrange the filled strands side by side, seam-side down. Beginning in the middle, cross one strand over the other to form an X-shape, being careful to keep the seams facing down. Starting from the middle cross, continue to cross the strands, one over the other in the same direction, until you reach the end. Pinch the ends together. Repeat with the other end. Coil it into a ring and transfer it to a parchment-lined baking sheet, seam-side down. Tuck one end under the second and pinch to seal tucked end. (**NOTE**: *At this point the ring can be refrigerated up to 24 hours. Remove from the refrigerator and let come to room temperature about 2 hours before baking.*)

Preheat the oven to 350°F.

Let the ring rise for about 1 hour in a warm, draft-free place, until doubled in size. Glaze with the egg wash and sprinkle with more seeds, if desired. Bake for 45 to 50 minutes. Rotate the baking sheet in the oven halfway through the baking. The bread should be golden brown and sound hollow when tapped. The internal temperature can be tested with an instant-read thermometer and should be 190°F.

Chocolate Crumb Babka

This is coffee cake par excellence for chocolate lovers. We have taken the same dough that we use to make challah and turned it into another sublime treat. The dough is layered with a chocolate schmear, cinnamon sugar, and chocolate chips to create a rich bread that is perfect for breakfast, brunch, or tea.

The word *babka* is derived from the Polish word *baba*, meaning old woman or grandmother. While many people are used to seeing babkas shaped like loaves, they were traditionally round and plump (like our bubbes!). We've returned to this shape, primarily because it is how our grandmothers served their babkas. We can still see one of our grandmothers "putting it to her coffee for breakfast" as she used to say.

MAKES 1 LARGE BUNDT BABKA

½ recipe Weekly Challah (page 23)

Chocolate Schmear

5 ounces bittersweet chocolate (preferably 65% cacao or higher), broken into small pieces

½ cup low-fat milk

8 tablespoons (1 stick) unsalted butter

2 tablespoons cocoa powder

¼ cup sugar

1½ teaspoons pure vanilla extract

Cinnamon Sugar

¼ cup packed brown sugar

2 teaspoons ground cinnamon

Crumb Topping

1 cup unbleached all-purpose flour

8 tablespoons (1 stick) chilled unsalted butter, cut into pieces

½ cup packed brown sugar

1 tablespoon ground cinnamon

1 to 2 teaspoons hot water

ingredients continue

Prepare the challah dough through its first rise (see page 23).

While the dough is rising, prepare the chocolate schmear. In a medium bowl, combine the chocolate pieces, milk, butter cocoa powder, and sugar. Place over a pot with simmering water (or in a double boiler) and melt slowly for about 10 minutes, stirring occasionally. Remove from the heat just before the chocolate has completely melted and stir in the vanilla. Set aside.

To make the cinnamon sugar, combine the brown sugar and cinnamon in a small bowl and set aside.

To make the crumb topping, combine the flour, cold butter, brown sugar, cinnamon, and hot water in the bowl of a food processor fitted with a metal blade. Pulse until the mixture is crumbly. (Or, you can place the ingredients in a bowl and cut the butter into the mixture with two knives.) Transfer the mixture to a bowl and squeeze it with your hands to form crumbly clumps. Set aside.

To make the chocolate drizzle, place the chocolate pieces in a small bowl over a pan with simmering water and, as they begin to melt, add the milk and sugar. Stir, and when the chocolate is completely melted, remove from the heat and set aside. NOTE: *This mixture is much thinner than the chocolate schmear.*

Grease a Bundt pan with 1 tablespoon softened butter, making sure to fully coat the grooves of the pan. Working on a lightly floured surface or on a piece of parchment paper, divide the dough portion in half. Knead each piece of dough a couple of times. If the dough is very sticky, sprinkle a little bit of flour over it, sparingly. With your hands, roll each piece of dough into a 14-inch-long strand. Cover each strand with a piece of parchment paper and, using a rolling pin, roll the dough into a 14 x 6-inch rectangle. The dough should be very thin, about ⅛ inch thin. Remove the top piece of parchment paper.

recipe continues

Chocolate Drizzle

2 ounces bittersweet chocolate, broken into small pieces

2 tablespoons low-fat milk

2 tablespoons sugar

1 tablespoon unsalted butter at room temperature to grease pan

1 cup bittersweet chocolate chips or pieces (optional)

½ cup pecans, broken into pieces (optional)

Spread half the chocolate schmear onto one piece of the dough, leaving 1 inch from the edges bare. Sprinkle with half the cinnamon sugar and half the chocolate chips if using. Roll the dough up like a jellyroll from a long side. Scrunch the roll and place it in the greased Bundt pan so that it fills only one half of pan—the roll will have an irregular wave shape.

Repeat the process of filling the remaining dough with the chocolate schmear, cinnamon sugar, and chocolate chips. Scrunch the roll and place snugly into the other half of the pan. Pinch the ends together to form a circle. Do not worry if some of the filling is oozing out.

Sprinkle the babka with the crumb topping. If you are using the pecans, sprinkle them over the top. Let it rise for 1½ hours at room temperature or place it in the refrigerator to rise overnight. (If you refrigerate overnight, you will need to remove the babka from the refrigerator and let it come to room temperature for 1 hour before baking.)

Preheat the oven to 350°F. Place the filled Bundt pan on a baking sheet. Bake for 45 to 50 minutes, until the top is golden brown. Remove from the oven and cool in the pan for at least 30 minutes. Loosen from the pan with a blunt knife. Invert the babka onto a plate and then flip it back over to serve. Using a spoon, drizzle it with the chocolate drizzle and serve.

VARIATIONS

You can also make two babka loaves with this recipe. Scrunch or twist each filled roll to fit into a 9-inch loaf pan. Bake both at 350°F for about 45 minutes. Then you can eat one and save one in the freezer for another delicious day.

Cinnamon Raisin Babka: For those who prefer cinnamon to chocolate, omit the chocolate schmear and the chocolate drizzle. Plump 2 cups of raisins in ¼ cup hot water for 10 minutes and then drain the raisins if the water is not completely absorbed. Double the cinnamon sugar. To assemble the babka, sprinkle each of the pieces of dough with half the cinnamon sugar and half the raisins. Sprinkle with the crumb topping if desired and scatter pecans on top.

Light and Easy Cornbread

A JCC Manhattan member who grew up in Atlanta gave us this recipe for cornbread. Her family, like so many Jewish families across the globe, absorbed local recipes and integrated them into their food traditions. Moist, crumbly, and delicious, this cornbread is also great when made into muffins. For a spicy variation, add two medium jalapeños, seeded and finely chopped, to the corn before sautéing. For a great crust, bake the cornbread in a 13-inch cast-iron skillet: Heat the pan and add a pat of butter for a little extra crispiness, then pour in the batter and bake for 40 to 45 minutes in a 375°F oven.

MAKES ONE 9 X 9-INCH BREAD OR 12 MUFFINS

Preheat the oven to 375°F. Line a 9 x 9-inch square pan with parchment paper or 12 muffin cups with liners.

In a small saucepan, melt 1 cup butter over medium-high heat and then allow to cool.

Melt the remaining 1 tablespoon butter in a medium skillet over medium-high heat. Add the corn kernels and sauté, stirring occasionally, until some of the kernels are beginning to brown, 5 to 7 minutes. Remove the corn from the heat and let it cool slightly.

In a large bowl, combine the flour, sugar, cornmeal, baking powder, and salt. In a separate medium bowl, combine the melted butter, cooked corn, milk, and eggs. Add the wet ingredients to the dry and mix until just combined. The batter will be very thick.

Transfer the batter to the pan or muffin cups, filling each cup three-fourths full. Place in the oven and after 5 minutes lower the heat to 350°F. Bake until the top is golden brown and a toothpick inserted in the middle comes out clean, about 45 minutes for the square bread, 30 minutes for the muffins.

1 cup (2 sticks) plus 1 tablespoon unsalted butter

1½ cups corn kernels, either fresh (from about 3 cobs) or frozen and defrosted

3 cups unbleached all-purpose flour

1 cup sugar

1 cup medium cornmeal

2 tablespoons baking powder

1½ teaspoons kosher salt

1½ cups low-fat milk

2 extra-large eggs

Fig and Fennel Bread

This impressively flavored loaf is quite easy to make. The fig and fennel combo is inspired—a little sweet, but savory too. Serve with soup, as a snack, or sliced thin and toasted with cheese. Resist eating it straight out of the oven and let the bread cool to achieve the perfect texture.

MAKES TWO 12-INCH LOAVES

1 package dry yeast (2¼ teaspoons)

1 tablespoon sugar

1¼ cups warm water (105°F)

3 cups bread flour

1 cup rye flour, light or medium

8 ounces dried Calimyrna figs, chopped (about 1½ cups)

2 tablespoons fennel seeds, crushed

1 tablespoon kosher salt

2 teaspoons grapeseed or olive oil

In a small bowl, sprinkle the yeast and sugar over the warm water. Let stand until the yeast activates (the mixture will bubble), about 10 minutes.

In the bowl of a standing mixer fitted with the paddle attachment, combine the bread flour, rye flour, ¾ cup of the figs, fennel seeds, and salt. Mix at the lowest speed, gradually adding the yeast mixture. Mix until all the flour is just incorporated. (To mix by hand, stir the mixture vigorously with a wooden spoon until the dough comes together.)

Replace the paddle with the dough hook and knead at a low speed until the dough is smooth and elastic, about 3 minutes. (To knead by hand, transfer the dough to a floured work surface and knead until smooth and elastic, about 5 minutes.)

Coat a large bowl lightly with oil. Transfer the dough to the bowl and turn to coat it. Cover the bowl with a damp kitchen towel. Let the dough rise in a warm, draft-free place until doubled in volume, about 1 hour.

Punch the dough down and transfer it to a lightly floured work surface. Knead gently until the dough is deflated and all air bubbles are worked out. Knead in the remaining figs. Halve the dough and shape each piece into a 12-inch-long loaf.

Preheat the oven to 375°F.

Line a medium baking sheet with parchment paper. Transfer the loaves to the baking sheet, leaving 4 inches between them. Cover the loaves with a damp kitchen towel and let the loaves rise in a warm, draft-free place until almost doubled in volume, about 35 minutes.

Bake the bread until the crust is golden and the loaves sound hollow when tapped (to an internal temperature of 190°F), about 45 minutes. Cool the bread on a large rack.

Grilled Rosemary Flatbread

Easy and adaptable, this flatbread is a real crowd-pleaser. The dough rises for a very short time (because we use instant or rapid-rise yeast) and is incredibly forgiving. It can be rolled and rerolled and left to rest. We like to have a big group over for a flatbread-making party where each guest gets their own grilled flatbread to top as they like. Our suggestions for toppings (see the box) are simply a starting point. This recipe is easily multiplied.

MAKES 6 FLATBREADS

1 package instant or rapid-rise yeast (2¼ teaspoons)

1 tablespoon sugar

1 cup warm (105°F) water plus ½ cup lukewarm water

3 cups bread flour or unbleached all-purpose flour, as needed, plus more for dusting

¼ cup extra-virgin olive oil, plus more for coating the bowl and brushing the breads

1 tablespoon chopped rosemary

1 teaspoon kosher salt

¼ cup coarse semolina flour, cornmeal, or additional bread flour

Coarse sea salt (optional)

Optional toppings (see box)

In a large bowl, combine the yeast, sugar, 1 cup warm water, and 1½ cups of the flour. Allow to rest in a warm place until the yeast activates (the mixture will bubble), 5 to 10 minutes.

Coat a medium bowl with olive oil. Set aside. Add the ½ cup lukewarm water, ¼ cup olive oil, rosemary, kosher salt, and 1 cup of the remaining flour to the yeast mixture and stir to mix well. Gradually add the remaining flour 1 tablespoon at a time and incorporate it by hand, until a soft dough is formed. Flour a work surface, transfer the dough to it, and knead until the dough is smooth, 5 to 10 minutes. Transfer the dough to the oiled bowl, turn to coat, and allow to rest in a warm, draft-free place until the dough doubles in size, about 20 minutes. (At this stage, the dough may be left for up to 2 hours.)

Punch down the dough and divide it into 6 equal pieces. Heat a grill pan over high heat.

Sprinkle a work surface with the semolina, cornmeal, or bread flour. Roll out the dough one piece at a time to make a ¼-inch-thick free-form shape. Brush the dough with olive oil and sprinkle with the sea salt, if using. Transfer to the pan and grill, turning once, until the flatbread is cooked through, 5 to 8 minutes. Repeat with the remaining flatbreads. Add toppings, if using. (NOTE: *If using a topping with cheese, transfer the flatbread to a 350°F oven to melt it.*)

Possible toppings include grated Parmesan, mushrooms sautéed with thyme and topped with grated Emmentaler, basil leaves and sliced plum tomatoes brushed with oil, and roasted red and yellow cherry tomatoes sprinkled with Parmesan.

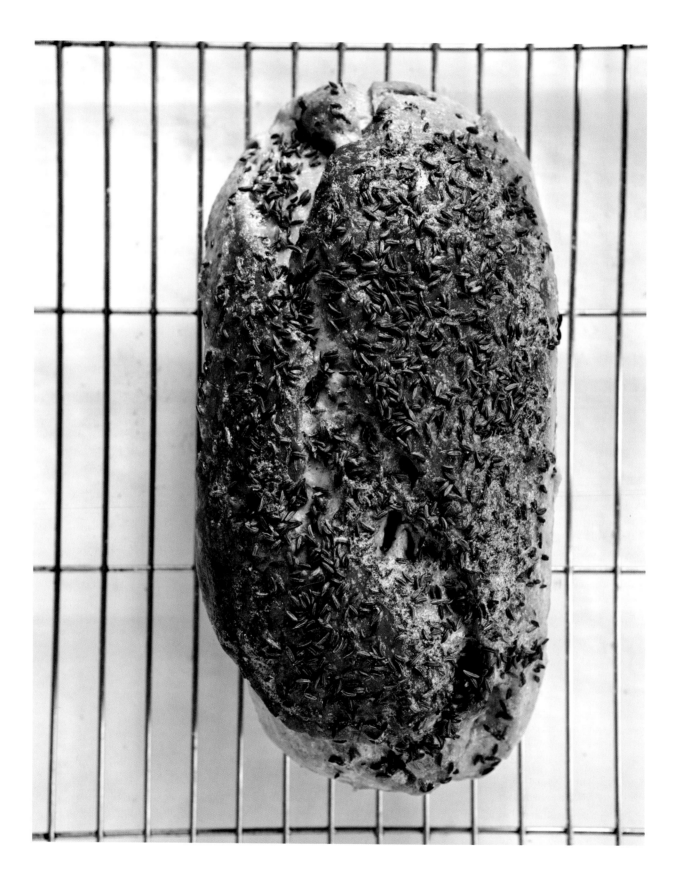

Rye Bread

When our grandparents and great-grandparents left the Old Country for the New, they brought their love of rye with them. Rye bread became a staple in Polish, Russian, and probably German Jewish homes for two main reasons: Rye flour was easy to find and it was less expensive than wheat flour. Thus the "Jewish rye" was born: specifically a rye seasoned with caraway seeds. All three of us remember going to the local Jewish bakery as kids and ordering two rye loaves—one seeded, one not.

Our recipe will remind you of your grandparents' rye—slightly sour, seeded, and with a great chew. The beer adds the Old Country fermented flavor, and since you only use 1 cup, the baker gets to finish the rest of the bottle. A QUICK NOTE: *Rye flour has significantly less gluten than wheat flour, so don't expect a light or airy dough. This bread slices easily and will keep very well for a few days.*

MAKES 2 MEDIUM LOAVES

In a large bowl, sprinkle the yeast and sugar over the warm water. Allow the yeast to activate (the mixture will bubble), 5 to 10 minutes.

Meanwhile, in a small saucepan, bring the beer to a simmer over medium heat. Remove from the heat and allow the beer to cool to room temperature (you want the beer to be flat.)

In a large bowl, combine the rye and all-purpose flour with the salt and stir. In the bowl of a standing mixer, combine the yeast mixture with the flat beer, honey, and oil. Switch to the dough hook. Mixing on low speed, begin adding the flour mixture 1 cup at a time, about 4 minutes. The mixture will become very stiff; you'll need to add the last of the flour by hand.

Transfer the mixture to a floured work surface and knead until the dough is smooth and no longer sticky. Spread the dough out and knead in the caraway seeds, 1 tablespoon at a time, until they are fully integrated.

Grease a large bowl with grapeseed oil. Roll the dough in the bowl so it's coated with oil. Cover with a damp towel and allow the dough to rise in a warm, draft-free place until it's doubled in size, 2 to 3 hours, depending on air humidity.

Punch the dough down, halve it, and form each half into an oval loaf. Line a baking sheet with parchment paper. Sprinkle semolina or cornmeal on the parchment to coat the bottom of the loaves. Place the loaves on the sheet at least 4 inches apart.

Whisk the egg white and water together and brush on the loaves to glaze. Allow to rise, uncovered, in a warm, draft-free place until the dough doubles again, 1 to 2 hours. For a shiny, firm crust, reglaze about every 30 minutes during this rise.

Preheat the oven to 400°F. Brush one last time with the egg wash and sprinkle the loaves with additional caraway seeds. Bake the bread for 15 minutes, lower the heat to 375°F, and bake until the loaves sound hollow when tapped (an internal temperature of 190°F), about 15 minutes. Cool the bread on a rack for 40 minutes.

1 package dry yeast (2¼ teaspoons)

1 tablespoon sugar

¾ cup warm (105°F) water

1 cup dark beer

3 cups medium rye flour

3 cups unbleached all-purpose or bread flour, plus more for dusting

1 tablespoon table salt

2 tablespoons honey

1 tablespoon grapeseed or canola oil, plus more for oiling the bowl

3 tablespoons caraway seeds, plus more for sprinkling

Semolina flour or cornmeal, for dusting

1 egg white mixed with 2 teaspoons cold water

Swedish Cardamom Ring

A good friend of JCC Manhattan who grew up in Sweden brought this recipe to our attention, variations of which are found in every Swedish household. It's the kind of bread that verges on breakfast pastry or dessert with its sweet and festive flavors. Swedish pearl sugar consists of hard, irregularly shaped grains that can withstand high baking temperatures and adds a pleasing crunchy texture to many baked goods. Don't be put off by the length of this recipe; the beautiful presentation and taste are well worth it. NOTE: *This bread freezes well.*

MAKES TWO 14-INCH RINGS

1 package dry yeast (2¼ teaspoons)

18 tablespoons (2¼ sticks) unsalted butter, 8 of the tablespoons at room temperature

2 cups 2% milk at room temperature

1 cup sugar

2 tablespoons ground cardamom or cinnamon

1 teaspoon kosher salt

6 cups unbleached all-purpose flour, plus more for dusting

1 extra-large egg, beaten

1 cup Swedish pearl sugar (optional)

1 cup slivered almonds (optional)

For Swedish holidays, it's traditional to add saffron to the bread instead of cardamom. To do this, add 1 tablespoon powdered saffron to the milk and yeast (and omit the cardamom added to the sugar). Then top the bread with raisins.

Place the yeast into a medium bowl. In a small saucepan, melt the 10 tablespoons of cold butter. Add the milk and remove from the heat. When the mixture has cooled to lukewarm (about 105°F), add to the bowl with the yeast.

In another small bowl, combine the sugar, cardamom, and salt. Add half the sugar mixture to the yeast mixture (reserve the rest). Mix until smooth.

Add the flour, ½ cup at a time, to the yeast mixture and stir with a wooden spoon. The dough will be lumpy at first but will become smooth as the flour is incorporated.

Knead the dough on a lightly floured work surface until smooth, light, and pliable. (You can also knead it in the bowl.) Return the dough to the bowl, cover it with a damp kitchen towel, and allow the dough to rise in a warm, draft-free place, about 45 minutes.

Line two baking sheets with parchment paper. Halve the dough with a knife. Roll the first half into a 24 x 15 x ⅛-inch rectangle. Spread half of the softened, room-temperature butter in a thin layer over the rectangle with a blunt knife, being careful not to tear the dough. Sprinkle half the remaining sugar-spice mixture over the dough (keep the rest for the second ring).

Starting from one long side, roll the dough tightly, ending with the seam side down. Join the two ends together to form a ring and pinch the ends tightly to close securely. Transfer the ring to the baking sheet. With a sharp paring knife, make cuts every 2 inches from the outside of the ring near to, but not through, the inside. Make sure to leave ½ inch of the inside of the ring intact. Give each section a quarter twist, always twisting in the same direction; the cut surface will now be uppermost. With your hands, nudge the dough slightly inward to tighten up the ring.

Repeat with the remaining dough and sugar mixture for the second ring.

Preheat the oven to 400°F. Allow the rings to rise 20 minutes more. Brush the tops and sides of the rings with the beaten egg. Sprinkle with the pearl sugar or almonds or both, if using, and bake until golden brown, 15 to 20 minutes. Transfer to a rack to cool.

VARIATION

To make 24 small buns, follow the recipe through rolling up the dough into a log, but don't join its ends to make a ring. Instead, cut the roll into 1½-inch sections. Place each section in a muffin liner, cut-side-up. Place on a baking sheet (you do not need to bake them in a muffin tin) and brush each one with the beaten egg. Sprinkle with either the pearl sugar or almonds or both, if using. Bake in a 400°F oven until golden brown, about 15 minutes. Transfer the buns to a rack to cool.

Morning Glory Muffins with Oat Flax Topping

These are an extra healthy version of the classic morning glory muffin. We're always trying to introduce whole-wheat or white whole-wheat flour into traditional recipes to make them more healthful and have found that a combination of flours makes for the best texture and flavor. We love the additional health benefits we get from the seeds and the whole wheat. The muffins can be frozen individually; take them out as needed and defrost on the counter.

MAKES 22 TO 24 REGULAR MUFFINS

To make the topping, combine the pecans, oats, flax seeds, and sugar in a medium bowl and mix well. Add the coconut oil, blend thoroughly, and set aside.

Preheat the oven to 350°F. Line two 12-cup muffin tins with paper liners.

To make the batter, in a very large bowl sift together the flours, sugar, baking soda, cinnamon, and salt. Stir in the carrots, dried fruit, pecans, coconut, apple, and chia seeds. Mix until thoroughly combined.

In a separate medium bowl, beat together the eggs, oil, and vanilla, then stir in the applesauce. Add the egg mixture to the flour mixture and stir until the batter is just combined. Spoon about ¼ cup of the batter into each muffin cup. Sprinkle with the topping. Bake until the muffins are springy to the touch, 25 to 30 minutes. Allow the muffins to cool in the pan for 5 minutes, then turn out onto a rack to cool.

Topping

½ cup chopped pecans

¼ cup uncooked rolled oats

2 teaspoons flax seeds

1 teaspoon sugar

1 heaping tablespoon solid coconut oil

Batter

1 cup unbleached all-purpose flour

1 cup whole-wheat flour

1¼ cups sugar

2 teaspoons baking soda

2 teaspoons ground cinnamon

½ teaspoon kosher salt

2 cups grated carrots (from about 6 large carrots)

½ cup raisins or dried cherries, cranberries, or diced apricots, or a combination

½ cup chopped pecans

½ cup unsweetened shredded coconut

1 apple, peeled, cored, and grated

2 teaspoons chia seeds

3 extra-large eggs

1 cup grapeseed oil

2 teaspoons pure vanilla extract

1 cup applesauce

Lemon Scones

Even the most adventurous cook can give birth to a finicky eater. One of our own, under the influence of her peers at JCC Manhattan's Day Camp at Pearl River, buckled down and tasted these scones, which were a new food for her. The rest is history—she loved them. While most would not be daunted by the prospect of a scone, this was her particular challenge and she met it. It's so true that kids will often try new things when they are away from their parents, and camp is a great opportunity for experimenting on many levels. We like to serve the scones with 1 cup Homemade Ricotta (page 67) mixed with 1 tablespoon honey and 2 teaspoons lemon zest.

MAKES 12 TO 16 SCONES

2½ cups unbleached all-purpose flour, plus more for rolling out the scones

1 tablespoon baking powder

½ teaspoon kosher salt

Grated zest of 2 lemons

8 tablespoons (1 stick) unsalted butter, cut into tablespoon-size pieces

¼ to ⅓ cup sugar

4 tablespoons fresh lemon juice

½ cup plus 2 tablespoons low-fat milk

1 cup confectioners' sugar

Preheat the oven to 425°F. Line a baking sheet with parchment paper.

In a large bowl, combine the flour, baking powder, and salt. Add the lemon zest and mix well.

Cut in the butter with a pastry blender, or rub it in with your fingers, until the mixture looks like coarse crumbs. Add sugar to taste and toss to mix. Add 3 tablespoons of the lemon juice and the ½ cup milk and stir with a fork until a soft dough forms. Shape the dough into a ball. Lightly flour a work surface, turn the dough onto it, and knead until it comes together, 10 to 12 times. Do not overwork it.

For triangular scones, halve the dough, knead each half lightly into a ball. Pat or roll each ball into a 6-inch circle. Cut each circle into 6 or 8 wedges. For round scones, roll all the dough to a thickness of about 1½ inches and cut out circles with a 2-inch round cutter. Reroll the dough scraps and repeat.

Transfer the wedges or circles to the baking sheet, setting them slightly apart. Bake until the edges of the scones are beginning to brown, about 12 minutes. Meanwhile, in a small bowl, combine the remaining 2 tablespoons milk and 1 tablespoon lemon juice with the confectioners' sugar to create a glaze. When the scones are done, move to a rack, drizzle the glaze over them, and allow to cool.

Homemade Pretzels

Riding the elevator at JCC Manhattan on any given day, you'll notice enticing smells coming from the second floor. This is the home of the Saul and Carole Zabar Nursery School, where the teachers use cooking as a way to hone motor skills (stirring, rolling, kneading) and teach basic math concepts (measuring, adding, subtracting), and as a way to help kids expand their palates. These pretzels are one of the most popular recipes at the nursery school.

NOTE: *We like to substitute whole-wheat flour for all-purpose flour whenever we can. This is a perfect recipe to do so, as it results in a pretzel much higher in fiber. You can try a combination of white (75%) and whole-wheat flour (25%) to get started. Increase the percentage of whole-wheat to white flour each time you make the pretzels until it suits your taste.*

MAKES 12 PRETZELS

Preheat the oven to 425°F.

In a large bowl, sprinkle the yeast and sugar over the warm water. Allow the yeast to activate (the mixture will bubble), 5 to 10 minutes. Add the salt and flour and mix.

Transfer the dough to a floured work surface. It will be very lumpy. Knead the dough until smooth, at least 5 minutes. Divide the dough into 12 equal pieces. Roll them into thin ½-inch-diameter ropes. For a traditional pretzel shape, take one strand and make a U-shape. Cross the two ends over each other, then fold them down and press into the bottom curve of the U. Or have fun shaping the dough into twists, spirals, or whatever shape you like (see photo, opposite).

Transfer the pretzels to a baking sheet. Brush them with the egg and sprinkle with salt, cinnamon, sugar, or za'atar, if using. Bake until golden brown, 12 to 15 minutes. Transfer to racks to cool.

2 packages dry active yeast (4½ teaspoons)

2 tablespoons sugar

1¼ cups warm (105°F) water

1 teaspoon kosher salt

4 cups unbleached all-purpose flour, plus more for dusting

1 large egg, beaten

Very coarse salt, ground cinnamon, sugar, or za'atar (optional)

Bubbe's Hungarian Sweet Cheese Hamantaschen

Any child who has gone to Hebrew school or day school will be familiar with the triangular filled cookies served for Purim called hamantaschen. These cookies are said to represent the three-cornered hat or three-cornered pocket of the Persian archenemy of the Jews, Haman. Ashkenazi Jews traditionally fill their cookies with poppy seeds, apricots, raspberries, or prunes. Today, hamantaschen can also be found filled with chocolate chips, peanut butter, or hazelnut spread.

This recipe evolved as two of us emailed back and forth comparing the sketchy notes of our Hungarian grandmothers' recipes for yeast-dough hamantaschen. We loved their soft and chewy treats, more "doughy" than the traditional bakery hamantaschen cookie. We've taken their "add a pinch" or "just add enough" and created a new recipe. Filled with honey-sweetened farmer cheese, they are the perfect breakfast with a cup of strong coffee on Purim morning, or any other time.

To make the dough, in a small bowl, sprinkle the yeast and ¼ teaspoon sugar over the warm water. Set aside and let the yeast activate (mixture will bubble), about 10 minutes.

In a large bowl, combine the ¼ cup sugar, flour, and salt. Mix to combine. Adding the soft butter and with your hand or the back of a wooden spoon, gently combine the butter into the flour mixture until it resembles coarse crumbs.

Pour the buttermilk into another small bowl. Add the egg and vanilla and beat to combine. Add the yeast mixture and stir to combine.

Make a well with your hands in the flour mixture. Pour the wet ingredients into the well and stir together with your hand or a wooden spoon, incorporating the flour slowly. Mix for 10 to 15 seconds, until a soft and smooth ball of dough is formed. If your dough is very sticky, add a bit more flour, 1 teaspoon at a time. Let the dough rise in the mixing bowl, covered with a damp cloth in a warm, draft-free place for 1 hour.

To make the filling, in a medium bowl, combine the farmer cheese, cream cheese, honey, milk, and lemon zest. Add the soaked raisins and walnuts, if using.

Preheat the oven to 325°F. Line baking sheets with parchment.

Roll the dough out on parchment paper until ⅛ inch thick. Cut out 3-inch circles with a round biscuit cutter or with an overturned glass. Set a small bowl of water on your work surface. Spoon 2 teaspoons filling into the center of a dough round. Wet your fingertips lightly and pinch the dough round into a triangle by folding and overlapping the edges of the dough and pinching at three corners. Repeat with the remaining dough and filling.

Place on the baking sheets and bake for 20 to 25 minutes, until golden brown. Cool on a rack.

Dough

1 package dry active yeast (2¼ teaspoons)

¼ teaspoon plus ¼ cup sugar

¼ cup warm water (105°F)

2½ cups all-purpose flour, plus more if needed

½ teaspoon kosher salt

12 tablespoons (1½ sticks) unsalted butter at room temperature

¾ cup buttermilk at room temperature

1 extra-large egg

½ teaspoon pure vanilla extract

Filling

8 ounces farmer cheese at room temperature

4 ounces whipped cream cheese at room temperature

2 tablespoons honey

1 tablespoon low-fat milk

½ teaspoon grated lemon zest

2 tablespoons golden raisins soaked in ¼ cup hot water (optional)

2 tablespoons chopped walnuts (optional)

STARTERS

21st-Century Whitefish Salad 53

Summer and Winter Vegetable Tarts 54

Buckwheat Buttermilk Blinis 57

Truffle Popcorn 59

Roasted Delicata Squash Rings 61

Crostini with Three Toppings 62

Yogurt Sauce Two Ways 65

Homemade Ricotta 67

Pickled String Beans and Baby Carrots 68

Savory Plum-Tomato Jam 71

Latkes Four Ways 72

Pickled Grapes with Rosemary 75

Black Bean Cakes with Tomato Salsa 76

Potato and Zucchini Egg Tart (Feinkochen) 79

Salmon-Halibut Gefilte Fish
with Apple Beet Horseradish Relish 82

21st-Century Whitefish Salad

Smoked whitefish salad is a quintessential Ashkenazi Jewish dish that is most commonly made with sour cream and mayonnaise. We've modernized the original salad by lightening the flavors and brightening it with fresh herbs. We've also reduced the fat by using 0% Greek yogurt, although you can use 2% or 4% for a richer version. But try it with the 0% first; we promise you won't miss the calories. Besides spreading on a bagel, you might try stuffing the salad into endive leaves and then topping with salmon caviar and dill—a great brunch dish.

SERVES 4 TO 6

Place the whitefish in a medium bowl and break it up with a fork. Remove any remaining bones.

Add the lemon juice, onion (to taste), celery, yogurt, cream cheese, mustard, parsley, and dill. Season with the salt and pepper, stir to blend, and serve as desired.

10 ounces smoked whitefish, bones removed

1½ tablespoons lemon juice

1 or 2 tablespoons chopped red onion

2 tablespoons chopped celery

2 tablespoons plain 0% Greek yogurt

2 tablespoons whipped cream cheese

½ teaspoon Dijon mustard

1 tablespoon chopped fresh flat-leaf parsley

1 teaspoon chopped fresh dill, plus more for garnish

Kosher salt and freshly ground black pepper

2 to 4 red Belgian endives (optional)

2 tablespoons salmon caviar (optional)

Summer and Winter Vegetable Tarts

We love a recipe that can transition across seasons, and this tart is a great example. We originally only made it in the summer, but we loved it so much that once the winter came around, we decided to adapt the vegetables with the season. No matter the time of year, you'll have a fresh, savory tart to kick off a meal or pass around at a party.

Frozen puff pastry is a great labor-saving find. Keep one or two boxes in your freezer; just remember it needs to defrost and soften for a couple of hours in the refrigerator before you can shape it. Once you have placed it on a lined baking sheet, you will need to par-bake it before you top it with either summer or winter vegetables. Then pop it back in the oven to finish it off.

BOTH RECIPES SERVE 6 AS AN APPETIZER OR MAKE
20 BITE-SIZE HORS D'OEUVRES

Puff Pastry Crust

Unbleached all-purpose flour, for dusting

1 (14-ounce) package frozen puff pastry, defrosted according to package directions

Preheat the oven to 350°F.

Place a sheet of parchment paper (about 15 x 18 inches) on a work surface and lightly flour the sheet. Top with 1 sheet of dough (if the package contains 2), lightly flour it, and top with a second piece of parchment. Roll the dough between the sheets to a rectangle that's about 12 x 15 inches.

Transfer the dough to a baking sheet and remove the top layer of parchment. Roll and crimp the edges to make a shell. Return the top parchment sheet and cover with pie weights or dried beans to prevent the pastry from puffing too much. Bake until the pastry is light golden brown, about 25 minutes. Remove the parchment with the weights. Place back in the oven for 5 to 10 minutes, until the center is a light golden brown. Set aside to cool.

recipe continues

Summer Tart

Summer Tart

Our summer tart contains zucchini, peppers, and eggplant. We prepare it with an under-layer of our homemade ricotta, but of course you can opt for the store-bought kind. Pesto can also be spread under the ricotta for another layer of flavor. This is also great made with any leftover grilled or roasted diced vegetables that are hanging around your fridge.

- 2 pounds any combination of zucchini, red and yellow peppers, or eggplant, cut into 1-inch cubes
- 2 small red onions, sliced ¼ inch thick (about ½ cup)
- 1 pint cherry tomatoes, halved
- ¼ cup olive oil
- ½ teaspoon kosher salt
- ½ teaspoon freshly ground black pepper
- 1 cup Homemade Ricotta (page 67) or fresh ricotta
- 1 par-baked Puff Pastry Crust (page 54)

Preheat the oven to 400°F.

In a large bowl, combine the vegetables and oil and toss lightly. Add the salt and pepper and toss. Spread the vegetables in a single layer onto 1 or 2 baking sheets and roast until lightly browned, 25 to 35 minutes. Leave the oven on.

Carefully spread the ricotta on the cooled crust. Top with the vegetables in a single layer. Bake until the tart is hot, about 15 minutes. Allow to cool slightly, then cut and serve.

Winter Tart

Butternut squash, sliced mushrooms, and melted cheese make this a perfect winter dish.

- 4 garlic heads
- ½ cup plus 3 tablespoons extra-virgin olive oil
  Kosher salt and freshly ground black pepper
- 1 large butternut squash (about 3 pounds), peeled, seeded, and cut into ¼-inch-thick slices
- 2 cups ¼-inch-thick sliced wild mushrooms, such as cremini, porcini, or baby bella
- 2 fresh thyme sprigs
- 2 leeks, white and light green parts only, sliced into ¼-inch rings (about 2 cups)
- 1 par-baked Puff Pastry Crust (page 54)
- 4 ounces shredded Gruyère, Fontina, or hard goat cheese

Preheat the oven to 375°F.

Cut ¼ inch off the top of the garlic heads to expose the cloves inside. Pour 2 tablespoons of the oil into the bottom of a small ovenproof pan. Place the garlic heads, cut side up, in the pan and drizzle with an additional 2 tablespoons oil. Season with salt and pepper, cover tightly with foil, and roast until the garlic is golden and softened, 45 minutes to an hour. Let cool. Squeeze the pulp from its skin into a small bowl, mash, and set aside. Turn the oven up to 400°F.

In a large bowl, toss the squash with 2 tablespoons oil. Transfer to a baking sheet in a single layer and roast, rotating the pan halfway through, until the squash has browned, about 30 minutes. Transfer the squash to a plate and set aside. Reduce the oven temperature to 375°F.

Meanwhile, heat 3 tablespoons oil in a large skillet over medium-high heat. Add the mushrooms and the thyme and cook, stirring, until just soft, 5 to 7 minutes. Transfer the mushrooms to a plate and set aside. Remove the thyme sprigs.

In the same pan, heat the remaining 2 tablespoons oil over medium-high heat. Add the leeks, reduce the heat to medium, and sauté until the leeks have softened, about 10 minutes. Transfer the leeks to a plate and set aside.

Using a knife, spread the garlic over the cooled crust and top with the leeks, mushrooms, and squash. Sprinkle with the cheese and bake until the crust is well browned and the filling is heated through, about 15 minutes. Cut and serve.

Buckwheat Buttermilk Blinis

Blinis are thin, elegant pancakes that can be topped with smoked salmon, crème fraîche, or even caviar if you're feeling very luxurious. We amped up the savory flavor here by adding dill seeds to the blini batter. Buckwheat, or kasha, has a flavor we associate with the Old Country. For the Jews of Russia, Lithuania, and Ukraine, buckwheat was second only to barley and they used it in many ways in their cooking. Despite the name, there's no wheat in buckwheat—it's a seed, not a grain—and it is enjoying renewed popularity today because it is gluten free.

MAKES FORTY 2-INCH BLINIS

In a large bowl, whisk together the flour, baking powder, baking soda, dill seeds (to taste), salt, and pepper.

Beat the 4 egg whites in a medium bowl to form soft peaks. In another medium bowl, whisk together the 2 yolks, the butter, buttermilk, yogurt, and water. Pour this into the flour mixture and stir until just combined; the batter may be lumpy, which is fine.

Preheat a flat griddle over medium heat. Fold one-third of the egg whites into the batter until completely incorporated. Fold in the remaining egg whites until just combined and there are no egg-white streaks. (Fold gently, so as not to deflate the whites.)

Heat 2 tablespoons oil or butter on the griddle. Drop the batter 1 tablespoon at a time on the griddle, about 2 inches apart. Cook until the cakes are lightly golden on both sides, about 1½ minutes per side. Repeat with all the batter. Serve immediately or keep warm in a 200°F oven. Transfer to plates, and serve with your choice of accompaniments.

1½ cups buckwheat flour

2 teaspoons baking powder

1 teaspoon baking soda

½ to 2 teaspoons crushed dill seeds

⅛ teaspoon kosher salt

¼ teaspoon freshly ground black pepper

2 extra-large eggs, separated, plus 2 egg whites

8 tablespoons (1 stick) unsalted butter, melted, plus more melted butter for the griddle

1 cup buttermilk

1 cup plain low-fat yogurt

¼ cup water

GLUTEN-FREE WAFFLES

You can also use this batter to make delicious waffles. Use your waffle iron to cook them and serve the waffles with blueberries and maple syrup to balance the savory flavor with sweetness.

COFFEE AND CONSONANTS

The Gift of Literacy was one of the first programs at JCC Manhattan. Begun in 1990, it was started as a response to President Clinton's call for volunteers to help underserved children learn to read. It began with one neighborhood elementary school, a few children whose parents couldn't speak English and therefore couldn't help with reading at home, and a few volunteers who loved children, loved reading, and wanted to help. The volunteers were trained, the children were selected, and before we knew it, a program was born.

Al Schwartz and Jack Speyer were two of the first volunteers to sign up. Friends since kindergarten, they would head up to PS 75 in upper Manhattan every Tuesday and Thursday afternoon. They read to Carlos and Lily, John and Taesha, and literally hundreds of second-graders over the next twenty years. Some days the kids were eager to read with the volunteers. Other times they were tired after a long day in school. There were setbacks with every child, the normal frustrations of learning a new language. But Al and Jack were not deterred. They celebrated the small victories over a cup of coffee after each session and pressed on because they deeply understood the power of reading to change a child's life. They came from a Jewish tradition that places high value on learning, studying in partnership with others, and giving of your time.

Since that initial program, the literacy program at the JCC has grown to include hundreds of volunteers working with thousands of children in seven public schools and community centers in Manhattan. Based on the successful model of the Gift of Literacy, the JCC recently began the Gift of Math for children struggling with arithmetic and other basic math skills.

Volunteers for these programs range in age from 12 to 92 and are teens, college students, stay-at-home moms, professionals with flexible schedules, and retired adults. Some volunteers bring therapy dogs that have been trained to listen to children read. Some volunteers bring special books or stickers to help with math. Always, they bring themselves, their own stories, and their generous hearts.

Truffle Popcorn

This is a simple but sophisticated snack that's also a great bite to serve at cocktail parties. Our kids love it, too. They take bags of it with them for snacking at school and after.

SERVES 6

Pop the kernels using a hot-air popper. Transfer the popcorn to a medium bowl, add the salt and oils, and toss. Serve immediately, or transfer to small containers.

½ cup popcorn kernels

¼ teaspoon truffle salt or kosher salt

2 teaspoons extra-virgin olive oil

2 teaspoons white truffle oil, or more extra-virgin olive oil

Make your own microwaveable popcorn: Place ½ cup popcorn kernels in an untreated brown or white lunch-size paper bag. Fold over the top two times (about ½ inch at each fold). Place in a microwave with the folded edge placed down. Cook on microwave popcorn setting.

Roasted Delicata Squash Rings

Finding the right snack to feed children after school is a challenge. Delicata squash, with its green stripes and edible skin, is the perfect solution when cut into rings and roasted until caramelized. It's a great source of beta-carotene, the compound the body converts to vitamin A, which is essential for good vision, healthy skin, and a strong immune system. Plus the low glycemic index (which measures how quickly your body converts food to glucose) keeps kids from having a low-sugar crash at their after-school sports practices, making them a favorite snack of JCC Manhattan's swim team. These rings are also wonderful as a side dish with almost anything.

To transport the squash, place the rings in covered containers with parchment paper between each layer.

SERVES 8

Preheat the oven to 375°F.

Slice both ends off the squash. Using a long spoon or knife, scrape out the seeds and stringy membrane from the interiors. Set the seeds aside to roast separately (see box).

Slice the squash into ½-inch-thick rings. Remove any fibers from the center of the slices that you may have missed. Transfer half the slices to a large mixing bowl and toss with ¼ cup of the oil. Repeat with the remaining squash and oil.

Place the slices in a single layer on baking sheets. Season with salt and pepper. Roast for 30 minutes. Turn the rings over with a metal spatula and continue to roast until soft and caramelized, 10 to 20 more minutes. Broil until brown, 2 to 3 minutes. Serve warm or at room temperature.

4 medium delicata squash, scrubbed

½ cup grapeseed or olive oil

Kosher salt and freshly ground black pepper

Don't discard the squash seeds, which are great for munching when toasted: Place on a baking sheet in a single layer and toast in a 350°F oven for about 10 minutes, until lightly golden.

Crostini with Three Toppings

Crostini—toasted or grilled bread with various toppings—is always a crowd-pleaser. The word means "little toasts" in Italian, and that's the guiding principle for us—a small bite of bread with a flavorful dollop on top. Here, we offer crostini with three different Jewish-inspired spreads—caponata alla Giudea, mushroom chopped "liver," and a bean purée. Caponata originated in Sicily and, according to Claudia Roden, was associated with the large Jewish community that lived on the island from Roman times until the beginning of the sixteenth century. Across the continent in Eastern Europe, chopped liver was one of the best-known Jewish foods. The first vegetable chopped "liver" may have come from kosher dairy restaurants, where meat was not served, but restaurateurs wanted to include a beloved dish on the menu. Our version, made with mushrooms, is much healthier than the liver-based original. Finally, we like to joke that our white bean purée is North American hummus. While we love the original chickpea hummus and make it all the time, it's also fun to experiment with all types of beans, including fava, cranberry, flageolet, and other beans native to Europe and the Americas.

For the toasts: Slice your favorite bread ¼ inch thin and cut it into pieces no larger than 2 inches across. You want the pieces to be bite size. Toast or grill and brush with olive oil, then top with the caponata, chopped "liver," or bean purée.

Caponata

The key to making this is to cut the eggplant small so that it cooks through evenly. If you undercook the eggplant, it will have a spongy consistency.

MAKES 8 CUPS

- 2 eggplants (about 2 pounds), peeled and cut into ¼-inch cubes
- 1 tablespoon kosher salt, plus more for seasoning
- ¼ cup pine nuts
- ½ cup extra-virgin olive oil
- 1 large onion, coarsely chopped (about 1 cup)
- 1 anchovy fillet, minced
- 1 (28-ounce) can tomatoes
- 2 celery stalks, thinly sliced
- ¼ cup red wine vinegar
- 2 tablespoons sugar
- 5 tablespoons tomato paste

- ¼ cup golden raisins
- 2 tablespoons capers, rinsed
- ½ cup pitted green olives, coarsely chopped
- 1 roasted red bell pepper, jarred or homemade (see page 116 for roasting instructions), coarsely chopped
  Freshly ground black pepper
- 2 tablespoons basil leaves cut into ribbons
- 2 tablespoons chopped fresh flat-leaf parsley

Place the eggplant in a colander set over a large bowl. Toss with the 1 tablespoon salt, top with a plate, and weigh it down with several cans. Let the eggplant drain for 1 hour. Rinse the eggplant and pat dry with paper towels.

Meanwhile, in a small dry skillet, toast the pine nuts over medium heat, watching closely and stirring often, until golden, about 3 minutes. Transfer to a bowl and set aside.

In a large skillet, heat 2 tablespoons of the oil over medium-high heat. Add one-third of the eggplant and cook, stirring, until golden brown, 7 to 8 minutes. With

recipe continues

a slotted spoon, transfer the eggplant to a medium bowl. Repeat in 2 batches with the remaining eggplant and 4 more tablespoons of oil.

Reduce the heat to medium-low, add the remaining 2 tablespoons oil, and heat. Add the onion and anchovy and sauté, stirring, until the onion is soft, about 15 minutes. Add the tomatoes and celery, increase the heat to medium, and cook, stirring, until the tomatoes release their juices, about 5 minutes. Add the vinegar, sugar, and tomato paste. Cook, stirring occasionally, until the mixture has thickened, about 3 minutes. Add the eggplant, pine nuts, raisins, capers, olives, and bell pepper.

Season with salt and pepper and cool to room temperature. Spread the caponata on the crostini and garnish with the basil and parsley.

Mushroom Chopped "Liver"

This is best made the day of, but it's also delicious prepared a day or two ahead. Keep it refrigerated, then bring to room temperature to serve. You can also use this as a crudité dip.

MAKES 2 CUPS

¼ cup dried currants

3 tablespoons cider vinegar or wine

⅓ cup olive oil

1½ cups chopped onions (about 2 medium onions)

1 tablespoon chopped garlic

1 pound domestic button mushrooms, trimmed and quartered

1 pound fresh wild mushrooms (any combination of maitake, beech, or other mushrooms), trimmed

1 teaspoon honey

Pinch of red pepper flakes

Kosher salt

Fresh thyme or oregano leaves (optional)

Place the currants in a small bowl, add the vinegar, and set aside to plump, about 10 minutes.

Heat the oil in a large skillet over low heat, add the onions and garlic, and sauté until soft and golden, 3 to 4 minutes.

Add the button mushrooms, sauté for 4 minutes, then add the wild mushrooms. Sauté until slightly cooked, 2 minutes more. Add the currants and vinegar, and stir to combine. Remove from the heat, add the honey and red pepper flakes, and season with salt and thyme and oregano, if using. Spoon into the bowl of a food processor fitted with a metal blade and pulse chop 7 times, until the mixture is coarse but spreadable. Serve warm or at room temperature on crostini.

White Bean Purée

Here's the reason to keep a few cans of organic white beans in your pantry at all times. This recipe is easy and flavorful. It also has endless uses in addition to topping crostini—you can, for example, serve it with crudités or use it as a sandwich schmear or to thicken a vegetable soup.

MAKES ABOUT 1½ CUPS

¼ cup extra-virgin olive oil, plus more for drizzling

1 teaspoon chopped garlic

3 rosemary sprigs at least 3 inches long

2 (15-ounce) cans white cannellini or great northern beans, drained and rinsed

2 tablespoons lemon juice

¾ to 1 teaspoon kosher salt, plus more if needed

¼ teaspoon freshly ground black pepper

1 to 2 tablespoons warm vegetable stock or water, if needed

In a small skillet, heat the oil over low heat. Add the garlic and sauté until golden, 3 to 5 minutes. Add the rosemary, remove the skillet from the heat, and set aside to steep, about 10 minutes. Remove sprigs.

In a food processor, combine the cooled oil mixture with the beans, lemon juice, and salt and pepper to taste. Pulse to chop, about 30 seconds, then process until the mixture is smooth, about 4 minutes. If needed, add vegetable stock to achieve a spreadable but not runny texture. Adjust the seasoning, transfer to a serving bowl, and drizzle with additional oil. Serve on crostini.

Yogurt Sauce Two Ways

Summer Herb Yogurt Sauce

Here's an opportunity to use summer's freshest herbs to make a sauce that goes beautifully with a crudité platter, white-fleshed fish, potatoes, or a roasted main course. We think these sauces are winners not only because they are delicious, but because yogurt is a low-calorie vehicle for showcasing many different flavors. In addition, the active cultures in yogurt provide you with the much-heralded probiotics, which are helpful for healthy digestion. The herb combinations and quantities are flexible, according to taste, but use the freshest herbs available.

MAKES ABOUT 2 CUPS

- 1 cup roughly chopped fresh dill
- ¼ cup roughly chopped fresh sorrel
- ¼ cup roughly chopped fresh mint
- ¼ cup roughly chopped fresh tarragon leaves
- ½ cup chopped fresh flat-leaf parsley
- 1 garlic clove, crushed
- 1 teaspoon kosher salt, plus more for seasoning
- 2 tablespoons extra-virgin olive oil
- 1½ cups 0% Greek yogurt
  Freshly ground black pepper

Combine the dill, sorrel, mint, tarragon, parsley, garlic, and salt in a food processor and purée until smooth. With the machine running, add the oil and yogurt and process until fully blended, making a beautiful green sauce. Season with additional salt, if needed, and pepper.

Winter-Spiced Yogurt Sauce

This is a great crudité dip or sauce for broiled or grilled fish. It keeps for a week refrigerated.

MAKES ABOUT 2 CUPS

- 1 tablespoon cumin seeds
- 1 tablespoon fennel seeds
- 1 teaspoon red pepper flakes
- 8 black peppercorns
- 2 tablespoons olive oil
- 4 garlic cloves, finely chopped (about 4 teaspoons)
- ¾ cup finely chopped shallots (about 4 large shallots) or red onion
- 2 to 3 teaspoons grated fresh ginger
- 2 tablespoons ground coriander
- 2 cups 0% Greek yogurt
- 1 cup packed cilantro leaves, chopped
  Kosher salt, if desired

Using a mortar and pestle or spice grinder, finely crush or grind the cumin and fennel seeds, pepper flakes, and black peppercorns together.

In a small saucepan, heat the oil over low heat. Add the garlic, shallots, and ginger and cook, stirring constantly, until the shallots are translucent, about 5 minutes (do not allow to color). Add the spice mixture and ground coriander. Sauté until the mixture becomes very fragrant, about 10 minutes. Cool to room temperature or refrigerate for 30 minutes. (The mixture will keep for 2 weeks or longer refrigerated.)

Spoon half the spice mixture into a medium bowl, add the yogurt and cilantro, and stir to combine. Continue to add the spice mixture until you have the desired flavor intensity and consistency you want. Season with salt, if desired, and serve.

Homemade Ricotta

As home chefs, we are committed to making whatever we can from scratch. Hence this recipe for delicious, easily made soft-curd cheese that is a cousin to ricotta. It has about a million uses, all of them tasty: As a starter with pears, crusty bread, and honey or our Savory Plum-Tomato Jam (page 71). Or spread it on crostini and sprinkle with cracked black pepper and lemon zest and drizzle with olive oil. It makes a great topping for pastas too. Our families have also been known to eat it straight out of the pot while it's still warm. The ricotta will last, covered in the refrigerator, for up to 4 days, if your family can resist it that long.

Buttermilk is used to curdle the milk to make the ricotta. But if you don't have buttermilk, you can make it yourself by pouring 1 tablespoon lemon or lime juice into a measuring cup, then adding low-fat or whole milk to the 1¼-cup line. Leave it for 5 to 10 minutes to let the ingredients react.

MAKES ABOUT 1 CUP

Combine the milks in a large heavy pot and bring to a slow boil over medium heat. Cook until the mixture reaches 180 to 190°F, or until you see steam rising from it.

The mixture will begin to separate into curds and whey. (The curds will collect in the middle of the pot. The whey liquid will migrate to the edges.) Once this happens, reduce the heat to as low as possible and stir the mixture gently once or twice. Cook for 2 minutes more, remove from the heat, and allow to rest for 15 to 30 minutes. (This helps the curds develop.)

Line a large strainer with a double layer of cheesecloth and set the strainer over a large bowl. Using a slotted spoon, gently ladle the curds into the cheesecloth—do not pour. Allow the curds to drain for at least 15 minutes or up to 1 hour. The longer you allow the cheese to drain, the firmer it will become.

When your desired firmness is reached, transfer to a bowl and add salt to taste. Serve or store in the refrigerator.

4 cups 2% milk (or for lower fat content, 2½ cups whole milk, 1½ cups skim milk)

1¼ cups buttermilk

Kosher salt

Pickled String Beans and Baby Carrots

Some of our favorite childhood food memories come from trips to the Lower East Side of Manhattan. Knishes, bialys, and pickles straight from the barrel rounded out a day of bargain hunting.

But for all those times when you can't get to the Lower East Side and you are craving a salty pickled taste, this recipe is a great substitute. Crisp, refreshing, and wonderfully simple to prepare, these pickled green beans and carrots are neither too sharp nor too salty. Both the beans and the carrots are ready in 48 hours, but will taste even better if left to pickle for a week. Serve as a munchy hors d'oeuvre or snack, or as a condiment with sandwiches.

MAKES 4 CUPS

Pickling Liquid
- 2 cups cider vinegar
- 1 cup dry white wine
- 1¼ cups water
- 2 tablespoons sugar
- 1 tablespoon kosher salt

- ½ pound string or wax beans, trimmed, or ½ pound baby carrots, halved lengthwise
- 2 garlic cloves, thinly sliced
- ½ teaspoon coriander seeds, crushed coarsely
- ½ teaspoon whole peppercorns
- 1 chile pepper, dried or fresh
- 2 bay leaves

To make the pickling liquid, in a medium saucepan, combine the vinegar, wine, water, sugar, and salt. Bring to a boil and boil for 1 minute.

Beans

In a quart-size glass container with a lid, combine the beans, garlic, coriander, peppercorns, chile, and bay leaves. Pour the pickling liquid over the beans. Cool completely at room temperature, cover, and refrigerate for at least 48 hours or up to 1 week.

Carrots

When the pickling liquid boils, reduce the heat to medium-low, add the carrots, and simmer until the carrots are crisp-tender, 2 to 3 minutes.

Transfer the carrots and pickling liquid to a quart-size glass container or jar and add the garlic, coriander, peppercorns, chile, and bay leaves. Cool completely at room temperature. Cover and refrigerate for at least 48 hours and up to 1 week.

For Pickled Grapes with Rosemary
(shown opposite, at right), see page 75

Savory Plum-Tomato Jam

This is ketchup for grown-ups, a sweet-savory mix with a dash of heat that's wonderful to have on hand. We've added lemongrass—a tangy note—to round out the flavors. We love it with scrambled eggs or omelets; with a hard, aged sheep-milk cheese; or with salty ricotta salata and toasted baguette slices. You can also put a dollop of it on a cucumber round and serve it as a canapé. Our families eat it on just about everything. It keeps for months when refrigerated. It also makes a great gift when presented in a beautiful glass jar.

MAKES ABOUT 3 CUPS

In a large heavy pot, combine the tomatoes, onion, honey, chile, coriander, cumin, bay leaf, vinegar, and lemon juice. Add salt and lemongrass, if using, to taste. Bring to a boil, reduce the heat to medium-low, and simmer until reduced, thick, and jammy, about 3 hours. Remove the bay leaf and lemongrass. Transfer to glass jars, cool, and refrigerate.

3 pounds plum tomatoes, coarsely chopped

1 small onion (about 8 ounces), chopped

¼ cup honey or packed light brown sugar

1 dried red chile pepper

¾ teaspoon ground coriander

½ teaspoon ground cumin

1 bay leaf

⅓ cup cider vinegar

2 tablespoons lemon juice

Kosher salt

1 to 2 lemongrass stalks, cut in 2-inch pieces, and bruised (optional)

Latkes Four Ways

Almost every ethnic group has their own version of potato pancakes. Eastern European Jews call theirs latkes. And of the many foods associated with specific Jewish holidays, latkes hold a special place in American and European hearts at Chanukah.

Latkes are very personal. How do you like them? Large or small, dense or lacey, spicy or sweet, with sour cream or applesauce—the possibilities are endless. Even among the three of us there's debate. Still, we came up with four latke recipes we all love, including one we think is the best basic latke recipe ever, and that you can also do ahead. One thing we do agree on is that smaller is better. Smaller latkes cook faster, absorb less oil, and are crispier. However, if you love 'em big, go for it. Just cook them at lower heat and increase the cooking time.

The Best Potato Latkes

After years of dealing with the discoloration that begins almost as soon as you grate the potatoes, we came up with a great technique so you can prepare the mixture hours ahead. We layer the latke components in a container with the potatoes at the bottom. This seals the potatoes away from exposure to air, preventing browning. Once refrigerated, the prepared ingredients can be stored for up to a day before frying. Mix the ingredients just before cooking.

MAKES FORTY-EIGHT 1½-INCH OR TWENTY-FOUR 3-INCH LATKES

- 3 pounds Yukon Gold potatoes, peeled and placed in a bowl of water to prevent discoloration
- 2 small onions
- 1 teaspoon kosher salt, plus more for seasoning
- 2 tablespoons matzah meal, unbleached all-purpose flour, or potato starch
- 1 to 2 tablespoons chopped fresh dill or flat-leaf parsley, or both
- 2 extra-large eggs, beaten
  Grapeseed oil for frying
  Freshly ground black pepper

With a box grater or a food processor, grate the potatoes and onions into the same bowl and mix to combine. With your hands or with a towel, squeeze out excess moisture and transfer the mixture to the bottom of a tall, narrow container. Sprinkle on the salt, matzah meal, dill, and parsley (to taste), covering the potato mixture completely. Pour the eggs on top and spread them with a spoon to fully cover the ingredients below them; don't mix. Cover with plastic wrap and refrigerate for up to 1 day, until ready to fry. Just before frying, mix ingredients to combine completely. Follow the cooking instructions on page 74 to fry in grapeseed oil, then season with additional salt and black pepper to taste.

Beet Latkes

The color of these latkes is as festive as the latkes are delicious. If you grate the beets by hand, wear gloves, as the beets will turn your hands pink. Serve with applesauce, yogurt, or sour cream.

MAKES THIRTY-TWO 1½-INCH OR SIXTEEN 3-INCH LATKES

- 2 pounds beets, peeled
- 1 small red onion
- ¼ cup unbleached all-purpose flour

recipe continues

4 extra-large eggs
¼ cup chopped fresh dill
Kosher salt and freshly ground black pepper
Grapeseed oil for frying

With a box grater or a food processor, grate the beets and onion into the same medium bowl to combine. Add the flour, eggs, and dill and mix together. Season with salt and pepper. Follow the cooking instructions below to fry in grapeseed oil.

Curried Sweet Potato Latkes

These latkes have become the most requested in our houses. Trust us on this one—the sweet and savory pancakes are real crowd-pleasers. The batter can be made a day ahead, as sweet potatoes do not oxidize: a big help! Serve with homemade Chutney (see page 188) and yogurt.

MAKES THIRTY-TWO 1½-INCH OR SIXTEEN 3-INCH LATKES

2 pounds sweet potatoes, peeled
4 extra-large eggs
⅓ cup chopped fresh cilantro
2 to 3 teaspoons curry powder
   Kosher salt and freshly ground black pepper
¼ cup cornmeal
2 to 3 tablespoons unbleached all-purpose flour
   Grapeseed oil for frying

With a box grater or food processor, grate the potatoes. In a small bowl, whisk the eggs. Add the cilantro and curry powder (to taste) and beat. Season with salt and pepper, add to the grated potatoes, and mix. Stir in the cornmeal and flour. Follow the cooking instructions at right to fry in grapeseed oil.

Parsnip and Potato Latkes

Parsnips and potatoes combine well, giving these latkes a hint of sweetness.

MAKES THIRTY-TWO 1½-INCH LATKES OR SIXTEEN 3-INCH LATKES

1 medium potato (8 to 10 ounces), peeled
2 medium parsnips (1 pound total), peeled
1 large carrot (about 4 ounces), peeled
1 tablespoon lemon juice
¼ cup unbleached all-purpose flour
2 extra-large eggs, lightly beaten
1 to 2 tablespoons minced fresh thyme
1 tablespoon minced fresh dill
¾ teaspoon kosher salt
¼ teaspoon freshly ground black pepper
   Grapeseed oil for frying

With a box grater or food processor, grate the potato, parsnips, and carrot into the same medium bowl to combine. With your hands or with a towel, squeeze out excess moisture and transfer the mixture to a large bowl. Add the lemon juice, flour, eggs, thyme (to taste), dill, salt, and pepper and stir to mix. Follow the cooking instructions below to fry in grapeseed oil.

Cooking Instructions

Prepare a baking sheet for draining the latkes by lining it with paper towels or parchment paper. Preheat the oven to 200°F.

Heat ½ inch of oil in a deep heavy skillet over medium-high heat until hot. (Test with a drop of batter—if the oil sizzles, it's hot enough. Taste this tidbit when cooked through to check salt and pepper seasoning. Adjust to taste before cooking rest of the latkes.) Spoon heaping tablespoons of the batter into the oil leaving ½ inch between pancakes and fry about 2 minutes. When the edges start to turn golden, flip the latkes once and then flatten slightly with the back of a spoon. Continue frying until golden brown, about 2 minutes. Transfer to the lined baking sheet to drain. Work in batches to fry the remaining batter, keeping the finished latkes warm in the preheated oven. Season with additional salt and black pepper to taste. Serve hot with accompaniments.

Pickled Grapes with Rosemary

Pickled grapes look like olives and are served like olives, but have a refreshingly unique, sweet-and-sour flavor with just a touch of heat. Serve with toothpicks as a cocktail nibble or toss them into salads. They're good for 1 week, refrigerated.

MAKES 4 CUPS

Pack the grapes into 1 quart-size or 2 pint-size glass jars or other glass containers with lids.

In a small saucepan, combine the vinegar, water, salt, sugar, garlic, rosemary, pepper flakes, and crushed coriander seeds. Bring to a simmer over medium heat. Remove from heat and let cool partially, about 20 minutes.

Pour the liquid into the jar(s), cover loosely, and allow to finish cooling, about 1 hour. Cover tightly and refrigerate for at least 4 hours.

3 cups stemmed mixed red and green seedless grapes, preferably organic (about 1 pound)

1½ cups white wine vinegar or white distilled vinegar

¾ cup water

1½ tablespoons kosher salt

1 tablespoon sugar

2 garlic cloves, lightly smashed
Leaves from 1 (3-inch) sprig fresh rosemary

⅜ teaspoon red pepper flakes or 1 teaspoon black peppercorns

1 tablespoon crushed coriander seeds

Black Bean Cakes with Tomato Salsa

Two of our daughters became vegetarians during their teenage years. While looking for an alternative to store-bought frozen veggie burgers, we were excited to find a class at JCC Manhattan's Patti Gelman Culinary Arts Center called Vegetarian Techniques. Their recipe for black bean cakes inspired this dish.

You can make these cakes whatever size you prefer—small, medium, or large. They can be served as hors d'oeuvres, as a plated first course, or as a main dish. We serve them with sliced avocado in addition to the salsa.

MAKES 12 LARGE, 24 MEDIUM, OR 36 BITE-SIZE CAKES

3 tablespoons extra-virgin olive oil

½ cup minced onion

½ cup minced red bell pepper

1 jalapeño pepper, seeded and minced

2 large garlic cloves, minced

1⅔ cups cooked soaked black beans, or canned

⅔ cup fine bread crumbs

⅓ cup fresh cilantro leaves, minced
Kosher salt and freshly ground black pepper

2 extra-large eggs or 3 egg whites, lightly beaten

¾ cup yellow cornmeal
Tomato Salsa (recipe follows)

In a medium skillet, heat 1 tablespoon of the oil over medium heat. Add the onion, red pepper, jalapeño, and garlic and cook, stirring occasionally, until softened, 2 to 3 minutes. Transfer to a food processor. Add the beans, bread crumbs, and cilantro to the food processor and season with salt and pepper. Add the beaten eggs and pulse twice to combine. Scrape down the bowl sides and transfer the mixture to a medium bowl.

Line a large plate with parchment paper. Spread the cornmeal on a second large plate. For large cakes, form the bean mixture into 3-inch round cakes; for medium, 2-inch cakes; for hors d'oeuvre size, 1-inch cakes. (The mixture will be wet and soft.) Gently dredge the cakes in the cornmeal and transfer to the lined plate. Refrigerate the cakes for at least 30 minutes or up to 12 hours.

Preheat the oven to 350°F.

Heat a large ovenproof skillet over medium-high heat. Add the remaining 2 tablespoons oil and cook the cakes, turning once, until browned, 2 to 3 minutes per side. Transfer the skillet to the oven and bake the cakes until cooked through, 18 to 20 minutes for 3-inch cakes; 10 to 15 minutes for 2-inch cakes; and 5 minutes for 1-inch cakes. Serve with the salsa.

Tomato Salsa

This superior salsa can accompany just about any southwest or Mexican dish. It keeps refrigerated for 5 or 6 days.

In a food processor, combine the chile peppers (to taste), onion, and garlic. Pulse until coarsely chopped. Add the tomatoes, cilantro, bell pepper, and lime juice (to taste) and pulse to combine all the ingredients. The salsa should be chunky; don't overprocess.

Transfer to a medium serving bowl and season with salt and pepper. Garnish with cilantro and serve.

MAKES 2 CUPS

1 to 2 fresh jalapeño or chipotle peppers, seeded

1 medium red onion, quartered

3 garlic cloves

3 large ripe tomatoes, quartered

½ cup cilantro leaves, plus more for garnish

½ red or yellow bell pepper, quartered, cored, and seeded

¼ to ½ cup fresh lime juice

Kosher salt and freshly ground black pepper

Potato and Zucchini Egg Tart (Feinkochen)

We love the combination of potatoes and eggs—it's so basic and comforting. Inspired by the classic Spanish tortilla (in Yiddish, *Feinkochen*), we've added sliced zucchini and grated Gruyère to our version. It's a perfect appetizer to serve at Shavuot, when it is traditional to eat dairy foods.

The tart works either as a plated appetizer served with mixed greens, or cut into squares as an hors d'oeuvre. Our Savory Plum-Tomato Jam (page 71) is a great garnish, but we've also included a recipe for a spicier condiment: Spanish *sofrito*, a classic Iberian sauce of aromatic ingredients cut into small pieces and sautéed in cooking oil. The egg tart can be served at room temperature.

SERVES 8 TO 10 AS AN APPETIZER OR MAKES 24 HORS D'OEUVRES

In a medium bowl, combine the potatoes and onion. In a broiler-safe 12-inch nonstick or cast-iron skillet, heat the oil over medium-low heat. Add the potato mixture, flatten as much as possible with a spatula, and cook until the potatoes are fork-tender but not brown, about 10 minutes. Shake the pan to make sure the whole mass isn't sticking and is cooking evenly. If the mixture starts to brown, lower the heat.

Place a colander over a bowl. Remove the pan from the heat and gently turn the potatoes and onions into the colander. Allow the oil to drain for at least 5 minutes. Season the mixture with 1 teaspoon of the salt while in the colander. Reserve the pan and the oil from the bowl. Use this oil to finish the dish and for the *sofrito*.

Pour off any additional oil left in the pan. In a large bowl, beat the eggs. Add the remaining 1 teaspoon salt and season with the pepper. Add the potato mixture and carefully combine. Let sit for at least 10 minutes to set.

Heat a grill pan over high heat until very hot. Brush the zucchini lightly with the reserved olive oil. Add the zucchini and grill until it has grill marks, 1 to 3 minutes. Flip the zucchini and repeat on the second side. Set aside.

Preheat the broiler. Heat 2 tablespoons of the reserved oil over medium heat in the broiler-safe skillet used previously. Add the egg mixture, sprinkle the cheese, and arrange the zucchini in a single layer over it. Cook until the eggs are cooked on the sides and partially set in the middle, about 5 minutes. Transfer the pan to the broiler and broil until the eggs are golden, 3 to 7 minutes.

Remove the pan from the broiler and let cool slightly. Run a knife or spatula around the edge and then under the egg tart to loosen it. Slide onto a serving plate or cutting board. Cut into slices, or into 2-inch squares to serve as hors d'oeuvres. Pass the *sofrito*, or add a small dollop to cut pieces.

1½ pounds Yukon Gold potatoes, halved and sliced paper thin

1 medium Vidalia onion, sliced paper thin (½ cup)

1 cup extra-virgin olive oil plus more for brushing

2 teaspoons kosher salt, plus more for seasoning

6 extra-large eggs
Freshly ground black pepper

10 ounces zucchini, sliced ⅛ inch thick

⅓ cup grated Gruyère or Parmesan cheese

Sofrito (recipe follows)

recipe continues

Sofrito

Sofrito is so delicious you may find yourself using it in various other ways—stirred into soups, spread on bread, and mixed in with grilled or roasted vegetables. Store in the refrigerator for at least two weeks.

Heat the oil in a medium skillet over medium heat. Add the onions, sugar, and salt. Reduce the heat to low and cook the onions, stirring occasionally, until caramelized, about 45 minutes. If the onions start to get very dark, lower the heat or add 1 tablespoon of water to slow down the cooking.

Add the tomatoes, paprika, and bay leaf and simmer over medium heat until the mixture gets very thick and the tomatoes start to separate from the oil, 10 to 15 minutes. Discard the bay leaf. Serve warm or at room temperature.

MAKES ABOUT 1 CUP

½ cup extra-virgin olive oil or oil reserved from the previous recipe

2 medium onions, minced (about 3 cups)

½ teaspoon sugar

1 teaspoon kosher salt

12 ounces canned diced tomatoes, drained

½ teaspoon smoked Spanish paprika or regular paprika

1 bay leaf

Salmon-Halibut Gefilte Fish with Apple Beet Horseradish Relish

We think of this recipe as our West Coast gefilte fish. Given to us by one of our sisters-in-law when we were lamenting the "smelly" task of making gefilte fish, this is a light, clean-tasting version of the traditional dish. It's also pretty and produces gefilte fish that taste and look more like ethereal French quenelles than the dish we know. We've come a long way since our grandmothers kept live carp in the bathtub for making gefilte fish!

Use the court bouillon (broth) immediately or let it cool completely, about 1 hour, before straining and storing it for later use. This recipe also doubles or triples nicely when feeding a big crowd. You can make it up to three days before serving.

MAKES 12 LARGE PIECES

Court Bouillon

- 4 quarts water
- ½ bunch fresh thyme
- ½ bunch fresh flat-leaf parsley
- ¼ teaspoon whole black peppercorns
- ¼ teaspoon whole fennel seeds
- 2½ cups dry white wine
- 1 medium onion, thinly sliced
- 1 medium carrot, peeled and sliced into ¼-inch rounds
- ½ lemon, cut into ¼-inch slices
- 2 bay leaves
- 1 tablespoon coarse salt

Fish

- 1½ pounds skinless filleted halibut
- 1½ pounds skinless filleted salmon
- 2 medium onions, grated (about 1 cup)
- 2 medium carrots, peeled and finely grated (about ½ cup)
  Finely grated zest of 1 lemon
- 1 tablespoon minced celery or minced fennel fronds
- 3 extra-large eggs
- 6 tablespoons matzah meal
- 6 tablespoons water
- 1 to 3 tablespoons sugar
- 1½ tablespoons kosher salt
- 1 teaspoon freshly ground black pepper
  Apple Beet Horseradish Relish (recipe follows)

For the court bouillon, fill a stockpot with the water. Place the thyme, parsley, peppercorns, and fennel seeds in a small piece of cheesecloth, knot to enclose, and add to the stockpot. Add the wine, onion, carrot, lemon, bay leaves, and salt. Cover the pot and bring to a simmer over medium-low heat. Remove the lid, and simmer gently 30 minutes. Remove and discard the cheesecloth package.

For the fish, cut the fillets into 1-inch pieces. Working in batches, pulse the fish in a food processor until roughly ground. Place the ground fish in a large bowl and add the onions, carrots, zest, celery or fennel fronds, eggs, matzah meal, water, sugar (to taste), salt, and pepper. Mix until just combined. Chill in the refrigerator for 30 minutes.

Fill a medium bowl with ice water. Wetting your hands in the water as you work, form ½-cup portions (3 to 4 ounces each) of the fish mixture into ovals. Bring the court bouillon to a gentle simmer. Add enough ovals to make one layer in the pot and poach until the ovals turn opaque and their shape is set, about 3 minutes. Add the rest. Simmer, continuing to poach the ovals until cooked through, 30 minutes. Remove the pan from the heat and allow the ovals to cool in the bouillon, about 20 minutes. Remove from the bouillon and transfer to a storage container. Ladle 2 tablespoons of the bouillon over the fish, cover, and chill. Serve with the horseradish relish.

Apple Beet Horseradish Relish

Refrigerate the relish until ready to use. It will last in the fridge for 2 months.

Preheat the oven to 400°F.

Coat the beets in olive oil and season with salt and pepper, then wrap in one or two foil packets. Place in a roasting pan and roast until fork-tender, about 60 minutes. Cool and peel.

In a food processor, combine the shallot, apple, and horseradish and pulse until coarsely chopped. Add the beets and parsley and pulse until coarsely chopped. Transfer to a medium bowl, add the vinegar and ¼ teaspoon salt, and mix.

MAKES 3 CUPS

2   to 3 beets (about 1 pound), stemmed and quartered

1   to 2 tablespoons olive oil
    Kosher salt and freshly ground black pepper

1   medium shallot, quartered

1   small Granny Smith apple, unpeeled, quartered, and cored

2   ounces fresh horseradish root, peeled and cut into ¼-inch pieces

⅓   cup fresh flat-leaf parsley leaves

2   tablespoons apple cider or sherry vinegar, or to taste

SOUPS

Yellow Cauliflower Soup with Parsley Oil 87

Stracciatella 89

Vegetarian Russian Borscht 90

Vietnamese Rice-Noodle Soup with Beef 93

Kasha and Mushroom Kreplach with Vegetable
Consommé 97

Tomato Soup with Gougères 99

Red Lentil Soup with Lime 102

Chicken Soup 106

Cilantro Matzah Balls 107

Fish Soup with Fennel and Saffron 109

Wild Mushroom Barley Soup 110

Yellow Cauliflower Soup with Parsley Oil

This soup might seem a bit ordinary because of the relatively few ingredients it calls for, but trust us, it's delicious. It's a great way to introduce cauliflower to a younger crowd, or to adults who are convinced they don't like it. If you can find yellow cauliflower, available in the fall at farmers' markets, by all means use it, as it makes the soup particularly beautiful. But don't hesitate to make it with everyday white cauliflower. You can also add roasted purple cauliflower flowerets as a garnish. The smooth texture of the soup belies the fact that this recipe doesn't have a drop of cream. The parsley oil can be made a few days ahead, as can the soup.

SERVES 8

In a large heavy-bottomed soup pot, heat the olive oil over medium heat. Reduce the heat to low, add the onions, and sweat until translucent, 15 to 20 minutes. Don't let the onions brown.

Add the cauliflower, season with salt, and add 1 cup of the water. Raise the heat slightly, cover the pot, and stew the cauliflower until tender, 15 to 18 minutes. Add the remaining 11 cups water; bring to a low simmer, and cook an additional 20 minutes uncovered.

Working in batches, transfer the cauliflower with its cooking liquid to a blender and purée to a very smooth, creamy consistency. Return the puréed soup to the pot. Let the soup rest for 20 minutes to allow the flavors to come together. (It will thicken slightly as it rests.)

Gently reheat the soup over low heat. If desired, thin the soup with ½ to 1 cup hot water. Ladle the soup into serving bowls, drizzle each portion with parsley oil, and season with pepper. Serve.

recipe continues

- 6 tablespoons extra-virgin olive oil
- 2 large onions (about 1¼ pounds), thinly sliced
- 2 heads yellow cauliflower or regular white cauliflower (about 3 pounds), broken into florets

  Kosher salt
- 12 cups cold water, plus more if needed
- ⅓ cup Parsley Oil (recipe follows) or olive oil

  Freshly ground black pepper

> If you don't have the time or inclination to make the parsley oil that garnishes the soup, here's a shortcut: Place ½ cup olive oil, parsley, and a pinch of salt in a food processor, pulse to finely mince the parsley, then process until the parsley colors the oil.

Parsley Oil

Did you ever wonder what those little green dots are that you find on the big white plates in elegant restaurants and cookbook photos? It's a green herb oil.

Fill a large bowl with water and add ice. Fill a very large pot with 2 quarts of water and bring to a boil. (A large pot ensures the water maintains a boil, which is essential for flash-cooking the parsley and preserving its color and taste.) Add the salt.

Place the parsley leaves and stems in a large strainer, lower it into the boiling water, and blanch the parsley until it's bright green, about 15 seconds. Immediately plunge the parsley into the ice bath. Drain the parsley and squeeze it dry in paper towels.

Put half the parsley leaves into a blender or a food processor. Add half the oil. Blend at medium speed, adding more oil if the blades are not turning freely, but reserving enough for the next batch. Increase the speed to high and continue blending until the oil is dark green, 2 to 4 minutes. Transfer to a bowl. Repeat with remaining parsley and oil, then combine both batches and quickly blend together.

Line a strainer with cheesecloth and strain the oil through it into a bowl, allowing the oil to drip slowly; don't squeeze the cheesecloth, as this will cloud the oil. For a deeper color and if you have the time, leave the purée in the fridge for 1 day before straining it. It can be stored in the refrigerator for up to 2 weeks.

NOTE: *This recipe can be made with other green herbs as well, such as basil, cilantro, dill, tarragon, or sorrel.*

MAKES ABOUT ⅓ CUP

½ cup kosher salt, plus more for seasoning

4 cups packed flat-leaf parsley leaves and thin stems

¾ cup grapeseed or olive oil

Stracciatella

In Italian, *stracciatella* means "little rags." This lovely soup was so named because of the raggedy egg strands running through it. In our preparation, we allow the eggs to set for a couple of minutes resulting in pillow-like strands. Chances are most of the ingredients are already in your pantry, which makes it an easy, any-time dish to put together. The classic is made with chicken stock, but our vegetarian version uses vegetable consommé.

SERVES 4

In a small bowl, whisk the egg and egg whites (or whites only) until frothy and well combined.

In a medium saucepan, combine the consommé and bay leaf and bring to a boil over high heat. Boil for 3 minutes and turn off the heat. Add the egg mixture all at once, immediately cover the pot, and allow the eggs to cook for 5 minutes. Don't stir the soup.

Using a small whisk, break up the egg strands. Stir in the spinach, parsley, and Parmesan. Cover the pan and allow the spinach to cook for 1 minute. Add salt and pepper to taste.

Remove and discard the bay leaf. Ladle the soup into 4 bowls, place a lemon half-moon in each bowl to garnish, and serve with additional Parmesan.

1 extra-large egg plus 2 whites, or 4 extra-large egg whites

6 cups Vegetable Consommé (page 98) or vegetable stock

1 bay leaf

2 cups packed baby spinach, stems removed, cut into thin ribbons

¼ cup chopped fresh flat-leaf parsley

⅓ cup grated Parmesan, plus more for serving

Kosher salt and freshly ground black pepper

½ lemon, sliced thinly

Vegetarian Russian Borscht

Borscht. The name itself takes you back to the Old Country. Whether or not your grandparents or great-grandparents came to this country from Russia, this updated, vegetarian version will warm your *kishkas*. Beets, the main ingredient, are known for their strong flavor, but here, long cooking mellows and sweetens them. We've added carrots and raisins for a touch more sweetness, plus potatoes and savoy cabbage, making this a substantial meal-in-a-bowl.

SERVES 8 TO 10

1 teaspoon caraway seeds

2 pounds beets, trimmed, peeled, and cut into ½-inch cubes (about 2 cups)

2 to 3 teaspoons kosher salt

9 to 10 cups vegetable stock or water or a combination

¾ pound Yukon Gold potatoes, peeled and cut in ½-inch cubes (about 1½ cups)

3 tablespoons unsalted butter

1 tablespoon extra-virgin olive oil

3 to 4 medium red onions, chopped (about 2 cups)

2 medium celery stalks, chopped

2 large carrots, peeled, sliced into ½-inch-thick half moons

1 pound cored savoy or green cabbage, chopped (about 4 cups)

2 to 4 tablespoons chopped fresh dill

2 to 3 tablespoons cider vinegar, plus more as needed

Juice of 1 lemon (2 tablespoons)

2 tablespoons plus 1 teaspoon honey

2½ cups tomato purée

1 to 2 tablespoons raisins (optional)

Freshly ground black pepper

Garnishes

Sour cream or yogurt

Chopped fresh dill

In a small skillet, toast the caraway seeds over medium heat, stirring, until lightly colored, 3 to 5 minutes. Transfer the seeds to a small bowl and set aside.

In an enamel or heavy-bottomed pot, combine the beets and 1 teaspoon salt with 8 cups (2 quarts) of stock and bring to a boil. Reduce the heat and simmer, partially covered, until the beets are tender, about 10 minutes. Add the potatoes and continue to simmer until the vegetables are fork-tender, 10 to 15 minutes. Using a slotted spoon, transfer the vegetables to a medium bowl and set aside. Reserve the cooking liquid.

In a heavy-bottomed soup pot, heat the butter and oil over medium heat. Add the onions, stir to coat with the oil, and sauté for 1 minute. Add the caraway seeds and 1 teaspoon salt to taste and continue to sauté until the onions are translucent, about 5 minutes. Add the celery, carrots, and cabbage. Add the reserved cooking liquid and bring to a boil. Reduce the heat and simmer until all the vegetables are fork-tender, 10 to 15 minutes. Add the reserved potatoes and beets, dill (to taste), vinegar (to taste), lemon juice, honey, tomato purée, and raisins (if using) and season with salt and pepper to taste.

Cover the pot and simmer slowly for 30 to 40 minutes. Add more stock as needed. Adjust the seasonings, adding more vinegar if needed. Transfer the soup to bowls, garnish with the sour cream and dill, and serve.

Vietnamese Rice-Noodle Soup with Beef

This recipe may seem like a bit of an outlier, but we are including it because it comes from a great class on Vietnamese cooking that is very popular at JCC Manhattan's Patti Gelman Culinary Arts Center. Many of us have had this wonderful soup—known as pho—in Vietnamese restaurants. Made from beef bones, onions, ginger, and lots of fragrant spices, it's delicate yet bracing—one of those dishes you can't get enough of. Everyone around the table gets to personalize their bowl since lots of garnishes, including basil, chiles, and lime, are passed around. Did we mention that thin slices of raw beef are cooked in each bowl by adding the hot soup just before serving?

This isn't a difficult dish to make, but it does require attention. Please read the recipe through before making it.

SERVES 8

Char the ginger and onions: Hold the ginger with tongs over an open flame or place it on a medium-hot electric burner. Char, turning, until the edges are slightly blackened and the ginger is fragrant, 3 to 4 minutes. Char the onions in the same way until blackened. Peel and discard the blackened skin of the ginger and onions, then rinse and set aside.

In a large stockpot, bring the water to a boil.

Meanwhile, place the bones and beef chuck in a second large pot and add water to cover. Bring the bones and chuck to a boil and boil vigorously for 5 minutes. (This cleans the bones and meat and reduces impurities that can cloud the broth.)

Using tongs, carefully transfer the bones and beef to the first pot of boiling water. (Discard the water in which the meat was cooked.) When the water in the first pot returns to a boil, reduce the heat to medium-low. Cook 5 to 10 minutes, skimming the surface often to remove any foam and fat until the broth is clear. Add the charred ginger and onions, soy sauce, and sugar. Simmer until the chuck is tender, about 40 minutes.

Remove 1 piece of the chuck from the simmering broth and submerge it in cool water for 10 minutes. (This prevents the meat from darkening and drying out.) Drain, transfer the chuck to a plate, cover with foil, and set aside.

Add the salt and continue to simmer the broth, skimming as necessary, for at least 1 hour.

Place the star anise and cloves in a spice bag, or secure them in a piece of cheesecloth. When the broth has been simmering about 1 hour, add the spices. Let the spices infuse the broth until it's fragrant, simmering about 30 minutes more. Remove and discard the spice bag.

2 (3-inch) pieces ginger with skin, halved lengthwise and bruised with the flat of a knife

2 large yellow onions (about 1½ pounds), unpeeled

6 quarts water

5 pounds beef marrow or knuckle bones

1 2-pound piece beef chuck, halved

¼ cup soy sauce

3 tablespoons sugar

1 tablespoon sea salt or kosher salt

10 whole star anise

6 whole cloves

1 pound dried 1/16-inch-wide rice-stick noodles

½ pound beef sirloin, slightly frozen

ingredients continue

recipe continues

Garnishes

- 1 pound bean sprouts
- 10 sprigs fresh Asian basil, Italian basil, or fresh tarragon
- 6 Thai bird chiles or 1 serrano chile, cut into thin rings
- 1 lime, cut into 6 thin wedges
- ½ onion, sliced paper thin
- 3 scallions, cut into thin rings
- ⅓ cup cilantro, chopped
  Freshly ground black pepper

Fill a large pot with water and bring to a boil. Remove the pot from the heat and add the noodles. Let stand until the noodles are tender-firm, 6 to 8 minutes. Drain well and rinse under cold water. Cover and set aside.

To serve, heat 8 soup bowls by stacking them in the oven at its lowest temperature (wear oven mitts when handling the hot bowls) or by pouring boiling water into them, then drying them well. Slice the reserved chuck thinly with the grain and shred with your fingers. Slice the partially frozen sirloin against the grain into paper-thin slices. Place the garnishes of sprouts, herbs, chiles, and lime wedges in small serving bowls.

Place the cooked noodles in the bowls. Divide the shredded chuck among the bowls and top with the raw sirloin. Bring the broth to a rolling boil and ladle 2 to 3 cups into each bowl. The broth will cook the raw beef instantly. Garnish with the sliced onion, scallions, and cilantro. Serve immediately, inviting guests to garnish the soup with the bean sprouts, herbs, chiles, squeezes of lime juice, and grindings of black pepper.

Kasha and Mushroom Kreplach with Vegetable Consommé

Italians have their tortellini, the Chinese have their wontons, and Jews have their kreplach: egg pasta shaped into triangular dumplings and traditionally stuffed with meat or chicken, but made here with mushrooms and kasha. These delicacies are usually eaten at the Jewish High Holidays, particularly at the meal before the fast of Yom Kippur. Among the many explanations for why we eat kreplach before Yom Kippur, one of our favorites is that we should eat stuffed foods to symbolize our wish for a full New Year. To cut down on the time and worry associated with creating a perfect kreplach, we suggest two shortcuts—wonton wrappers and an inexpensive dumpling press.

This is a great vegetarian alternative to chicken soup. The consommé is very light and it works well with traditional accompaniments, such as matzah balls (page 107).

The broth alone is an essential base recipe in our kitchen, used as a stock for other soups and sauces. You can vary the vegetables according to season or what you have on hand. When we're doing a big dinner, and prepping a lot, we fill a stockpot and add all the saved potato skins, scallion tops, herb stems, carrot peels, zucchini ends, leek greens, etc., to create our own clear, clean-tasting broth. Or you can stockpile trimmings in a resealable plastic bag and store in the freezer for another day. If you don't have trimmings, add 2 cups of roughly chopped non-cabbage-family vegetables for the best stock flavors.

Kasha and Mushroom Kreplach

Kasha, or buckwheat groats, and mushrooms pair perfectly to create a hearty, meaty filling for these dumplings. These can and should be made ahead of time and stored. You can freeze them for 2 months in plastic containers between layers of parchment or wax paper. Refrigerated, they last 4 days. The crumbled dried mushrooms are available at many markets. You can also use porcini powder and skip the straining of the broth.

MAKES ABOUT 50 KREPLACH

- 2 cups Vegetable Consommé (page 98), vegetable stock, or mushroom broth
- 2 tablespoons crumbled dried mushrooms, any kind
- 1 tablespoon extra-virgin olive oil
- 2 medium onions, finely chopped (about 2 cups)
- 1 egg white, beaten until frothy
- ½ cup whole or medium buckwheat groats
- 2 cups finely chopped fresh mushrooms, cremini or white button
- 2 medium carrots, peeled and finely chopped (about ½ cup)
- ¼ cup finely chopped fresh dill
- ½ teaspoon kosher salt
- ½ teaspoon freshly ground black pepper
- ½ teaspoon truffle oil (optional)
- 1 (10-ounce) package round gyoza or wonton wrappers
  Olive oil, for the steamer

Bring the stock to a boil in a medium saucepan. Add the dried mushrooms and remove the pan from the heat. Allow the mushrooms to soften, about 20 minutes.

Using a slotted or mesh spoon, remove the mushrooms and set aside. Allow the stock to rest about 5 minutes, then slowly strain it through a fine-mesh sieve. Return the soaking liquid to the saucepan.

recipe continues

In a large skillet, heat the olive oil over medium heat. Add the onions and cook, stirring, until they begin to caramelize, 10 to 12 minutes. Remove the onions from the pan and set aside, reserving the skillet. Return the stock to a boil.

In a small bowl, combine the egg white and groats and blend with a fork. Transfer the mixture to the skillet and cook over medium heat, stirring to break up the groats, until they begin to brown, about 4 minutes. Return the onions to the skillet and mix until the groats are well separated and dry. Add the reserved dried mushrooms and the fresh mushrooms and mix well, about 2 minutes. Add the boiling stock and continue mixing. Reduce the heat to low, cover, and simmer for 10 minutes. Remove the skillet from the heat and stir in the carrots, dill, salt, pepper, and truffle oil, if using. Adjust the seasoning.

To form the kreplach, fill a small bowl with warm water. Place 1 wrapper on a flat surface and use a finger or pastry brush dipped in the water to moisten the edge. Place 1 heaping teaspoon of the filling in the center.

Fold in half to make a half moon or triangle (depending on the wrapper shape) and seal the edges by pressing them together all along their edges with the prongs of a fork. (You can also use a dumpling press to do this.) Place the formed kreplach on a parchment-lined baking sheet, making sure that they do not overlap. At this point, you can freeze them or store them in the refrigerator for later use, separating the layers with parchment paper.

Use a bamboo steamer or a roasting pan with a fitted rack to steam the kreplach: Lightly oil the steamer basket or rack. If using the roasting pan, fill it with ½ inch of water and bring the water to a simmer over medium heat. Working in batches, place as many kreplach in the steamer or on the rack as will fit without touching each other. Cover the bamboo basket or cover the pan with foil and steam until the edges are tender, 3 to 5 minutes. Repeat with the remaining kreplach.

Transfer the kreplach to the hot soup or place them on platters and keep them warm in a 200°F oven.

Vegetable Consommé

Combine all the ingredients except the salt and kreplach in a large stockpot.

Bring to a boil, reduce the heat, and simmer for 1½ hours.

Allow the stock to cool in the pot. Strain out the vegetables and peppercorns. Add the salt, taste, and adjust the seasoning, if needed. Serve with the kreplach.

MAKES 2 QUARTS

4 quarts water

3 medium leeks, white and light green parts, trimmed, halved lengthwise, and cut into 2-inch lengths

4 large carrots, cut into 2-inch pieces (about 1 cup)

1 large onion, root end removed, skin left on, quartered

2 large parsnips, peeled, cut into 2-inch pieces (about 1 cup)

1 small celery root, peeled and cut into eighths

1 bunch fresh dill (stems included)

4 medium celery stalks, cut into 2-inch pieces (about 1 cup)

1 bunch fresh flat-leaf parsley (stems included)

4 sprigs fresh thyme, about 2 inches each (optional)

8 whole black peppercorns

2 to 3 cups vegetable trimmings, such as mushroom stems, pea pods, zucchini ends, potato skins, parsley root, onion skins, squash skins, tomato trimmings, or chopped assorted vegetables (non-cabbage-family)

1 teaspoon kosher salt, plus more if needed

Tomato Soup with Gougères

The recipe archive of the Patti Gelman Culinary Arts Center at JCC Manhattan has nineteen tomato soup recipes. We added eight more to the group from our personal recipe collections. After weeks of testing, this version emerged as our favorite. Nothing is more satisfying than a bowl of tomato soup with a cheesy bite. Grilled cheese is tried and true but our *gougères*, cheese-flavored puffs, are a real crowd-pleaser. The soup is best made during the summer when tomatoes overflow on market tables or are hanging from the vine. But because this soup is requested so often in our homes, we started making it during the winter with two 28-ounce cans of plum tomatoes with juice, which works beautifully with an added pinch of sugar and ½ cup of 2% milk.

SERVES 8

In a large heavy-bottomed pot, heat the oil over medium heat. Add the onions and cook, stirring, until softened, 3 to 5 minutes. Add the garlic, season lightly with salt, and sauté until the onions are translucent and the garlic is softened, about 3 minutes.

Transfer about one-third of the mixture to a bowl and set aside. Tie basil stems into a bunch with unbleached kitchen twine. Add the tomatoes and basil stems to the pot, reduce the heat, and simmer until the mixture is sauce-like, about 15 minutes. Remove and discard the stems. Transfer the mixture to a food processor, blender, or food mill, purée, and return to the pot.

Add the reserved onion mixture to the pot. Chop 1½ cups of the basil leaves and stir them into the soup, adding a little more oil, if you like. Adjust the seasoning. Garnish each portion with a drizzle of olive oil, Parmesan if you like, and additional basil. Pass the gougères separately.

recipe continues

1 cup extra-virgin olive oil, plus more for serving

2 large onions, finely chopped (about 2½ cups)

8 to 12 garlic cloves, minced (about 3 tablespoons)

Kosher salt

1 bunch fresh basil, stems and leaves separated (approximately 2 cups leaves)

4 pounds very ripe tomatoes, peeled, cored, and roughly chopped

½ cup freshly grated Parmesan (optional)

Gougères (recipe follows)

To make this soup into a *pappa al pomodoro*—tomato bread soup— stir 1 cup of dried ciabatta or baguette crumbs into the soup just before serving. Then sprinkle each portion with a drizzle of olive oil, additional bread crumbs, a basil leaf, and grated Parmesan.

Gougères

Elegant yet simple, these cheesy puffs are made by adding cheese to a basic French *pâte à choux* (cream-puff pastry). Once you've conquered this recipe, you can experiment with the dough: profiteroles, éclairs, and beignets all lie ahead. You'll feel like a real French chef!

Preheat the oven to 375°F. Line a baking sheet with parchment paper.

In a small heavy skillet, toast the dill seeds over moderate heat, stirring, until fragrant and slightly darker, 3 to 4 minutes. Be careful not to burn them. Transfer seeds to a small bowl and cool. With a mortar and pestle or in an electric spice grinder, grind seeds coarsely. Set aside.

To make the *pâte à choux*, combine the water, salt, and butter in a medium saucepan. Bring to a boil over high heat, stirring frequently. Remove the pan from the heat and add the flour all at once. Beat with a wooden spoon to create a smooth dough. Return the pan to medium heat and stir until the dough forms a ball.

Transfer the dough to the bowl of an electric mixer fitted with the paddle attachment. (A medium bowl with handheld mixer may also be used.) With the mixer on medium speed, add 2 eggs, one at a time, waiting until the first has been incorporated before adding the second. The batter should be stiff enough to hold soft peaks and fall softly from a spoon. If the batter is too stiff, beat another egg in a separate bowl and add to the batter, beating on high speed until you obtain the desired consistency. Stir the cheese and 1 teaspoon of the ground dill seeds into the mixture.

Use two spoons to shape the dough into 1-inch drops on the baking sheet, spacing them about 1 inch apart. Sprinkle the puffs with the remaining dill seeds.

Bake the puffs until golden brown, 20 to 25 minutes. Cool on the pan or on a rack. They are best served fresh out of the oven with the soup.

MAKES ABOUT 20 GOUGÈRES

2 teaspoons dill seeds

½ cup water

¼ teaspoon kosher salt

4 tablespoons (½ stick) unsalted butter, cut into ¼-inch cubes

½ cup unbleached all-purpose flour

2 or 3 extra-large eggs

¾ cup grated Gruyère or Cheddar cheese

Red Lentil Soup with Lime

Lentils have played an important role in Jewish history, dating back to the book of Genesis when Esau traded his birthright to Jacob in exchange for a bowl of "red stuff," which we're pretty sure was a red lentil stew. Many soups, especially ones that use legumes or beans as their main ingredient, take a long time to cook. But lentils are a cook's shortcut to a healthy, protein-laden soup. Once you have the vegetable or chicken stock made, you can make this soup in less than 40 minutes.

SERVES 6

3 tablespoons extra-virgin olive oil, plus more for drizzling

1 large onion, chopped (about 1¼ cups)

2 garlic cloves, minced (about 2 teaspoons)

1 tablespoon tomato paste

1 teaspoon ground cumin

¼ teaspoon kosher salt, plus more if needed

¼ teaspoon ground black pepper

Pinch of ground cayenne or chili powder, plus more to garnish

1 quart chicken stock or vegetable stock

2 cups water

1 cup red lentils, rinsed and picked over

1 large carrot, peeled and diced (about ¼ cup)

Juice of ½ lime, plus more if needed

3 tablespoons chopped fresh cilantro

1 lime, cut into 6 wedges

In a large, heavy-bottomed pot, heat the oil over high heat. Add the onion and garlic and sauté until golden, about 4 minutes. Stir in the tomato paste, cumin, salt, pepper, and cayenne or chili powder and sauté for 2 minutes.

Add the stock, water, lentils, and carrot. Bring to a simmer, partially cover the pot, and reduce the heat to medium-low. Simmer until the lentils are soft, about 30 minutes. Adjust the seasoning with salt, if necessary.

Using a blender or food processor, purée half the soup then return it to the pot. The finished soup should be somewhat chunky.

Reheat the soup if necessary. Stir in the lime juice and some of the cilantro right before serving. Transfer the soup to bowls, serve with a drizzle of oil, the lime wedges, and the remaining cilantro, and dust lightly with additional cayenne or chili powder.

OPERATION CHICKEN SOUP

Operation Chicken Soup is a key program of JCC Manhattan. For the last fifteen years, teens have gathered on Tuesdays and Wednesdays after doing their homework (or maybe instead of doing their homework) to cook. They are cooking not for themselves, but for their neighbors and those in need. In the beginning, they made actual chicken soup every week to serve to the homeless in the neighborhood. Lately, recipe selections have evolved to include all sorts of new dishes, but Operation Baked Ziti doesn't have the same ring to it, and certainly doesn't speak to the core of what Operation Chicken Soup is all about. Teenagers join the program for many reasons but mostly it boils down to this: They cannot reconcile the poverty they see on the streets or on the news with their own good fortune.

What never ceases to amaze us is the magic that happens when the teenagers come to cook. They listen, learn, ask questions, share stories, and feel their own incredible power to make a difference in their world, in their neighborhood, in the life of a single person who might otherwise not have had a meal to eat that very night.

Chicken Soup

To quote food critic Mimi Sheraton, chicken soup is the "panacea for all ills whether physical or emotional." When the three of us think of the food we most connect with nurturing, it is homemade chicken soup that comes to mind. Whether it is the aroma of chicken soup simmering in preparation for Shabbat, or a container of soup that travels up to our kids' universities, or a warm bowl to soothe your soul on a blustery day, chicken soup is a universal comfort food.

SERVES ABOUT 12

6 pounds chicken parts; or 2 whole chickens, including backs, wings, and necks, cut into eighths

About 6 quarts water, as needed

3 medium leeks, white and light green parts only, halved

2 medium parsnips, peeled and cut in 3 chunks each

1 large onion, quartered

1 bunch fresh dill including stems, tied with kitchen twine

1 bunch fresh flat-leaf parsley including stems, tied with kitchen twine

8 medium carrots, peeled

6 celery stalks

1 small celery root, peeled and cut into 2-inch chunks (optional)

20 peppercorns

4 small carrots, peeled and cut into matchsticks (about 1 cup), for garnish (optional)

Kosher salt and freshly ground black pepper

Rinse the chicken under cold water. Remove any excess fat.

Place the chicken in a large stockpot. Add the water to cover the chicken by at least 4 inches and bring to a boil. Reduce the heat to low and simmer, using a skimmer to remove surface foam as it forms, about 30 minutes.

Add the leeks, parsnips, onion, dill, parsley, whole carrots, celery, celery root, if using, and peppercorns. Simmer until the chicken has begun to fall from the bones and the vegetables are very soft, 1 to 1¼ hours.

Using a slotted spoon, remove the chicken and set it aside for another use. Strain the soup using a fine metal or *chinois* strainer and either keep the vegetables for serving or discard. Discard the herbs. (For a very clear soup, strain the soup through cheesecloth.) Set the soup aside to cool.

After the soup has cooled, remove any remaining fat from the surface. The broth can be kept in the refrigerator for up to 4 days or stored in the freezer for up to 6 months. Before serving, heat the soup over low heat. Add the matchstick carrots, if using, and simmer until the carrots are tender-crisp, 3 to 5 minutes. Season with salt and pepper and serve with Cilantro Matzah Balls (page 107) or Kasha and Mushroom Kreplach (page 97), and additional vegetables and chicken from the soup, if desired.

Here's a tip from Jewish cookbook writer Helen Nash: If you don't have the time to cool your soup completely, you can still remove the excess fat. Wet a paper towel and draw it through the soup. The fat will remain on the cloth. (Don't wring out the cloth over the soup!)

Cilantro Matzah Balls

Cilantro in matzah balls? And a touch of jalapeño? You won't be surprised that this recipe comes by way of Mexico City. In 1900, there were only around 100 Jews living in Mexico. Today the number is somewhere around 60,000. This vibrant community is made up of both Ashkenazim and Sephardim, so it makes perfect sense that a traditional Ashkenazi delicacy is laced with local flavors. Green flecks of cilantro impart a bright citrus note. And the jalapeño adds a touch of spice—similar to the way some Hungarian Jews spiced their matzah balls with hot paprika. The color and flavors are perfect allusions to spring at your seder table, or all year-round. We find these matzah balls land directly in the middle of the floater vs. sinker debate—an ideal balance.

Serve the matzah balls in Chicken Soup (page 106) or Vegetable Consommé (page 98) with carrot sticks or carrot rounds (traditional for the Jewish New Year to symbolize a full and round year) and additional chopped cilantro.

NOTE: *We call for chicken fat or oil as our grandmothers swear that it's the chicken fat that makes the best matzah balls. The easiest way to get pure chicken fat is to skim it off your chicken soup pot. Just keep the fat in a container and place it in the freezer for later use. But rest assured, for those of you who cringe at the thought of using schmaltz (chicken fat), these matzah balls are also delicious made with grapeseed oil.*

MAKES 24 SMALL MATZAH BALLS

In a blender or food processor, combine the eggs, fat or oil, cilantro leaves and stems, and jalapeño. Blend until smooth. Transfer to a medium bowl and add the matzah meal, seltzer, salt, and pepper. Stir until well combined. Cover and refrigerate for 1 hour.

Bring a large pot of stock or generously salted water to a boil. Using wet hands, gently shape the matzah meal mixture into walnut-size balls. Drop the balls into the boiling water a few at a time. Once all the balls are in the pot, return to a boil, and reduce the heat to a simmer. Cover and cook until tender, about 30 minutes. Turn off heat and leave them in the hot cooking liquid for 15 minutes for extra fluffiness, or transfer to the chicken soup immediately.

4 extra-large eggs

¼ cup chicken fat, or grapeseed oil, or combination

½ cup cilantro leaves, plus tender stems

¼ jalapeño pepper, seeds removed

1 cup matzah meal

½ cup seltzer

1 teaspoon kosher salt

½ teaspoon freshly ground black pepper

Chicken stock or water for cooking

Fish Soup with Fennel and Saffron

Fish with fennel and saffron is a mainstay of French Mediterranean cooking. If you can't hop on a plane to France, the aromas created while this soup simmers will transport you across the Atlantic. Serve with crusty bread, a light salad, and a glass of wine, and you'll have a luxurious meal. This is also a great one-pot meal for lunch or dinner during Sukkot, the Jewish harvest festival. In the Northeast, it's often chilly in the sukkah—the small huts built in the fall in observance of the holiday—and this is a perfect soup to keep you warm.

SERVES 4 AS A MAIN, 8 AS A FIRST COURSE

Tie the bay leaf, ½ teaspoon fennel seeds, coriander seeds, and white peppercorns in cheesecloth and set aside.

In an enamel or heavy-bottomed stockpot, heat the oil over medium heat. Add the onions and sauté for 3 to 5 minutes. Add the garlic and sauté until the onions are translucent, 2 to 3 minutes. Add the wine and bring to a boil. Add the spice bundle, crushed fennel seeds, fennel, tomatoes, and stock. Return to a boil, reduce the heat to low, and simmer for 15 minutes.

Season the fish with salt. Add the fish, saffron threads, and thyme to the soup and simmer until the fish is cooked through, about 25 minutes. Discard the spice bundle and thyme sprigs. Season with salt and pepper. Add the parsley and serve.

- 1 bay leaf
- ½ teaspoon fennel seeds plus 2 tablespoons crushed fennel seeds
- ½ teaspoon coriander seeds
- 6 white peppercorns
- 3 tablespoons olive oil
- 3 medium onions, finely diced (about 1 cup)
- 2 garlic cloves, minced
- ¼ cup dry white wine
- 2 medium fennel bulbs, halved and sliced ⅛ inch thick (about 2 cups)
- 4 cups roughly diced tomatoes, fresh or canned
- 2 quarts fish stock or vegetable stock
- 1½ pounds firm white fish, such as halibut, haddock, or cod, preferably a combination, cut into 8 equal chunks
  Kosher or sea salt
- ½ teaspoon saffron threads
- 4 fresh thyme sprigs
  Coarsely ground black pepper, to taste
- ¼ cup chopped fresh flat-leaf parsley

Wild Mushroom Barley Soup

This light, tomato-based barley soup uses a variety of mushrooms and allows you to experiment with many different types. Almost every farmers' market has a mushroom stand and local supermarkets now carry a full array of wild and cultivated mushrooms. We've especially loved discovering Japanese enoki mushrooms, which are particularly tasty when frizzled and used as a garnish, as we do here. We cook the components of the soup separately then assemble them just before serving to ensure a clear, clean modern flavor. You can enrich the flavor by adding butter to the soup just before serving—but, of course, this is optional.

SERVES 8

To cook the barley, bring 1½ cups water to a boil. Add the barley, reduce to a simmer, and cook for 30 to 40 minutes. Transfer to a medium bowl and set aside.

Fill a medium pot with 2 quarts water and add the dried mushrooms. Bring to a boil, turn off the heat, and allow the mushrooms to rehydrate, about 30 minutes. Spoon out the mushroom pieces, chop, and set aside. Strain the cooking water to remove all the sediment and set aside.

In a heavy-bottomed pot, heat 2 tablespoons of the olive oil over medium-low heat. Add the leeks and shallots and sauté until they begin to color, about 5 minutes. Add the celery root, carrots, and garlic and sauté until the vegetables soften, 5 to 7 minutes. Add the soaked mushrooms, their soaking water, the tomatoes, stock, and thyme. Simmer for about 30 minutes, until the broth is flavorful and the soaked mushrooms are tender. Discard the thyme sprigs.

Meanwhile, heat 1 tablespoon of the olive oil in a large skillet over medium-high heat. Add one-third of the wild mushrooms and sauté until golden, 3 to 4 minutes. Repeat twice with oil and the remaining mushrooms. Add the salt and pepper and set aside.

If using the enoki mushrooms, heat 1 teaspoon olive oil in the same skillet over high heat. Add the enoki and cook, stirring, until frizzled and golden, about 3 minutes. Set aside for garnish.

Add the sherry and the barley to the soup pot and simmer. It will take about 10 minutes to reheat. Just before serving, add the wild mushrooms, half of the parsley, and the butter, if using. Ladle into bowls when piping hot, sprinkle with the remaining parsley, garnish with enoki, if using, and serve.

½ cup pearled barley

2 quarts plus 1½ cups water

2 ounces dried porcini mushrooms

6 tablespoons extra-virgin olive oil, plus 1 teaspoon if needed

3 leeks, white and light green parts only, washed, halved, and sliced into ⅛-inch half circles

6 medium shallots, diced (about 6 tablespoons)

1 cup celery root, peeled and chopped

3 medium carrots, peeled, cut into ½-inch discs (about ¾ cup)

1 medium garlic bulb, cloves separated and minced

8 plum tomatoes, seeded and diced; or 1 (28-ounce) can diced tomatoes, drained, juice reserved for another use

2 quarts vegetable stock

6 fresh thyme sprigs, tied with unbleached kitchen twine

3 pounds assorted wild mushrooms, such as shiitake, cremini, oyster, chanterelle, and maitake, sliced thin or torn into pieces

1 tablespoon kosher salt

1 teaspoon freshly ground black pepper

2 ounces enoki mushrooms, for garnish (optional)

1 cup dry sherry or dry white wine

½ bunch fresh flat-leaf parsley, chopped

2 tablespoons unsalted butter (optional)

SALADS

Orange, Frisée, and Radish Salad

We love radishes of all kinds, and the variety available today is so much more extensive than what we had growing up. They add crispness and bite to this salad, which also features frisée lettuce and juicy orange segments. You'll need to cut the oranges into pithless segments called *supremes*, a task that's easy to do (see box). You can do this a day ahead, which makes putting the salad together even easier. This makes a lovely main course if you add sliced poached chicken breast (page 120) or shredded leftover chicken.

SERVES 4 TO 6 AS A SIDE

In a large bowl, combine the frisée, radishes, oranges, chives, and tarragon.

In a small bowl, whisk together the orange juice, olive oil, vinegar, and shallots. Add the salt and season with the pepper.

Add the dressing to the salad, toss, and serve.

CITRUS *SUPREMES*

To cut oranges or other citrus fruit into *supremes*, first cut off both ends deeply enough to reveal the fruit. Place the fruit on one end and, with a sharp knife, remove the peel and pith by cutting from the top to bottom. The white lines of the membranes will now be visible. Working over a bowl to catch the juice, insert your knife as close to a membrane as possible and make a slice parallel to it, right to the center of the fruit. Find the membrane on the other side of that fruit section and make another slice down to the center of the fruit. Remove and reserve the tender, juicy segment. (The membranes will remain attached to the core of the fruit.) Continue in this way until you've removed all the segments.

Salad

4 cups frisée torn in pieces; or 8 medium endives, cut in ¼-inch slices

2 cups thinly sliced assorted radishes, such as watermelon, lime, breakfast, or red radishes

Supremes from 6 naval or blood oranges (see box)

12 to 15 chives, cut into 1-inch lengths

2 tablespoons snipped fresh tarragon leaves

Dressing

¼ cup orange juice

½ cup extra-virgin olive oil

⅓ cup sherry wine vinegar or apple cider vinegar

1 tablespoon chopped shallot

Pinch kosher salt

Freshly ground black pepper

Roasted Red Pepper, Tomato, and Parsley Salad

Here is a new way to prepare and combine some typical salad ingredients. We roast the peppers to achieve a smoky flavor that pairs well with the tomatoes. Then we use whole Italian flat-leaf parsley leaves as lettuce greens. This may seem unusual to you, but trust us. Finally, sautéing the garlic in oil mellows its flavor, while the toasted crushed cumin seeds add zest to the dressing. Gaeta or Niçoise olives and feta cheese are wonderful optional additions.

SERVES 6 AS A SIDE

10 plum tomatoes, halved lengthwise; or 4 pints grape or cherry tomatoes

¼ cup plus 1 tablespoon extra-virgin olive oil

Kosher salt and freshly ground black pepper

10 large bell peppers, red, yellow, and/or orange

1 teaspoon cumin seeds, toasted

3 to 4 garlic cloves, thinly sliced

3 cups fresh flat-leaf parsley leaves

2 to 3 tablespoons lemon juice

Preheat the oven to 450°F. Line a medium baking pan or baking sheet with parchment paper.

In a medium bowl, combine the tomatoes with the 1 tablespoon oil and toss. Season with salt and pepper. Place the tomatoes cut-side up on the sheet (or spread out the whole grape tomatoes). Roast until the tomatoes have browned, 40 to 50 minutes. Set aside.

Meanwhile, char the peppers over an open burner flame, turning as the skin blisters, 12 to 15 minutes. Or preheat the broiler and place the peppers on a large baking sheet and broil close to the heat source, turning every 10 minutes or so, until the peppers are charred on all sides and very soft, 30 to 35 minutes. Place the roasted peppers in a paper bag and close the bag. The steam created inside the bag will help loosen the skins, making peeling the peppers easier. Let them cool long enough so you can handle them, then peel them. Halve the peppers and discard their peel, seeds, and stems. Cut each half lengthwise into thirds and set aside.

Meanwhile, toast the cumin seeds in a small pan over low heat, stirring occasionally, until lightly colored and fragrant, 3 to 5 minutes. Transfer the seeds to a small bowl and set aside. Add the ¼ cup oil to the pan and sauté the garlic over low heat, stirring occasionally, until the garlic begins to color. Remove from the heat and set aside.

Using a mortar and pestle, partially crush the cumin seeds. You can also grind them coarsely in a spice grinder.

Pile the parsley leaves on a platter. In a large bowl, combine the tomatoes, peppers, garlic with its oil, crushed cumin, and lemon juice and toss. Season with salt, transfer onto the parsley leaves, and serve.

Plum and Spinach Salad

These days, our recipes need to be adapted for people with various food restrictions and preferences. The traditional preparation of spinach salad with bacon doesn't work for our kosher and vegetarian diners. So instead, we rely on plums and soy bacon. Deep purple or yellow plums or a combination of both work beautifully in this salad. This is a great do-ahead and assemble-just-before-serving recipe. It's also perfect for picnics, barbecues, or a light summer meal with a rosé.

SERVES 8 AS A SIDE

In a medium bowl, combine the onion with 1 cup hot water and soak for 30 minutes (this mellows the flavor).

Meanwhile, to make the dressing, whisk together the oil, mustard, and vinegar in a small bowl. Season with the salt and pepper.

Drain the onions and transfer them to a large salad or mixing bowl. Add the spinach, bacon, eggs, and chives. Add the dressing and toss. Add the plums and toss again gently. Adjust the seasoning and serve.

Salad

1 small red onion, halved lengthwise and sliced paper thin

1½ pounds baby spinach, washed and tough stems removed

6 strips soy bacon, cooked crisp and crumbled

5 hard-boiled eggs, whites chopped with 2 of the yolks (save the remaining yolks for another use)

1 bunch fresh chives, cut into ¼-inch lengths

6 plums, pitted and sliced thinly

Dressing

⅔ cup extra-virgin olive oil

2 tablespoons Dijon mustard

¼ cup red wine vinegar

   Kosher salt and freshly ground black pepper

Tahini-Dressed Chicken Salad with Arugula

Many people are first introduced to tahini as the sauce that's drizzled on falafel, the Israeli street food. Made from ground sesame seeds, it is often served as a condiment in Middle Eastern cuisine as well as mixed into salads. In this chicken salad we are using tahini as an alternative to mayonnaise; thus updating an important American classic. Chicken is poached on the bone for a moist and delicate flavor, while the peppery flavor of the arugula balances the richness of the tahini.

SERVES 4 AS A MAIN

Poached Chicken

10 sprigs fresh flat-leaf parsley
2 sprigs fresh thyme
1 small onion, halved
1 small carrot, peeled and halved
1 celery stalk including the leafy top, cut into chunks
3 pounds bone-in chicken breasts, halved and fat trimmed
5 to 6 cups chicken stock, vegetable stock, or water

Dressing

⅓ cup tahini paste
2 tablespoons lemon juice
2 teaspoons pomegranate molasses
¼ cup fresh flat-leaf parsley leaves
   Coarse salt and cracked black pepper
   Up to ½ cup warm water (if needed)

Salad

2 bunches arugula (about 4 cups)
2 Persian, 3 Kirby, or 1 English cucumber, sliced ⅛ inch thick
1 cup fresh pomegranate seeds (see page 129)
6 scallions, white and green parts, thinly sliced

To poach the chicken, in a medium saucepan, combine the parsley sprigs, thyme, onion, carrot, celery, and chicken breasts. Add stock to cover and bring to a boil. Lower the heat to very low and cover. Poach the chicken until just firm to the touch, about 20 minutes. Remove the pan from the heat, uncover, and cool the chicken in the liquid for 30 minutes.

Transfer the chicken to a cutting board. Bone and skin the chicken and cut the meat into ¼-inch slices. Discard the bones and skin.

To make the dressing, in the bowl of a food processor, combine the tahini, lemon juice, pomegranate molasses, and parsley leaves. Process until smooth. Season with salt and pepper.

To assemble the salad, place the arugula leaves on a platter. Top with the chicken slices, and surround with the cucumber slices. Drizzle on the dressing (if the dressing has thickened, whisk in a little hot water). Garnish with the pomegranate seeds and scallions and serve.

The chicken poaching liquid can be reused. Once it's strained, it can be saved for 3 days in the refrigerator or a few months in the freezer. You can substitute it for chicken stock or water. Remember to remove any fat from the surface of the broth before using.

Fennel, Green Apple, and Pecorino Salad

It's traditional to eat apples during the Jewish High Holiday season and this salad incorporates them in a surprising way. The fennel provides alluring licorice-like notes that are offset by the sweet-tart-salty combination of apple and pecorino cheese. This can be served as a first course or as one of many salads at a tapas-style meal. It can also be held up to an hour before serving.

NOTE: *To get the apple and fennel slices paper thin, use a mandolin, the largest slicing slit on a box grater, or a food processor with a fine slicing disc.*

SERVES 6 AS A SIDE

In a large bowl, combine the fennel, apple, and pecorino and toss.

To make the dressing, combine the oil and lemon juice in a small bowl. Season with salt and pepper.

Add the chopped fennel fronds and parsley to the fennel mixture, pour the dressing over the salad, and toss. Adjust the seasoning and serve.

Salad

1 large fennel bulb, halved and sliced paper thin, fronds chopped

1 large Granny Smith apple, cored, quartered, and sliced paper thin

1 (4-ounce) piece pecorino Romano, thinly shaved

1 cup packed fresh flat-leaf parsley leaves or baby arugula leaves

Dressing

3 tablespoons extra-virgin olive oil

3 tablespoons lemon juice

Kosher salt and freshly ground black pepper

Summer Corn, Cucumber, and Tomato Salad

Nothing says summer like corn, cucumbers, and tomatoes, and this quickly thrown together salad celebrates that trio. The corn is raw, so, for the best taste, make sure to buy it when it is perfectly in season. Leftover corn from the barbecue the night before, while changing the texture and flavor of the salad, is also delicious. Using a variety of tomato shapes makes this salad aesthetically pleasing, and a touch of old-fashioned distilled white vinegar gives it a nice, bright flavor.

SERVES 8 TO 10 AS A SIDE

Dressing

2 to 3 tablespoons distilled white vinegar

1 tablespoon safflower oil

2 teaspoons coarse-grain mustard
   Kosher salt and freshly ground black pepper

Salad

6 ears fresh corn

4 small seedless cucumbers, cut into small dice

1 pound tomatoes, assorted types and sizes, roughly cut into slices and medium wedges

½ Vidalia or other sweet onion, sliced paper thin

1 bunch watercress, mâche, or purslane

12 fresh basil leaves, plus more for garnish (optional)

To make the dressing, whisk together the vinegar (to taste), oil, and mustard in a small bowl. Season with salt and pepper.

Slice the kernels from the cob and transfer to a large bowl. Add the cucumber, tomatoes, onion, and watercress.

Pour the dressing over the salad and toss.

Snip the basil leaves into thin ribbons and mix in gently. Garnish with additional basil leaves (if desired) and serve.

Kale, Farro, and Carrot Salad

Kale is abundant at farmers' markets in early spring, the fall, and early winter. Like Brussels sprouts, kale develops its best flavor after the first cold snap. And it's beautiful. We especially love Tuscan (lacinato) kale, with its dark, blue-green color. When shopping, choose bunches with dark, unblemished, crisp leaves. Here, we use it raw, tenderized by removing the central stem, and shredded. The farro adds heartiness and the dried wild blueberries, soaked in *verjus* (see box), give the salad a delicate, subtle hint of sweetness. We adapted the recipe from a salad created at Blue Hill at Stone Barns in New York. The dried wild blueberries and Parmesan cheese make this version our own.

To make the farro, heat the oil over medium heat in a medium saucepan. Add the onion, celery, and carrot and sauté until the vegetables are lightly browned, about 5 minutes. Add the farro, stir, and reduce the heat to low. Toast, stirring occasionally, for about 2 minutes. Add the water and bay leaf, and bring to a boil. Cover, lower the heat, and simmer until the farro is tender and almost all the liquid has been absorbed, about 25 minutes (or follow package directions). Using a colander, drain any remaining liquid and transfer the farro to a shallow bowl. Discard the bay leaf. Let cool.

Meanwhile, make the salad. Soak the blueberries in the ¼ cup *verjus* or orange juice until plumped, about 30 minutes (if using currants, they can be soaked overnight). Drain and set aside berries. Toast the pine nuts in a small skillet over low heat, watching carefully and stirring often, until golden, about 3 minutes. Transfer to a small bowl and set aside.

In a large bowl, combine the kale with the 2 tablespoons *verjus* or vinegar, season with salt and pepper, and toss. Set aside for at least 15 minutes.

In a second large bowl, combine the farro, blueberries, pine nuts, grated carrots, shallots, and pepper flakes. Add the olive oil and toss well. Add the kale and toss again. Sprinkle with the Parmesan (to taste) and chives, and drizzle with the lemon juice. Adjust the seasoning and serve.

VERJUS

Literally meaning "green juice," *verjus*, the pressed juice of unripened grapes, is actually red or white depending on the grape it comes from. It's similar to vinegar, but has a gentler flavor with a sweet-tart taste because it isn't fermented. We enjoy using it in salad dressings, especially on heartier greens like kale and arugula. Once opened, it will keep in the refrigerator for 2 to 3 months.

Farro

- 1 tablespoon grapeseed or canola oil
- ½ cup finely chopped onion
- ¼ cup finely chopped celery
- ¼ cup finely chopped carrot
- 2¼ cups (14 ounces) pearled or semi-pearled farro
- 3 cups water
- 1 bay leaf

Salad

- 1 cup dried wild blueberries or currants
- ¼ cup *verjus* (see box) or orange juice
- 1 cup pine nuts or shelled pumpkin seeds
- 2 bunches lacinato kale, center ribs and stems removed, finely shredded (about 4 cups)
- 2 tablespoons *verjus* (see box), sherry vinegar, or balsamic vinegar

   Kosher salt and freshly ground black pepper
- 2 medium carrots, peeled and shredded or grated (about 1 cup)
- 2 medium shallots, finely chopped (about 2 tablespoons)
- ½ teaspoon red pepper flakes
- ½ cup extra-virgin olive oil
- ½ to ¾ cup shaved Parmesan
- 3 tablespoons snipped fresh chives or coarsely chopped fresh flat-leaf parsley
- 2 tablespoons lemon juice

Karpas Salad

We've dubbed this our *karpas* salad, named after the spring herbs and bitter greens served at a Passover seder, but we make it all year-round. It also features dates, pine nuts, pomegranate seeds, and a bright lemon dressing—a terrific mix.

SERVES 8 AS A SIDE

In a small skillet, toast the pine nuts over low heat, watching carefully and stirring often, until golden, about 3 minutes. Transfer to a small bowl and let cool.

In a large bowl, combine the arugula, parsley, cilantro, and chives. Add the pine nuts and dates and toss.

To make the dressing, whisk the lemon juice (to taste) and olive oil together in a small bowl. Season with salt and pepper. Just before serving, toss the salad with the dressing. Sprinkle with the pomegranate seeds and dill to garnish. Adjust the seasoning, and serve.

Salad

½ cup pine nuts

6 ounces baby arugula

Leaves from 2 bunches fresh flat-leaf parsley (about 4 cups)

Leaves from 1 bunch cilantro (about 2 cups)

½ cup fresh chives cut into ⅛-inch lengths

¾ cup dried pitted dates, thinly sliced

1½ cups pomegranate seeds (about 2 pomegranates)

Fresh dill to garnish.

Dressing

2 to 3 tablespoons lemon juice

3 tablespoons extra-virgin olive oil

Kosher salt and freshly ground black pepper

SEEDING A POMEGRANATE

To peel the pomegranate and get to its seeds, gently score the leather-like skin into quarters, and then place the entire pomegranate in a large bowl filled with water. Keeping your hands under the water, gently pull off the skin and remove the seeds, which will fall to the bottom. Carefully drain the water, discard the outer skin and fibers, and dry the seeds.

COLORS OF KINDNESS

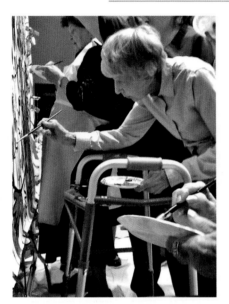

A healthy community is composed of individuals who share common interests and goals. Their contributions can be varied, but when people work together as a community something magical happens. Just consider the *Colors of Kindness* mural, created by the Jewish Community Center of Metropolitan Detroit. The goal of the project was simple: to emphasize the importance of collaboration.

The mural project was a carefully orchestrated symphony conducted by a local Michigan artist who knew exactly how to get many different people to create a cohesive, unique work of art. The crowds would arrive at the JCC's campus in Oak Park. Inside, hundreds of chairs were set up on one side of the hall, and a large white canvas was stretched along the opposite wall. Each volunteer artist would receive a number, and as the numbers were called, four to five members would work and paint together.

No one was told what part of the mural to work on—volunteers could choose for themselves. The only instruction the artist gave to his painters throughout the process was: Don't worry. There are no mistakes. Just have fun with your own small part of the mural and enjoy the act of creating something larger than yourself.

This kind of approach to collaboration is seen at JCCs nationwide and serves to create a warm, nurturing community.

Syrian Potato Salad (Salata Batata)

Spice up classic American potato salad with this Syrian version. The potatoes are lightly dressed with olive oil and lemon juice and seasoned with allspice, evoking the pungent, complex aromas of a bustling Middle Eastern *shuk* (marketplace), like the one in Jerusalem. You'll need to start this salad ahead of time, as the potatoes require thorough cooling in the fridge. But your patience will be rewarded when you serve the salad to your family or guests.

SERVES 8 TO 10 AS A SIDE

Bring a large pot of water to a boil. Add the potatoes. When the water returns to a boil, reduce the heat to medium-high and cook, uncovered, until the potatoes are tender when pierced gently with a fork, 20 to 30 minutes. Don't let the potatoes become mushy. Drain, transfer the potatoes to a large bowl, and cover with cold water.

When the potatoes are cool enough to handle, in 5 to 10 minutes, drain, peel, and return them to the bowl. Add fresh water to cover the potatoes. Cover the bowl with plastic wrap and refrigerate until completely cool, about 45 minutes.

Meanwhile, to make the dressing, in a jar or other container with a tightly fitting top, combine the dressing ingredients. Shake well and set aside.

Drain and halve the potatoes lengthwise. Halve each slice lengthwise again, then crosswise into ¼-inch-thick pieces, so each potato gives you 8 to 16 pieces, depending on the size.

Transfer the potatoes to a large bowl. Pour the dressing evenly over them, add the scallions, and mix gently to coat. Chill thoroughly, about 4 hours.

When ready to serve, garnish the potatoes with the eggs, allspice (to taste), and olives, if using.

8 medium potatoes (about 3 pounds), Yukon Gold or Red Bliss

Dressing

⅔ cup olive oil

½ cup fresh lemon juice

1 to 1½ teaspoons ground allspice (to taste)

1 teaspoon sugar

1 teaspoon kosher salt

Freshly ground black pepper

Salad

1 cup finely chopped scallions, white and green parts

2 large hard-boiled eggs, cut in eighths

1 to 1½ teaspoons ground allspice

6 to 8 pitted Kalamata or Gaeta olives (optional)

Cold Minted Pea Salad

Peas, mint, and a tart citrusy dressing make for a light and refreshing spring salad. This salad is delicious with grilled, smoked, or steamed salmon (page 165). It's best to use fresh peas, available at farmers' markets in early spring. If, however, you can only find frozen peas, buy various brands; you'll get a visually pleasing variety of pea sizes. The sumac adds a bright, acidic touch without the use of citrus juice, which would discolor the peas and mint.

SERVES 8 AS A SIDE

Salad

3½ pounds fresh peas in the pod, shelled; or 28 ounces frozen peas, defrosted

½ pound fresh sugar snap peas, sliced diagonally into thin strips

1 cup fresh mint leaves cut into thin ribbons

Dressing

¾ cup Greek yogurt

¼ cup extra-virgin olive oil

2 teaspoons Dijon mustard

¼ to ½ teaspoon sumac

1 teaspoon kosher salt, plus more for seasoning

Freshly ground black pepper

Grated zest of 1 lemon

If using fresh peas, bring salted water to a boil in a large saucepan. Fill a large bowl with ice and add enough water to make an ice bath. Add the peas to the boiling water and cook until bright green and crisp-tender, 1 to 3 minutes. Drain the peas and transfer to the ice bath. When cold, drain thoroughly and transfer to a large bowl. If using frozen peas, simply rinse under cool water, drain, and transfer to a bowl. Add the sugar snap peas and mint and toss.

To make the dressing, in a medium bowl, whisk together the yogurt, oil, mustard, sumac (to taste), salt, and pepper. Add the dressing to the salad and toss. Add the zest, toss, adjust the seasoning, and serve.

Moroccan Carrot Slaw

This slaw is delicious when it is first made and better after it has marinated for a few hours. Harissa is a North African hot chile paste, which is readily available in many grocery stores. The salad can be served at room temperature or chilled.

SERVES 6 TO 8 AS A SIDE

In a large bowl, combine the carrots, cilantro, oil, lemon juice, garlic (to taste), cumin, paprika, harissa (to taste), and salt and toss. Cover with plastic wrap and marinate, refrigerated, for at least 30 minutes or up to 3 days. Right before serving, garnish with cilantro and serve.

1 pound carrots, peeled and coarsely grated (about 4 cups)

¼ cup chopped fresh cilantro, plus additional for garnish

¼ cup extra-virgin olive oil

3 tablespoons lemon juice

2 to 3 garlic cloves, minced or pressed

1 teaspoon ground cumin

1 teaspoon sweet paprika

½ to 1 teaspoon harissa, or ¼ to ½ teaspoon cayenne

Pinch kosher salt

PASTA, POLENTA & RISOTTO

Gemelli with Mushroom Bolognese

Jews have lived and cooked in Italy for over 2,000 years, and both cultures share a love of family and food. A cherished staple of Italy's Emilia Romagna region, bolognese sauce is a deliciously rich meat sauce. Our version replaces the meat with mushrooms to make this a vegetarian—but still hearty and deeply flavorful—dish. The vegetables and the mushrooms must be cut small so that they almost melt in the sauce to achieve the traditional texture. For a super-rich sauce, add a little bit of cream and grated cheese to finish it. Gemelli—twisty pasta spirals—are a perfect vehicle for the sauce.

SERVES 6 TO 8

½ cup vegetable stock

⅓ cup crushed dried wild mushrooms, such as porcini

¼ cup extra-virgin olive oil

1 small onion, finely chopped (about ⅓ cup)

2 medium carrots, peeled and finely chopped (about 1 cup)

2 medium celery stalks, finely chopped (about ½ cup)

2 teaspoons minced garlic

¾ pound mushrooms, such as porcini or cremini, cut into thin strips

1 to 2 teaspoons chopped fresh thyme leaves

3 tablespoons tomato paste

½ cup dry red wine, such as cabernet or barolo

2 large ripe tomatoes, peeled, seeded, and chopped (about 1 cup), or 1 (14-ounce) can of diced tomatoes

Kosher salt and freshly ground black pepper

1 pound gemelli pasta

¼ cup chopped fresh flat-leaf parsley

In a small saucepan, heat the stock over medium heat just until hot. Transfer to a medium bowl and add the dried mushrooms. Allow the mushrooms to soak until rehydrated, 20 to 30 minutes. Drain the mushrooms, chop finely, and set aside. Strain the liquid through a paper towel–lined sieve, and reserve the liquid.

Bring a large pot of salted water to a boil.

In a large heavy sauté pan, heat the oil over medium heat. Add the onion, carrots, celery, and garlic and sauté until soft and golden, 10 to 15 minutes. Add the fresh mushrooms and thyme and sauté until the mushrooms soften, 10 minutes. Add the tomato paste and wine and cook for 10 minutes. Add the soaked, chopped dried mushrooms with their liquid and the tomatoes. Reduce the heat to medium-low and cook until the mixture has thickened, 15 minutes. Season with salt and pepper.

Add the gemelli to the boiling water and cook until al dente, about 11 minutes (or follow package directions). Drain, reserving some of the cooking water.

Add the pasta to the sauce and toss until the flavors have blended, 2 to 3 minutes. If the sauce seems dry, add some of the pasta cooking water. Transfer to a platter, season with pepper, sprinkle with the parsley, and serve.

Spaghettini with Garlic and Oil

Sometimes the quickest preparations are the most beloved. For those of us who keep kosher kitchens, this pasta makes adults and kids equally happy when we are serving a non-dairy meal. To dress up the simple pasta, include the optional cherry tomatoes and the gremolata.

SERVES 8 AS A SIDE

Bring a large pot of salted water to a boil.

In a large skillet, heat the oil over medium heat. Add the garlic and cook, stirring occasionally, until just golden, 3 to 5 minutes. If using tomatoes, add them now and cook 2 minutes, until they have begun to wilt. Remove the pan from the heat and set aside.

Cook the pasta in the boiling water until slightly undercooked, 5 to 6 minutes (or follow package directions). Drain the pasta, reserving 1 cup of the cooking water.

Transfer the pasta and 3 tablespoons of the water to the pan with the garlic. Toss over low heat to finish cooking the pasta. Add the parsley, season with the salt, pepper, and red pepper flakes or gremolata, if using. Toss again and serve.

⅓ cup extra-virgin olive oil

3 medium garlic cloves, minced

1 pint cherry or grape tomatoes, halved (optional)

1 pound dry spaghettini

2 to 3 tablespoons chopped fresh flat-leaf parsley

Kosher salt and freshly ground black pepper

Crushed red pepper flakes (optional)

Gremolata (recipe follows, optional)

Gremolata

Combine the zest, garlic, and parsley in a small bowl.

Grated zest of 1 medium lemon, preferably organic (about 1 tablespoon)

1 teaspoon minced garlic

2 tablespoons finely chopped fresh flat-leaf parsley

Whole-Wheat Pasta with Caramelized Red Peppers

When we have kids coming home late from swimming or gymnastics practice, spouses getting stuck in the office, and we're juggling it all, this is the perfect dish to prepare quickly. It's done, start to finish, in about 20 minutes. Serve with a salad and you're good to go. And once you taste this hearty vegetarian pasta, you'll make it again and again. The nutty whole-wheat pasta complements the fresh flavor of the sweet peppers beautifully. If you can find farro pasta, by all means use it—it takes the whole-wheat pasta experience to another level.

SERVES 4 TO 6

Bring a large pot of salted water to boil. Add the pasta and cook until al dente, 10 to 12 minutes (or follow package directions).

Meanwhile, in a large skillet, heat the oil over medium heat. Add the garlic and sauté until just beginning to color, about 4 minutes. With a slotted spoon, immediately transfer the garlic to a small bowl and set aside.

Add the peppers to the pan and sauté over medium heat until soft and slightly wilted, about 5 minutes. Return the garlic to the pan and season generously with salt and pepper. Add the pasta to the pan and heat through. Transfer to a serving dish and toss with the Parmesan and basil. Serve with more Parmesan.

1 pound whole-wheat (or farro) penne or any other sort of tubular pasta

3 tablespoons extra-virgin olive oil

2 to 3 medium garlic cloves, thinly sliced

4 large or 5 medium red bell peppers, stemmed, seeded, and sliced about ¼ inch thick

Kosher salt and freshly ground black pepper

½ cup grated Parmesan, plus more for serving

1 cup fresh basil leaves cut into thin ribbons

Pappardelle with Lamb Ragù

This is our version of ethnic fusion—East (Morocco) meets West (Italy). It is a perfect hearty winter pasta sauce that also works exceptionally well when served over steamed spinach instead of pasta.

SERVES 6

2 tablespoons extra-virgin olive oil

2 medium carrots, peeled and finely chopped (about 1 cup)

1 medium onion, finely chopped (about 1 cup)

2 celery stalks, finely chopped (about ⅔ cup)

1½ pounds ground lamb

2 teaspoons ground coriander

1 teaspoon fennel seeds, crushed

1 teaspoon chopped fresh rosemary

1 teaspoon chopped fresh thyme leaves

½ teaspoon ground cumin

Kosher salt and freshly ground black pepper

2 tablespoons tomato paste

½ cup dry red wine

1 (28-ounce) can diced tomatoes

1¼ cups chicken stock

Pinch red pepper flakes (optional)

1 pound pappardelle pasta

2 tablespoons chopped fresh mint

In a Dutch oven or enamel pot, heat the olive oil over medium heat. Add the carrots, onion, and celery and sauté until softened, about 5 minutes.

Turn up the heat to high. Add the lamb, coriander, fennel seeds, rosemary, thyme, and cumin. Sauté, breaking the meat up while browning it, for 4 to 5 minutes. Season with salt and pepper. Add the tomato paste and wine and simmer until the liquid has evaporated, about 5 minutes.

Add the tomatoes with their juice and the stock and bring to a boil. Cover the pan partially and simmer over medium-low heat until the liquid is slightly reduced, 25 to 30 minutes. Adjust the seasoning and add the red pepper flakes, if using.

Meanwhile, bring a large pot of salted water to a boil. Cook the pasta until al dente, 8 to 10 minutes (or follow package directions). Drain well, transfer the cooked pasta to the sauce, and toss over low heat. Transfer the pasta onto a large serving platter, sprinkle with the mint, and serve.

Summer Pappardelle with Corn and Tomatoes

We're always looking for new ways to pair three favorites from the farmers' market—corn, tomatoes, and basil—and this recipe is perfection. Long flat pasta is ideal here, but it also might be fun to use shells to catch the corn and tomato bits inside. The sautéed vegetables alone, without the pasta, also make a great side dish.

SERVES 4 TO 6

Bring a large pot of salted water to a boil. Add the corn and cook until just tender, about 3 minutes. Remove the corn and reserve the cooking water in the pot. When the corn has cooled slightly, cut the kernels from the cobs. Set aside.

In a large skillet, melt 2 tablespoons butter over medium heat. Add the tomatoes, salt, and pepper. Cook, stirring occasionally, until the tomatoes begin to burst, about 5 minutes. Add the garlic and cook for 1 minute. Add the wine and cook until reduced by half, 4 to 6 minutes. Add the vegetable stock and corn, reduce the heat to low, and simmer about 3 minutes. Remove from the heat.

Meanwhile, return the corn cooking water to a boil. Add the pasta and cook until al dente, about 3 minutes if using fresh pasta, about 9 minutes if using dry pasta (or follow the package directions). Reserve 1 cup of the cooking water and drain the pasta.

Return the skillet to the burner and heat the sauce over medium heat. If the sauce gets too thick, add the reserved pasta water as needed. Transfer the pasta to the skillet, add the scallions and Parmesan, and stir to coat. For a richer sauce, add an additional tablespoon of butter. Remove the pasta from the heat and season with salt and pepper. Fold in the basil and serve with additional Parmesan.

2 large ears of corn

2 or 3 tablespoons unsalted butter

2 pints grape or cherry tomatoes

1 teaspoon kosher salt, plus more for seasoning

½ teaspoon freshly ground black pepper, plus more for seasoning

2 garlic cloves, minced

½ cup dry white wine, such as chardonnay or sauvignon blanc

½ cup vegetable stock

1 pound fresh or dry pappardelle, fettuccine, or shells

1 small bunch scallions, white and green parts, sliced thin (about 1 cup)

½ cup grated Parmesan, plus more for serving

Basil leaves, cut into thin ribbons

Egg Noodles with Savoy Cabbage and Sausage

In the Old Country, homemade *lokshen* (egg noodles) were once a criterion by which a Jewish woman's worth was measured. Even in the New Country, women continued to make homemade noodles on the Lower East Side of Manhattan and other places Jews settled. One of our great-aunts would make *lokshen* at home on Thursday nights in preparation for Shabbat, and over the course of the evening, members of the family would trickle in. Each one took home a care package filled with noodles and strudel.

In this recipe, we've paired wide egg noodles with a classic Eastern European combination of cabbage and spicy chicken sausage. This is a wonderful winter pasta dish, or for any time you are in the mood for something hearty and satisfying. The sauce can be prepared hours, or even a day, ahead.

SERVES 6

1 savoy cabbage (about 1 pound), cored and quartered

3 tablespoons extra-virgin olive oil

1 medium onion, chopped (about ½ cup)

2 medium carrots, peeled, finely chopped (about 1 cup)

2 garlic cloves, finely chopped (about 2 teaspoons)

2 teaspoons crushed fennel seeds

8 ounces hot Italian chicken sausage, casings removed and meat crumbled

½ cup dry white wine

Up to 2 cups chicken or vegetable stock

12 ounces wide egg noodles

¼ cup finely chopped fresh flat-leaf parsley

½ to 1 teaspoon freshly grated nutmeg

Freshly ground black pepper

Using a steamer, steam the cabbage quarters until fork-tender, about 15 minutes. When cool enough to handle, slice thinly.

In a large heavy skillet, heat the oil over medium-low heat. Add the onion, carrots, and garlic and sauté until the onion is translucent and has begun to soften, about 7 minutes. Add the fennel seeds and sausage meat, increase the heat to medium-high, and cook, stirring, until the meat is browned evenly, about 5 minutes.

Add the cabbage, wine, and 1 cup stock to the meat mixture. Reduce the heat to low and simmer until the cabbage is cooked, about 20 minutes. Add more stock, a few tablespoons at a time, if needed to keep the mixture moist.

Meanwhile, bring a large pot of salted water to a boil. Add the noodles and cook until very al dente, about 8 minutes (or follow package directions). Drain the noodles, return them to the pot, and add 1 cup of the sauce. Toss over high heat for 1 minute. Stir in the parsley, nutmeg, and pepper (to taste). Transfer to a serving platter or shallow wide bowl, top with the remaining sauce, and serve.

Nokedli (Hungarian Spaetzle)

Affectionately called "Knuck-a-Knuck" by one of our families, these small egg noodle dumplings, Austro-Hungarian in origin, are the ideal comfort food. They are the perfect way to soak up pan juices or they can be tossed with loads of butter and cheese. The original version calls solely for all-purpose flour, but we suggest a combination of half all-purpose and half whole-wheat to make a heartier dish.

SERVES 6 AS A SIDE

Bring a large pot of salted water to a boil.

In a medium bowl, beat the eggs with a fork until smooth. Add the water and salt and beat to combine. Gradually beat in the flours ¼ cup at a time to make a soft, sticky dough. The dough will be very stretchy. If the dough is dull looking, continue beating until it shines. Let the dough rest for 10 minutes.

Spoon half the dough onto a dinner plate. With a blunt knife, move some dough towards the edge of the plate and spread it until it is about ¼ inch thick. Use the knife to scrape tiny bits of the dough off and flick them into the pot of boiling water. Dip the knife blade frequently into water to help the batter slip off. The dough will grow as it cooks, so cut very small (about ¼-inch) rectangular pieces; this is just a guideline, you can experiment with the size and shape until you find the ones that you like best. (Or use a very simple inexpensive spaetzle maker; they are easy to find online and at gourmet kitchen stores.) Make sure the water stays at a boil. After cutting in about half of the dough, cover the pot partially and boil 10 to 20 minutes, until tender throughout, depending on the size you cut. Remove from the water with a slotted spoon, and drain in a colander. Repeat with remaining dough. Salt to taste.

5 extra-large eggs

¼ cup water

1 teaspoon kosher salt

1 cup unbleached all-purpose flour

1 cup whole-wheat flour

Two-Grain Saffron Couscous

We love the size and flavor variation of the two types of couscous in this recipe. Lebanese large-pearl *moghrabieh* couscous, which is made from semolina wheat, is paired with small-size whole-wheat Moroccan *m'hamsa* couscous. The size variation is texturally interesting as well as visually beautiful. If you have trouble finding these specific types of couscous, see our variation that follows to use Israeli and instant couscous. Flavored with saffron and colored by the bright yellow turmeric, this dish is excellent served alongside tagines, broiled meats, and stews.

To turn this into a great dish for Tu B'Shevat, we like to add ingredients to represent each of the Seven Species that the Bible describes as being abundant in the land of Israel. Top the couscous with sliced pitted dates and figs, some pomegranate seeds, and a dressing made with olive oil, wine vinegar, and a touch of barley malt syrup and you have a Seven-Species dish.

SERVES 6 TO 8

6 cups vegetable, chicken, or beef stock, or water

½ teaspoon ground turmeric

½ teaspoon kosher salt

Pinch saffron threads

1 bay leaf

1 cup Lebanese (*moghrabieh*) couscous

1 cup whole-wheat Moroccan (*m'hamsa*) couscous

2 tablespoons extra-virgin olive oil

2 tablespoons chopped fresh flat-leaf parsley or cilantro (optional)

In a medium saucepan, combine the stock, turmeric, salt, saffron, and bay leaf and bring to a boil over high heat.

Add the Lebanese couscous, reduce the heat to low, and simmer, uncovered, for 25 minutes. Add the Moroccan couscous and olive oil and stir. Increase the heat to high and bring to a boil. Cover, remove from the heat, and allow to rest until the liquid is absorbed, 10 to 12 minutes. Discard the bay leaf, fluff with a fork, stir in the parsley, if using, and serve.

NOTE: *You can make this dish using Israeli and instant couscous. Substitute the Israeli for the Lebanese couscous and cook for only 7 minutes. Add the instant couscous and the olive oil, and stir. Bring to a boil, cover, and remove from the heat. After 5 minutes, fluff with a fork, stir in the parsley, if using, and serve.*

Risotto with Salmon, Leeks, and Peas

Risotto is traditionally served as a first course. Here we've broken with tradition on a few fronts. By incorporating vegetables and fish, we transform the creamy rice into a main course. We've also added Parmesan, not usually a seafood partner. But Italians, who should know, have acknowledged the tastiness of Parmesan with some fish dishes. While we're happy to experiment with flavor, some things—such as risotto technique—are best done the traditional way. According to the late Marcella Hazan, the secret to good risotto is fresh ingredients and elbow grease. So be ready to stir with vigor and take your time.

Serve this on Shavuot, the holiday when we traditionally eat dairy foods.

SERVES 4

Bring the stock to a boil in a medium saucepan. Reduce the heat, cover the pan, and simmer gently.

If using fresh shelled peas, blanch them in boiling water in a medium saucepan for 2 to 4 minutes, until bright green and partially cooked. Drain and run under cold water to stop cooking. Set aside.

Meanwhile, in a large saucepan, melt half the butter with the oil over low heat. Add the leek and sauté until softened, 5 to 6 minutes. Add the wine, turn up the heat to medium, and cook until the alcohol has evaporated, about 2 minutes. Season with salt.

Add the rice, stir well, and pour in just enough of the simmering stock to cover. Cook, stirring constantly, until all the liquid has been absorbed. Make sure to maintain an active simmer. Stirring constantly, continue to add more stock, about ½ cup at a time as each addition has been absorbed, until the rice is approaching tender-firm, about 12 minutes. As you cook, be sure to scrape the bottom of the pan to prevent the rice from sticking.

Add the salmon to the saucepan and stir until the rice is tender and the salmon is cooked through, about 5 minutes. Stir gingerly to avoid breaking up the salmon pieces. After 3 minutes, add the peas and stir through. Remove the pan from the heat and stir in the remaining butter and the Parmesan, if using. Season with salt and pepper. Sprinkle with the lemon zest and serve immediately.

5 to 6 cups fish or vegetable stock

1 cup shelled fresh peas or defrosted frozen peas

3 tablespoons unsalted butter

2 tablespoons extra-virgin olive oil

1 cup thinly sliced leek, white and light green parts only

⅔ cup white wine
   Kosher salt

1½ cups Arborio rice

6 ounces salmon fillet, skin removed, cut into ½-inch cubes

½ cup grated Parmesan (optional)
   Freshly ground black pepper
   Grated zest of 1 small lemon

This recipe is a blueprint for making risotto. Once you've mastered the technique, feel free to experiment with seasonal vegetables as substitutes for the fish. Two of our favorites are asparagus or fava beans with a garnish of tarragon.

Buckwheat Noodles with Grilled Hen-of-the-Woods Mushrooms

While buckwheat and mushrooms were both staples in an Eastern European diet, this Asian-inspired recipe reflects the way we like to cook now. We have paired buckwheat noodles, with their deep nutty flavor, and hen-of-the-woods mushrooms (also known as maitake), which are grilled until they become crunchy on the outside and chewy-tender within. A garlicky dressing made with yuzu juice (see page 173 for a description) and a sprinkling of toasted sesame seeds finish this delicious dish. Soba noodles can also be gluten free. Please check the package labels.

Hen-of-the-woods mushrooms have great health benefits and are thought to boost the immune system. Store them, like all mushrooms, in a paper bag in the refrigerator. If they're wrapped in plastic they become soggy and won't yield the best result. Look for hen-of-the-woods at farmers' markets and gourmet food stores, but if they aren't available, substitute shiitake mushrooms.

SERVES 4

1 tablespoon sesame seeds

6 tablespoons grapeseed oil, plus more for brushing

¼ cup yuzu juice or lime juice

5 teaspoons soy sauce

½ teaspoon finely minced garlic

½ teaspoon freshly ground black pepper, plus more for seasoning

¾ pound hen-of-the-woods mushrooms, separated into about 8 clusters

Kosher salt

½ pound soba noodles

1 to 2 tablespoons toasted sesame oil

2 tablespoons roughly chopped fresh flat-leaf parsley or cilantro

1 lime, quartered

Pea shoot tendrils, for garnish (optional)

In a small sauté pan, toast the sesame seeds over medium heat, stirring occasionally, until golden, about 3 minutes. Transfer to a small bowl and set aside.

In a small bowl, whisk together the oil, juice, soy sauce, garlic, and ½ teaspoon pepper. Set the dressing aside.

Heat a grill pan over high heat. Brush the mushrooms with grapeseed oil and season with salt and pepper. Working in batches, grill the mushrooms, turning occasionally, until browned and crisp, about 4 minutes per side. Transfer the mushrooms to a plate.

Bring a large pot of salted water to boil. Cook the noodles according to the package directions, usually 6 to 8 minutes. Toss with the sesame oil (to taste) and transfer to a platter.

Toss the noodles with the grilled mushrooms and sprinkle with the toasted sesame seeds and parsley. Drizzle on some dressing. Serve with the lime wedges and the remaining dressing, and garnish will pea shoots, if using.

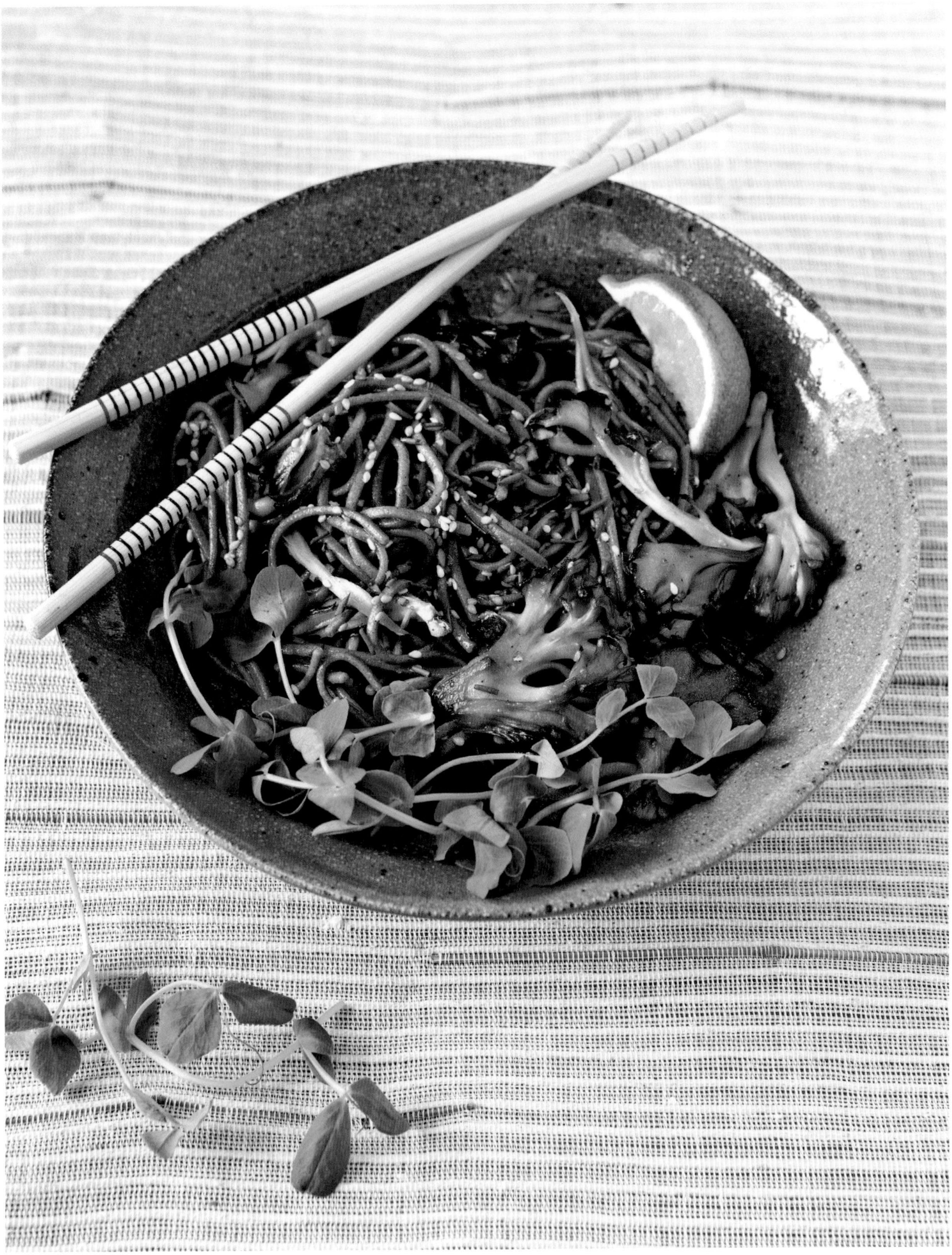

Barley Risotto with Zucchini

Barley is one of our favorite ancient grains and we regularly use it in place of rice, potatoes, or pasta. It's known as a "superfood" because of its low glycemic index and because it is packed with vitamins, minerals, fiber, and antioxidants. When used to make risotto, as we've done here, barley is less finicky than the traditional Italian Arborio rice. This is also a great way to incorporate zucchini into a dish when, by the end of summer, there's so much on hand.

SERVES 4

7 cups chicken or vegetable stock

2 tablespoons extra-virgin olive oil

3 medium shallots, finely chopped (about 3 tablespoons)

1 cup pearled or semi-pearled barley

⅔ cup white wine, or more as needed

3 cups diced zucchini (2 or 3 small zucchini)

¾ cup freshly grated Parmesan (optional)

1 tablespoon unsalted butter (optional)

Kosher salt and freshly ground black pepper

Bring the stock to a boil in a medium saucepan. Reduce the heat, cover the pan, and simmer gently.

Heat the olive oil in a heavy-bottomed skillet over medium heat. Add the shallots and sauté until softened, 4 to 5 minutes, taking care not to let them brown. Add the barley and stir until the grains are well coated with the oil and begin to have a toasty smell, about 2 minutes. Add the wine and cook until it's fully absorbed, 2 to 3 minutes. Start adding the stock, 1 cup at a time, while stirring. Allow each cup to be absorbed before adding the next. As you cook, be sure to scrape the bottom of the pan with your spoon to prevent the barley from sticking. After about 25 minutes taste the barley; it should be al dente and chewier than a risotto made with rice. If the barley is still hard, continue to add stock ½ a cup a time, stirring consistently and reserving ½ cup for the last step.

Add the zucchini and ½ cup of the stock. Cook until the zucchini is tender, 5 to 7 minutes. Remove from the heat, stir in the Parmesan and butter, if using, and season with salt and pepper. Serve immediately.

Polenta with Winter Greens

A cooking class at Blue Hill at Stone Barns in Westchester, New York, provided the springboard for this recipe. Kale is sautéed with currants, capers, pine nuts, and a hint of hot pepper and served on Asiago-flavored polenta. The result is a perfect balance of sweet, salty, bitter, spicy, and creamy.

If you belong to a CSA (community supported agriculture) or have access to various greens from a farmers' market, experiment with whatever is available. (If you're using very bitter greens, such as mustard or turnip greens, you may want to blanch them first to remove any harsh bitterness.) We also like to serve the polenta with Warm Mushroom Sauté (page 260).

SERVES 4

In a small bowl, combine the currants with hot water to cover. Allow the currants to plump, at least 20 minutes. Drain. In a small skillet, toast the pine nuts over medium-low heat, watching carefully and stirring, until golden, about 3 minutes. Transfer to a small bowl and let cool. Add the currants, anchovies, and capers, if using, and combine.

In a large skillet, heat the oil over medium heat. Add the garlic and shallots and sauté until just beginning to color, 4 to 5 minutes. And the currant mixture and sauté until combined, 1 minute. Increase the heat to high and add the kale. Cook, stirring, until the kale has wilted, about 5 minutes. Season with salt and pepper, add the zest and red pepper flakes, and toss to mix well.

To make the polenta, oil an 8 x 10-inch stoneware or glass baking dish. In a large pot, bring the stock and milk with the bay leaf to a boil. Reduce the heat to a slow simmer and, whisking continuously, add the cornmeal in a steady stream. When all the cornmeal has been added, continue whisking frequently until the polenta has thickened and begins to pull away from the side of the pot, about 40 to 45 minutes. Remove from the heat and stir in the butter and cheese. Season with salt and pepper to taste. Transfer the polenta to the dish and top with the greens. Serve immediately.

½ cup currants

2 tablespoons pine nuts

3 anchovy fillets, minced

1 tablespoon nonpareil capers (optional)

¼ cup extra-virgin olive oil

2 large garlic cloves, thinly sliced

4 large shallots, thinly sliced (about ½ cup)

1 pound baby kale or other greens

Kosher salt and freshly ground black pepper

Grated zest of 1 lemon

¼ teaspoon red pepper flakes

Polenta

Olive oil, for oiling the baking pan

3 cups vegetable stock or water

4 cups low-fat milk

1 bay leaf

2 cups coarse cornmeal

4 tablespoons unsalted butter

1½ cups Asiago cheese or Parmesan

1 teaspoon kosher salt and freshly ground black pepper

DO-AHEAD POLENTA

To make the polenta up to 2 hours in advance, follow directions above but cook the polenta for only 30 minutes, then spoon the polenta into the prepared dish. Set aside at room temperature. Finish cooking in a 250°F oven for 1 hour. The top of the polenta will get a slight crust and the center and bottom will remain soft.

Israeli Couscous Risotto

Legend has it that Prime Minister David Ben-Gurion asked the owners of the Osem food company to create a wheat-based rice substitute when rice was hard to come by during Israel's early years. Known as "Ben Gurion rice," this originally rice-shaped dish has morphed into the round-shaped product we know today as "Israeli couscous." Larger beads than traditional couscous, Israeli couscous is very popular and widely available outside of Israel and we love making risotto with it. It's not as temperamental as Arborio rice and we enjoy its al dente, pasta-like texture. Toasting the couscous first (as we often recommend with grains) gives it a delicious nutty flavor, and the sun-dried tomatoes add a bright note to the dish.

SERVES 4 TO 6

Bring the stock to a boil in a medium saucepan. Reduce the heat, cover the pan, and simmer gently.

In a large skillet, melt 1 tablespoon of the butter over low heat. Add the leek and gently sauté until soft and translucent, 5 to 6 minutes. Add the couscous and stir continuously with a wooden spoon for 1 minute.

Increase the heat to high and pour in just enough of the simmering stock to cover the couscous. Cook, stirring constantly, until the liquid has been absorbed. Make sure to maintain an active simmer. Stirring constantly, continue to add more stock, about ½ cup at a time, until each addition has been absorbed and the couscous is approaching tender-firm, about 12 minutes. As you cook, be sure to scrape the bottom of the pan with your spoon to prevent the couscous from sticking. When all the stock has been added, the couscous should be al dente. If not, continue to cook, adding stock or water, until it is.

Add the tomatoes, spinach, and basil, and stir until the spinach is wilted. Stir in the remaining 2 tablespoons butter and the Parmesan. Season to taste with salt and pepper and serve.

4 cups vegetable stock, plus more if needed

3 tablespoons unsalted butter

1 leek, white part only, thinly sliced (reserve greens for making stock, see page 98)

2 cups Israeli couscous

1 cup sun-dried tomatoes, packed in oil, drained, and cut into thin strips

5 ounces baby spinach

2 tablespoons basil leaves cut into thin ribbons

1 cup grated Parmesan

Kosher salt and freshly ground black pepper

FISH

Fish Tacos with Orange Chipotle Sauce and
Jicama-Grapefruit Slaw 161

Grilled Halibut Kebabs with Marcona Almond
Sauce 162

Steamed Salmon on Chard Leaves 165

Turkish Roasted Whole Fish 166

Lemon Cardamom Halibut 169

Pan-Seared Branzini 170

Simple Sole with Three Sauces 172

Red Snapper Layered with Tomatoes and
Pickled Jalapeños 174

Fish Tacos with Orange Chipotle Sauce and Jicama-Grapefruit Slaw

People search high and low for great fish tacos. No need to go any further. This recipe was inspired by a class at the Patti Gelman Culinary Arts Center at JCC Manhattan. The school frequently teaches courses dedicated to fish since so many people are looking for alternatives to meat. You'll never miss the beef in these flavorful tacos. The slaw is also a delicious, refreshing side and pairs well with grilled meat, fish, or poultry.

SERVES 4

To make the sauce, combine the orange juice, vinegar, and chipotles in a small saucepan and bring to a boil. Reduce the heat and simmer, stirring occasionally, until reduced to ⅓ cup, about 20 minutes. Remove from the heat and allow to cool.

To prepare the fish, in a medium shallow bowl, combine the cumin, coriander, chili powder, pepper, and salt and stir to mix. Brush the fish on all sides generously with the olive oil. Coat the fish with the spice mixture. Set aside.

To make the slaw, combine the jicama, cabbage, cilantro, grapefruit and its juice, and lime juice in a medium bowl. Season with salt, to taste, and toss.

Preheat the oven to 250°F. Wrap the tortillas in foil and warm in the oven, about 10 minutes. Halve, pit, and peel the avocado, then cut it into ¼-inch slices.

To cook the fish, heat a medium skillet over medium-high heat. Add the fish and cook, turning once, until golden and cooked through, about 4 minutes per side. Break fish into bite-size pieces.

Place a tortilla on each person's plate. Spread the sauce on the tortillas and layer with the fish, slaw, and avocado. Fold and serve.

Sauce

- 1 cup orange juice
- 1 tablespoon white vinegar
- 1½ teaspoons seeded and minced canned chipotles in adobo

Fish

- 1½ teaspoons ground cumin
- 1½ teaspoons ground coriander
- 1 teaspoon chili powder or ground dried chile pepper
- 1 teaspoon freshly ground black pepper
- 1½ teaspoons kosher salt, plus more for seasoning
- 1 pound snapper fillets
- 1 tablespoon olive oil

Slaw

- 8 ounces jicama, cut into very thin strips
- 6 ounces napa cabbage, thinly sliced
- ¼ cup chopped cilantro
- 1 ruby red grapefruit, cut into *supremes* (see page 115), extra juice reserved
- Juice of 2 limes
- Kosher salt

Tacos

- 8 small flour tortillas
- 1 avocado

Grilled Halibut Kebabs with Marcona Almond Sauce

One of our all-time favorite recipes, this is a surprisingly simple dish to make, given how delicious and elegant the results are. The tangy and sublime sauce—the invention of one of our sons—features Spanish Marcona almonds, which have a sweet and delicate taste. The sauce can be partially prepared a day ahead. Adding lemon juice to the sauce just before serving ensures that the tastes and colors stay bright.

SERVES 4

16 (8-inch) wooden skewers, soaked in water for 30 minutes, or 16 (8-inch) metal skewers

Almond Sauce

⅔ cup Marcona almonds

4 teaspoons coriander seeds

¼ cup extra-virgin olive oil

1 tablespoon Dijon mustard

Grated zest and juice of 2 small lemons, preferably organic (about 4 tablespoons juice, 2 tablespoons zest)

2 tablespoons chopped cilantro leaves

Kosher salt and freshly ground black pepper

Kebabs

2 (2-inch-thick) halibut steaks, boned and skinned (1¾ to 2 pounds total), cut into twelve 2-inch cubes

5 tablespoons extra-virgin olive oil

2 garlic cloves, pressed or minced (about 2 teaspoons)

Kosher salt and freshly ground black pepper

3 lemons or limes, sliced into ¼-inch rounds

16 fresh small figs (optional)

To make the almond sauce, toast the almonds in a small skillet over medium heat, stirring, until golden, 3 to 5 minutes. Roughly chop and transfer the nuts to a small bowl. In the same skillet, lightly toast the coriander seeds over medium heat, stirring, until just fragrant, 1 to 2 minutes. Coarsely crush the seeds using a mortar and pestle or with a rolling pin, between 2 pieces of parchment paper.

In a small bowl, whisk together the crushed coriander, olive oil, mustard, and lemon zest until thoroughly combined. (Set the lemon juice aside until just before serving.) Stir in the toasted almonds and cilantro and season with salt and pepper. Set aside.

To make the kebabs, combine the halibut with 3 tablespoons of the oil and the garlic and place in a large glass baking dish. Season with salt and pepper and toss. Cover with plastic wrap and marinate for 10 minutes.

Assemble the skewers, alternating the fish cubes, lemon or lime rounds, and figs, if using. Use 2 parallel skewers per kebab to ensure that the fish doesn't spin around a skewer when you are turning the kebabs.

Heat an outdoor grill or grill pan. Brush the kebabs with the remaining 2 tablespoons oil. Grill the kebabs, turning once, until the fish is opaque but not dry, 3 to 4 minutes per side.

Pour the almond sauce into a medium skillet and gently heat. Stir in the lemon juice. Serve the sauce with the kebabs.

Steamed Salmon on Chard Leaves

Steaming salmon fillets is a quick and healthy technique that results in deliciously fresh-tasting fish. We've incorporated garlic scapes into this recipe as a fun seasonal addition. Scapes are the curling tops of growing garlic plants and are edible, tender, and tasty. In the Northeast, the scapes appear for a short period of time in green markets in late June and early July. Buy them when you see them, as they keep for many months in the refrigerator; otherwise, scallions will do the job beautifully. We suggest using a bamboo steamer with two stacking baskets for this.

SERVES 4

To make the sauce, combine the ginger, rice wine vinegar, soy sauce, and honey in a small bowl. Set aside.

Line a bamboo steamer basket with 6 of the chard leaves.

Rinse the salmon and pat dry. Place the fish in a large bowl and rub with the sesame oil and pressed garlic. Season with salt and pepper.

Fill a pot that the steamer basket will fit over snugly with 2 inches of water and bring to a boil. Add the fish to the chard-lined basket. Sprinkle with scapes or scallions and cover. Place the basket over the pot and steam the fish for 4 minutes. Add the remaining chard leaves to a second basket. Place the second basket on top of the fish basket, cover it, and continue to steam for 4 to 6 minutes, until firm. (The fish will continue to cook after you remove it from the steam.)

Remove the baskets from the steamer. Drizzle the fish with the sauce and serve with the additional chard.

Sauce
- ½ teaspoon grated fresh ginger
- ⅓ cup rice wine vinegar
- 1 tablespoon soy sauce
- 1 teaspoon honey

Salmon
- 16 tender red or rainbow Swiss chard leaves (about ½ pound), tough stem portions removed
- 1½ pounds center-cut salmon fillet, cut into 4 equal pieces
- 2 teaspoons toasted sesame oil
- 2 garlic cloves, pressed
  Kosher salt and freshly ground black pepper
- 3 garlic scapes or 5 scallions, chopped

FISH CAKES

When you have a lot of leftover cooked fish, such as halibut, sole, snapper, salmon, or cod, use it to make delicious fish cakes: In a medium bowl, combine about 1 pound of flaked fish with 2 roughly mashed boiled, peeled medium potatoes, 2 eggs, 1 tablespoon of whatever fresh green herbs you have (such as parsley, dill, or cilantro), and 1 tablespoon grated or minced onion. Season with salt and pepper. Gently shape the mixture into 3-inch cakes (or make them bite size for serving as an hors d'oeuvre) and dredge them in cornmeal. Brown in butter or oil over medium heat. (You can also freeze them before cooking. Just put them in a warm skillet without defrosting.) Serve with Tartar Sauce (page 173).

Turkish Roasted Whole Fish

Who knew that to jump-start a big project, and inspire and unite a group, all we needed to do was prepare this dish? Flavored with Turkish spices and an herbed tomato paste, this fish was served in one of our homes at the launch of JCC Manhattan's new-building capital campaign. Everyone left raving about the idea for the building *and* begging for the recipe, now dubbed Capital Campaign Fish.

We use red snapper because its size is manageable at home, but you can easily double the recipe to serve a crowd by using a large sea bass. Count 1 pound of whole fish per person, and bake 10 minutes per inch of fish thickness.

To make the herbed tomato paste, place the sun-dried tomatoes in a small glass bowl, add the hot water, and soak the tomatoes until softened, 10 to 20 minutes. Drain. Combine the spice mixture, the sun-dried tomatoes, and the remaining paste ingredients in a food processor. Pulse 6 or 7 times to combine and then continue to process until you make a smooth paste. Set aside.

To make the filling, chop the fennel fronds; set aside 2 tablespoons for garnish. Combine ½ cup of the remaining chopped fronds, the sliced fennel bulb, lemon slices, and red onion and season with salt and pepper in a medium bowl. Set aside.

Preheat the oven to 500°F.

Place the fish on a large sheet of heavy-duty foil. Season both sides of the fish generously with salt and pepper. Rub the inside of the cavity with half of the herbed tomato paste. Place the filling inside the snapper (you may have more filling than fits inside the fish). Pat the remaining paste under and outside the fish to coat it. Strew any remaining filling (lemon, fennel, onion) around the fish.

Gently transfer the fish on the foil to a baking sheet and pour the wine around it. Enclose the fish in the foil, making a seam at the top. Bake for 15 minutes. Carefully open the package and continue to bake the fish until crispy and cooked through, about 15 minutes. Be careful not to overcook.

Carefully transfer the fish with two spatulas to a warmed serving platter. Pour the fish juices into a small saucepan. Bring to a simmer over medium heat, adding a little more wine if more liquid seems to be needed. Whisk in the butter one piece at a time, add the parsley, and transfer to a sauceboat. Garnish the fish with the reserved chopped fennel fronds and serve with the sauce and lemon wedges.

Turkish Spice Mixture

You can put this spice mixture on any fish or chicken as a rub. If using fresh herbs, it will keep for 2 weeks in the fridge. If you make it with all dried herbs it will keep on your shelf for up to 4 months.

To make the Turkish spices, combine all the ingredients in a medium bowl and stir to blend.

1½ teaspoons ground cumin

1½ teaspoons paprika

1½ teaspoons sumac

1½ teaspoons dried mint

½ teaspoon dried oregano or thyme; or 1 teaspoon fresh chopped oregano or thyme leaves

¼ teaspoon kosher salt

¼ teaspoon freshly ground black pepper

Herbed Tomato Paste

2 ounces sun-dried tomatoes (not packed in oil)

¼ cup hot water

Turkish Spice Mixture (see below)

1 tomato (about 4 ounces), diced

2 cups fresh flat-leaf parsley leaves

Leaves from 2 (3-to-4-inch-long) fresh rosemary sprigs

2 garlic cloves, peeled

1 shallot, halved

Grated zest and juice of 1 lemon

2 tablespoons extra-virgin olive oil

1 heaping teaspoon Dijon mustard

1 teaspoon honey

¼ teaspoon freshly ground black pepper

Filling

1 small fennel bulb, sliced very thin (fronds reserved)

1 small lemon, sliced very thin

1 small red onion, sliced very thin (about ½ cup)

Kosher salt and freshly ground black pepper

1 whole red snapper or sea bass (about 5½ pounds), head, tail, and skin left on, butterflied and boned

Kosher salt and freshly ground black pepper

½ cup white wine, plus more if needed

2 tablespoon unsalted butter, cut into small pieces and frozen

¼ cup chopped fresh flat-leaf parsley

6 lemon wedges

THERAPY ON THE FLY

It's a cold, winter day in Manhattan and on the third floor of JCC Manhattan a group of war veterans are casting their fly-fishing lines across the gymnasium. They are part of a therapeutic fly-fishing program to help them heal from post-traumatic stress disorder and they needed a place to practice in the winter. Where could they practice? Enter the JCC and its commitment to repairing the world (*tikkun olam*). They asked and we said yes.

Tikkun olam is everyday fare at JCC Manhattan. Each Saturday morning, hundreds of underserved children learn to swim and play basketball, dance and prepare for exams through our Saturday Morning Community Partners program. Working with large and small social service agencies throughout the city, the JCC opens its doors and its facilities for free, knowing that it takes a whole city to raise all of our children to be safe and healthy.

While there are many ongoing programs and projects at the JCC that address the neediest members of the community, sometimes a crisis hits and we have to rally support. JCCs are frequently the central address in any community to respond to urgent needs. And people know it. When the devastating superstorm Sandy hit New York in 2012, hundreds of people poured into the JCC with clothing, food, and cash, realizing that though they were fortunate enough not to be affected, thousands of people needed their help. One woman and her son bought out every toothbrush in the neighborhood because they knew that often it's life's smallest items that matter the most.

People came and cooked thousands of meals and then traveled to Brooklyn, Staten Island, and Queens to serve them. They sorted clothing; they went door-to-door to make sure people were okay.

Whether it's fly-fishers in the gym, city children learning how to swim in the pool, or people sharing Thanksgiving dinner after the storm, what binds us together is the understanding that we need one another and that when we come together as a community, there's no stopping us.

Lemon Cardamom Halibut

Halibut is a dense, hearty fish that stands up to lots of flavoring. Here, the fish is marinated in a green cardamom–based mixture inspired by Indian flavoring without being too spicy or overpowering. The marinade was made one evening to serve to guests after they returned from a trip to India and were still craving those aromas and flavors. You can make the marinade, which also works well with other firm or flaky white fish (or even chicken), one or two days ahead. Serve the halibut with basmati or black rice and Chutney (see page 188).

SERVES 4

Combine all the marinade ingredients in a large glass bowl and whisk to blend.

Add the fish pieces to the marinade, turn to coat, and marinate at room temperature for 20 minutes.

Preheat the broiler. Transfer the fish to a rimmed baking sheet and broil 3 inches from the heat source until cooked through, 8 to 10 minutes. (You can keep the cooked fish in a 250°F oven for 10 minutes before serving.) Transfer to a serving dish, drizzle with any extra marinade from the pan, and serve with lemon quarters.

Marinade

⅓ cup olive oil

Grated zest and juice of 1 lemon

2 medium shallots, chopped (about 2 tablespoons)

2 garlic cloves, pressed or finely chopped (about 2 teaspoons)

2 teaspoons chopped fresh ginger

1 teaspoon madras curry powder

¼ teaspoon coriander

⅛ teaspoon ground cloves

6 green cardamom pods, crushed

1½ pounds halibut or cod fillet, cut into 4 equal-size pieces

1 lemon, quartered and seeded

Pan-Seared Branzini

This simple, bright dish allows us to pretend we're on the Mediterranean in Italy or Greece. The fish, flavored with fennel, lemon, and herbs, is pan-seared, oven-finished, and then drizzled with olive oil—that's it. You'll need one large ovenproof heavy skillet—well-seasoned cast-iron is best—or two smaller ones. Make sure you have enough room in the pan or pans so the fish can sear without steaming. Don't fret if the fish skin tears a bit when you turn it in the pan. With a bit of practice, and a thorough brushing of olive oil, it will get easier. This is great served with Celery Root and Potato Purée (page 264), Garlic Mashed Potatoes (page 280), or barley risotto (page 154).

SERVES 4

4 branzini (about 1 pound each) with heads and tails on, scaled and gutted

Kosher salt and freshly ground black pepper

2 medium fennel bulbs, very thinly sliced, fronds reserved

2 lemons, halved lengthwise, each half cut into eight slices

¼ to ½ cup chopped fresh flat-leaf parsley

Leaves from 4 fresh thyme sprigs

1 to 2 tablespoons extra-virgin olive oil, plus more for brushing and drizzling

½ to 1 cup white wine

Preheat the oven to 375°F.

Wash and dry the fish well. Cut 3 diagonal slits into 1 side of each fish. Season the inside of the fish with salt and pepper. Place 2 to 4 fennel slices and a few whole fronds inside the cavity of each fish. In each slit insert a lemon wedge, some parsley, and a few leaves of the thyme.

Brush both sides of the fish well with olive oil then lightly season the skin with salt and pepper.

Preheat one 14-inch ovenproof skillet (or 2 smaller ones, each large enough to hold 2 fish) over medium-high heat. When the skillet is hot, add just enough oil to coat the bottom, 1 to 2 tablespoons. Carefully place the fish in the skillet, slit sides down, alternating head to tail. (If using 2 pans, divide the oil between both and place 2 fish in each.) Leave the fish untouched until the skin is nicely browned, about 5 minutes. Carefully turn the fish using 2 spatulas if necessary. Cook on the other side until browned, 3 to 4 minutes.

Remove the skillet(s) from the heat. Add enough of the wine to just cover the bottom of the skillet(s), avoiding the crisped skin as you pour. Transfer the skillet(s) to the oven to finish cooking, about 5 minutes (the fish will feel firm to the touch).

Remove the skillet(s) from the oven and let sit for 5 minutes. Drizzle with additional olive oil and serve from the skillet(s).

Simple Sole with Three Sauces

We think of sole as a great blank canvas, a mild but flavorful vehicle for sauces and other accompaniments. Here, we're suggesting three terrific sauces and two methods of cooking. Choose the sauce you want to make on any given night: The red pepper sauce is savory and rich; the tartar sauce uses fat-free Greek yogurt instead of mayonnaise for a lighter but still luscious result; and the yuzu sauce adds Asian soy-citrus notes to the fish. And choose between the two ways to cook sole or other white fish like lemon sole or flounder: Pan-searing is great, but if you're cooking for a crowd, you may want to broil the fish, as you can cook more pieces at the same time.

SERVES 4

1 tablespoon extra-virgin olive oil

1 tablespoon unsalted butter or additional olive oil

1 garlic clove, pressed or thinly sliced (optional)

4 (6-to-8-ounce) pieces fillet of sole, skinned

Kosher salt and freshly ground black pepper

2 lemons, halved

Sauce of choice (recipes follow)

For pan-searing: Heat a large heavy skillet over medium-high heat. Add the oil, butter, and garlic, if using, and heat until the butter is melted and the oil is hot. Season the fish with the salt and pepper. Add the fish and cook for 2 minutes. Turn and cook until the fish is opaque and browned on the edges, about 2 minutes more. Squeeze the lemon over the fish while it's still warm.

For broiling: Preheat the broiler and line the broiler pan with foil. Transfer the fish to the pan, brush both sides with 2 tablespoons oil and season with salt and pepper. Top with the garlic, if using, and squeeze the lemon over the fish. Broil until the fish is opaque and browned on top, about 2 to 4 minutes.

Transfer the fish to plates and serve with sauce of your choice.

Roasted Red Pepper Sauce

This sauce is also great under grilled eggplant or zucchini slices, topped with crumbled feta cheese, and served at room temperature.

Preheat the oven to 450°F. Lightly oil a large baking sheet with olive oil.

Arrange the tomatoes, pepper, and garlic on the baking sheet and drizzle with 6 tablespoons of the oil. Season with salt and pepper and toss to coat. Roast until the vegetables are soft and brown around the edges, 45 to 50 minutes.

Squeeze the garlic pulp from the skin into a food processor. Add the tomatoes and pepper and process until smooth.

Heat the remaining 2 tablespoons olive oil in a medium saucepan over low heat. Add the puréed vegetable mixture, thyme, and vinegar and cook, stirring until the sauce has heated through, 2 to 3 minutes. Adjust the seasoning and serve.

MAKES ABOUT 1½ CUPS

Olive oil, for oiling the baking sheet

½ pound plum tomatoes, quartered lengthwise

1 large red bell pepper (about 12 ounces), quartered and seeded

4 medium garlic cloves, unpeeled

8 tablespoons extra-virgin olive oil

Sea salt and freshly ground black pepper

1 tablespoon minced fresh thyme leaves

1 tablespoon red wine vinegar

Tartar Sauce

This can be made 3 to 4 days ahead of time and stored in the fridge. You can substitute mayonnaise for some of the yogurt for a richer sauce.

In a medium bowl, combine all the ingredients and whisk until well blended.

MAKES 1 CUP

2 medium shallots, diced (about 2 tablespoons)

1 garlic clove, minced

¼ cup capers, chopped

1 cup 0% Greek yogurt

1 tablespoon dried tarragon, crushed

½ cup chopped cornichons

1 teaspoon lemon juice

Tabasco sauce, to taste

Kosher salt and freshly ground black pepper

Yuzu Sauce

Yuzu, a very aromatic yellow citrus fruit that grows wild in China and Tibet, has made solid inroads into American cooking. Its flavor is tart and similar to that of grapefruit mixed with mandarin orange. Not eaten as a fruit by itself, its juice is used mostly as a seasoning.

In a medium bowl, combine all the ingredients and whisk until well blended.

MAKES 2 CUPS

1 tablespoon chopped fresh ginger

2 medium shallots, chopped (about 2 tablespoons)

1 cup soy sauce

1 cup orange juice

½ cup yuzu juice or sauce (available at Japanese markets) or lime juice

¼ cup honey

¼ teaspoon fresh thyme leaves

Red Snapper Layered with Tomatoes and Pickled Jalapeños

This special dish—perfect for a festive lunch or dinner—is based on a recipe we learned in a Jewish-Mexican cooking class taught by chef and restaurateur Roberto Santibañez. It takes a while to assemble, but is well worth the effort. You can, however, put it all together a day in advance, refrigerate it, then pop it into the oven before serving. Just leave out the step of marinating the fish in lime juice and squeeze the juice over the top right before baking.

The recipe calls for pickled jalapeños, which are a tasty surprise—briny with just a small kick (if you remove the seeds and membranes). Pickle lovers will particularly enjoy them. They can also be served with sliced cheese alongside salsa and chips.

SERVES 4 TO 6

4 (8-ounce) red snapper fillets, skinned

2 limes, halved

Kosher salt

4 large ripe tomatoes (about 2 pounds)

1 large onion, halved and thinly sliced

6 bay leaves

½ cup chopped cilantro

12 fresh thyme sprigs

3 Pickled Jalapeños (recipe follows), chopped and seeded

12 garlic cloves, peeled

½ cup small Spanish or green olives

1 tablespoon nonpareil capers (optional)

3 tablespoons extra-virgin olive oil

Place the snapper fillets in a 9 x 13-inch baking dish. Squeeze the juice from one of the limes over them and season with salt. Turn the fillets once or twice in the seasonings and marinate at room temperature for 30 minutes, or cover and refrigerate for up to 4 hours.

Bring a large saucepan of water to a boil. Fill a large bowl with ice and add water. Core the tomatoes and cut a shallow X in the intact end. Slip the tomatoes into the boiling water and leave until their skins start to peel away, about 10 seconds depending on ripeness. Remove the tomatoes with a slotted spoon and transfer to the ice bath. When cool enough to handle, peel. Cut the tomatoes into ½-inch slices.

Preheat the oven to 425°F.

Make a layer of half the onion in a separate 9 x 13-inch baking pan. (You can use a different pan size, but make sure the fillets will fit snugly in it with just a small bit of overlap.) Place slightly less than half the tomatoes on top of the onions. Top with the bay leaves, scatter with half of each of the cilantro, thyme, and pickled jalapeños (reserve the remaining for garnish). Season with salt.

Tuck the garlic under the vegetables at the edges of the dish. Squeeze the juice from the remaining lime over the vegetables and top with the fillets, spacing them evenly (they can overlap if necessary). Scatter the olives and the capers, if using, over the fish, then top with the remaining tomatoes and onions. Drizzle with half of the oil. Cover tightly with foil.

Bake the fish for 20 minutes. Uncover and bake until the juices bubble up around the fish and it is cooked through, 15 to 20 minutes more. Sprinkle with the remaining cilantro, thyme, and jalapeños, drizzle with the remaining olive oil, and serve.

Pickled Jalapeños

With a paring knife, cut 2 vertical slits in the jalapeños on opposite sides, beginning about ½ inch from the stem end and stopping about 1 inch above the tapered end. (**NOTE**: *Jalapeños are among the moderately spiced peppers and the heat resides primarily in the seeds and white membranes. We suggest washing your hands with warm soapy water immediately after handling the peppers.*)

In a heavy saucepan, heat the oil over medium-low heat. Add the jalapeños, onion, carrot, and garlic and cook, stirring often, until the vegetables are softened but not browned, about 10 minutes. Add the vinegar, water, sugar, mustard, lime, bay leaves, thyme, marjoram, allspice, salt, and pepper. Bring to a boil, reduce the heat, and simmer until the vegetables are cooked through, about 15 minutes. Taste and add water if the brine seems too sharp; it will mellow as it sits. Let the mixture cool to room temperature.

Pack the vegetables and their liquid into a quart-size glass canning jar. Make sure the vegetables are completely submerged in their liquid and refrigerate.

10   medium jalapeños (about ¾ pound)
¼   cup extra-virgin olive oil
1   medium onion, cut into 2-inch chunks
1   large carrot, peeled and cut into ½-inch rounds
12   garlic cloves, peeled
½   cup cider vinegar
½   cup water, or more as needed
¾   tablespoon sugar
1   teaspoon Dijon mustard
½   lime, cut into ½-inch-thick slices
2   bay leaves
2   fresh thyme sprigs
2   fresh marjoram sprigs
6   allspice berries, coarsely crushed
1½   tablespoons kosher salt
¼   teaspoon coarsely ground black pepper

POULTRY

Farmhouse Chicken

Since we started writing this cookbook, we haven't been able to stop making this chicken. Inspired by French country cooking, it's crispy and moist. You'll be pleasantly surprised to see that you can make this year-round since frozen artichoke hearts are a great stand-in for fresh. If you don't have artichokes, no worries, the star of this dish is the chicken.

NOTE: *If you'd like a light sauce with this, after plating the chicken and artichoke mixture, add an additional ¼ to ½ cup chicken stock, depending on how much sauce you want, to the skillet and deglaze over low heat. Serve the sauce separately in a gravy boat.*

SERVES 4 TO 5

Preheat the oven to 450°F.

In a small bowl, combine the garlic, mustard, wine, 2 tablespoons of the oil, the balsamic vinegar, sriracha, if using, rosemary, fennel seeds, and ½ teaspoon of salt.

Heat a large, heavy, ovenproof skillet (preferably cast-iron) over high heat. Spread half the mustard mixture on the underside of the chicken. Transfer the chicken to the skillet, breast side up, and spread the remaining mustard mixture on top. Cook the chicken until the bottom begins to brown, about 5 minutes. Transfer the skillet to the oven and roast until the skin has browned and the chicken is cooked through (to an internal temperature of 160°F), about 25 minutes.

Meanwhile, heat a grill pan over high heat. In a medium bowl, combine the artichokes and lemon slices with 1 to 2 tablespoons of the oil, as needed to coat them evenly, and sprinkle with the remaining salt. Transfer the artichokes and lemon to the grill pan and cook, turning once, until grill marks are visible, 7 to 10 minutes on the first side and 5 to 7 minutes on the second.

Transfer the artichokes, lemon, and olives, if using, to the skillet with the chicken. Add the stock and roast with the chicken for 5 minutes more. Remove the skillet from the oven and allow the chicken to rest for 5 minutes. Cut into 4 or 8 pieces. Transfer the chicken and artichoke mixture to a platter, sprinkle with the herbs, and serve.

3 garlic cloves, coarsely chopped (about 3 teaspoons)

3 tablespoons Dijon mustard

2 tablespoons dry white wine

3 to 4 tablespoons extra-virgin olive oil

1 tablespoon balsamic vinegar

1 teaspoon sriracha or Tabasco sauce (optional)

1 teaspoon fresh rosemary leaves or ½ teaspoon dried rosemary

½ teaspoon fennel seeds

1½ teaspoons kosher salt

1 (4-pound) chicken, butterflied, backbone removed (ask your butcher to do this)

10 ounces fresh baby artichokes, trimmed to tender, inner leaves halved; or defrosted frozen artichokes, drained and dried well

2 lemons, sliced ⅛ inch thick (10 to 12 slices)

½ cup pitted picholine olives, drained (optional)

¼ cup chicken stock

2 tablespoons mixed fresh chopped herbs, such as parsley, tarragon, chervil, and thyme

Grilled Chicken Paillards for Four Seasons

If you run out of chicken ideas, here's a template that will keep you creative throughout the year, thanks to the four recipes for seasonal salad toppings that follow. Taking the time to pound the chicken cutlets very thin and uniform, when making paillards, is worth the effort and critical to ensure quick and even grilling. Indoors or out, grilling is based on dry heat from below, so whether you use a backyard grill or a grill pan on your stovetop, you can always cook the perfect chicken paillard. Each of these salad toppings is wonderful on its own.

SERVES 4

4 boneless, skinless chicken breasts

3 tablespoons extra-virgin olive oil

2 tablespoons lemon juice

4 garlic cloves, minced (about 4 teaspoons)

¼ teaspoon kosher salt

¼ teaspoon freshly ground black pepper

Salad of choice (recipes follow)

Place each breast between 2 pieces of parchment paper and pound until ¼ inch thick (about 6 x 8 inches).

In a medium bowl, combine the olive oil, lemon juice, garlic, salt, and pepper. Place the chicken in the bowl and coat evenly in the marinade. Cover and marinate for at least 30 minutes or up to 1 hour. In hot weather, refrigerate while marinating. (NOTE: *The acidity of the juice will begin to "cook" the chicken and it may begin to turn it opaque.*)

Preheat an outdoor grill or grill pan over high heat. Add 1 or 2 paillards, depending on the grill's capacity, and grill until three-quarters cooked through, about 2 minutes. Using tongs, gently turn the chicken and grill about 2 minutes more, making sure that the paillards don't dry out. Repeat with the remaining paillards, placing each on a platter when done. Top with the seasonal salad of your choice and serve.

recipe continues

Spring Asparagus Salad

To make the dressing, whisk together the olive oil, avocado oil, vinegar, lemon juice, garlic, and sugar in a small bowl. Season with salt and pepper.

Using a vegetable peeler, shave the asparagus to make long ribbons. In a large skillet, heat the olive oil over high heat. Add the asparagus and cook, tossing continuously, until warm and bright green, 1 to 2 minutes. Add the radishes and stir. Remove from the heat and stir in the dill, chives, and tarragon. Drizzle with some of the dressing and toss.

Place the chicken paillards on a platter or individual serving plates, top with asparagus mixture, and serve with the remaining dressing.

SERVES 4

Dressing

¼ cup extra-virgin olive oil

2 tablespoons avocado oil or additional extra-virgin olive oil

2 tablespoons rice vinegar or white wine vinegar

2 tablespoons lemon juice

2 garlic cloves, pressed (about 2 teaspoons)

¼ teaspoon sugar

Kosher salt and freshly ground black pepper

Salad

2 pounds large asparagus, tough ends removed

2 teaspoons extra-virgin olive oil

1 bunch radishes, tops and roots trimmed, thinly sliced

½ cup chopped fresh dill

¼ cup snipped fresh chives

¼ cup snipped fresh tarragon

Summer Tomato Salad

In a large bowl, combine the tomatoes, arugula, onion, parsley, and oregano. Gently toss with the olive oil.

Place the chicken paillards on a platter or individual serving plates. Just before serving, add the lemon juice and salt to the tomato mixture, season with the pepper, and gently toss. Divide the salad over the paillards and garnish with the basil. Pass the balsamic vinegar, if using, to drizzle over the chicken.

SERVES 4

VARIATION
You may be surprised how delicious this preparation is if you try thinly sliced summer-ripe peaches instead of the tomatoes.

2 pints assorted tomatoes, cut into bite-size pieces

4 cups baby arugula leaves

½ small red onion, sliced paper thin (about ⅓ cup)

½ cup packed torn fresh flat-leaf parsley leaves

½ teaspoon fresh chopped oregano, or to taste

4 teaspoons extra-virgin olive oil

Juice of 1 lemon

½ teaspoon kosher or sea salt

Freshly ground black pepper

¼ cup small fresh basil leaves, for garnish

Good-quality balsamic vinegar, for drizzling (optional)

Fall Squash Salad

Preheat the oven to 450°F.

Line a baking sheet with foil or parchment paper and spread the squash on top. Drizzle with the olive oil and turn to coat. Roast for 10 minutes, shake the pan to shift the cubes, and continue to roast until fork-tender and brown-edged, 20 to 25 minutes.

In a medium skillet, toast the pumpkin seeds over medium heat, stirring, until golden, 6 to 8 minutes. Set aside.

In a small saucepan, warm the cider vinegar over medium heat. Remove from the heat, add the currants, and allow them to plump, about 10 minutes. Set aside.

Stack the kale leaves on top of one another, hold firmly, and slice into thin ribbons. Transfer to a large bowl.

In a small bowl, combine the pears with the lemon juice and toss.

To make the dressing, in another small bowl, whisk together the walnut oil, olive oil, cider vinegar, and lemon juice. Season with salt and pepper to taste.

To the bowl with the kale, add the squash, pears, drained currants, and half the dressing and toss vigorously. Allow to marinate for at least 15 minutes or as long as 1 hour. For a more tender kale, marinate longer.

Place each paillard on a dinner plate. Divide the salad mixture over the paillards. Sprinkle with the pumpkin seeds and serve with the remaining dressing.

SERVES 4

2 pounds butternut squash, peeled, seeded, and cut into 1-inch cubes

1 tablespoon extra-virgin olive oil

½ cup shelled pumpkin seeds

2 tablespoons cider vinegar

¼ cup dried currants

2 bunches Tuscan kale (about 1½ pounds), stems and ribs removed

2 firm pears, red skinned if possible, cored and cut into ½-inch dice

1 teaspoon lemon juice

Dressing

¼ cup walnut or pumpkin seed oil

2 tablespoons extra-virgin olive oil

2 tablespoons cider vinegar

4 teaspoons lemon juice

Kosher salt and freshly ground black pepper

Winter Endive and Radicchio Salad

In a medium skillet, heat the olive oil over medium heat. Add the leeks and sauté until softened, about 5 minutes. Add the chestnuts, stir to combine, and transfer to a large bowl. Add the endives, radicchio, clementines, vinegar, and thyme. Season with salt and pepper.

Spoon the salad over the paillards and serve.

SERVES 4

3 tablespoons extra-virgin olive oil

3 cups ¼-inch-thick sliced leeks, white and light green parts only

¾ cup jarred chestnuts, cut into ½-inch slices

3 endives (about ¾ pound), sliced ½ inch thick

1 small radicchio (about 3 ounces), halved, cored, and thinly sliced

2 clementines, peeled, sliced into quarters, and separated into sections

2 tablespoons rice vinegar

½ teaspoon fresh thyme leaves, chopped

Kosher salt and freshly ground black pepper

Fall Squash Salad

Roasted Chicken Paprikash

Chicken paprikash is a quintessential Hungarian dish that was made by every Hungarian bubbe. While we still love the stovetop version, we find that we more often want to eat roasted chicken these days. Hence the birth of this dish—a roasted chicken with all the paprika flavor of the original. You can serve this with wide egg noodles or ready-made spaetzle, but we love making our own *nokedli,* the Hungarian spaetzle.

SERVES 4

In a large glass bowl, combine the garlic, 1 tablespoon of the olive oil, the tomato paste, thyme, sweet and smoked paprika, and black pepper. Combine to make a paste. Add the chicken pieces and rub the mixture over the pieces, making sure to coat them well. Cover and marinate in the refrigerator, for 1 hour or as long as overnight.

Preheat the oven to 400°F.

Place the chicken pieces, skin side up, in a large baking pan in a single layer. Roast the chicken for 20 minutes. Turn the chicken pieces over and roast for 20 minutes more.

Meanwhile, toss the red peppers and leeks in a medium bowl with the remaining 2 tablespoons olive oil and salt and pepper to taste. Turn the chicken skin side up again and scatter the peppers and leeks around the chicken, making sure not to cover the chicken (so as to allow it to crisp). Drizzle the stock around the edges of the pan, and return the pan to the oven. Finish roasting the chicken until its juices run clear when pierced with a fork and the vegetables are frizzled and caramelized, about 20 minutes.

Platter the chicken and vegetables together. Toss the *nokedli* with the chicken pan juices. Drizzle the chicken with any remaining juices from the pan and garnish with chopped parsley or more thyme leaves. Serve with the *nokedli.*

NOTE: *If you want more pan sauce, add an additional ⅓ cup stock to the pan after you have plattered the chicken and the vegetables. Pour stock and drippings into a small saucepan, warm thoroughly, and pass at the table.*

6 garlic cloves, pressed (about 6 teaspoons)

3 tablespoons olive oil

2 tablespoons tomato paste

1 tablespoon fresh thyme leaves, or 1 teaspoon dried thyme

1 tablespoon sweet paprika

2 teaspoons smoked paprika

¼ teaspoon freshly ground black pepper

1 (3-pound) chicken, cut into eighths

3 red bell peppers, stemmed, seeded, and sliced very thinly

2 cups thinly sliced leeks, white and light green parts only (about 4 medium leeks)

Kosher salt and freshly ground black pepper

¾ cup chicken or vegetable stock

Nokedli (Hungarian Spaetzle, page 149)

Chopped fresh flat-leaf parsley or additional thyme leaves, for garnish

Green Masala Chicken

We are often inspired by the culinary traditions of diverse Jewish communities. Jews have lived in India for thousands of years—plenty of time to assimilate Indian flavors and spices such as masala, a spice mixture that is ground into a paste. Masala chicken is traditionally made with heavy cream, but we use unsweetened coconut milk to lighten it up. You can make the paste in about 20 minutes and then refrigerate it for a day or two before you want to cook the chicken. Then it takes just 25 minutes to finish. Serve with basmati rice, Sautéed Greens with Shallots (page 281), and Chutney (see box).

SERVES 4 TO 6

Masala Paste

- 2 cups packed cilantro leaves
- 1 cup packed fresh mint leaves
- 1 jalapeño pepper, coarsely chopped
- 4 to 5 garlic cloves (about 4 to 5 teaspoons)
- ½ cup water

Chicken

- 2 tablespoons extra-virgin olive oil
- 1 medium onion, finely chopped (about 1 cup)
- 8 skinless, boneless chicken thighs (about 1¾ pounds), cut into 1-inch pieces
- 2 teaspoons turmeric
- ½ teaspoon ground cinnamon
- ½ teaspoon ground cardamom
- ⅛ teaspoon ground cloves
- 1 cup unsweetened coconut milk
- ½ cup lemon juice
  Kosher salt and freshly ground black pepper

To make the paste, combine all the ingredients in a food processor or blender and purée until smooth. (If making the paste a day in advance, transfer to a bowl, cover, and refrigerate.)

In a large deep skillet, heat the oil over medium heat. Add the onion and cook, stirring frequently, until softened, about 5 minutes. Add the chicken, turmeric, cinnamon, cardamom, and cloves and cook, stirring occasionally, until the chicken has begun to turn golden, about 7 minutes. Add the masala paste, coconut milk, and lemon juice and bring to a boil. Reduce the heat and simmer until the chicken is tender, about 15 minutes. Season with salt and pepper and serve.

CHUTNEY

Here's a great, easy fruit chutney that will keep for months in your refrigerator: Place 2 cups currants, 2 cups minced peaches (or apples or mangoes), 1 cup minced onion, 2 stalks minced celery, ¼ cup finely chopped ginger, ½ cup mustard seeds, 2 cups packed dark brown sugar, 2 tablespoons molasses, 2 cups apple cider vinegar, and 1 tablespoon *each* cayenne, salt, turmeric, ground cardamom, and curry powder in a large heavy pot and bring to a boil. Reduce the heat and simmer until thickened, about 30 minutes.

Chicken and Apple Round "Sausages"

This is one of our favorite recipes to come out of JCC Manhattan's Patti Gelman Culinary Arts Center. We call the patties "sausages" because of the traditional sausage spices used—sage, allspice, garlic, and fennel seed. Using dark meat chicken only, they are moist and tender. When you're looking to cut down on red meat, this is a terrific hamburger alternative. By the way, when testing this recipe, we tried using fresh apples and found that the dried apples actually yielded a more intense flavor.

SERVES 6

In a medium saucepan, combine the apples and cider and simmer over medium heat until the liquid becomes syrupy, about 10 minutes. Transfer to a food processor and pulse to chop.

Transfer the mixture to a large bowl and add the ground chicken, egg, garlic, sage, fennel seeds, allspice, salt, and pepper and combine thoroughly with your hands. Make six patties with the mixture.

In a large skillet, heat the oil over medium heat, or brush a grill pan with oil and heat. Add the patties and cook, turning once, until just cooked through, 3 to 5 minutes per side.

Place a burger on one half of each bun. Top with the lettuce, onion, and the remaining bun half. Serve garnished with the cornichons.

> For the purist, you can grind the chicken yourself at home using a food processor or the grinder attachment of a standing mixer.

1 cup packed dried apples

1 cup apple cider

2 pounds ground chicken thigh meat

1 extra-large egg, lightly beaten

3 garlic cloves, finely chopped (about 1 tablespoon)

2 tablespoons finely chopped fresh sage

1 tablespoon fennel seeds, crushed

¼ teaspoon ground allspice

2 teaspoons kosher salt

½ teaspoon freshly ground black pepper

1 to 2 tablespoons olive or grapeseed oil

6 hamburger buns, rolls, or pita breads

6 leaves red-leaf or Boston lettuce

1 small red onion, thinly sliced

Cornichons, for garnish

Spicy Chicken Stir-Fry with Greens and Cashews

The Jewish love for Chinese food is renowned. Did it start with the proximity of the two communities on New York City's Lower East Side? Who knows. Regardless, when you find a Jewish community, inevitably you will find a Chinese restaurant nearby. Here's our take on a classic American-Cantonese stir-fry. We've spiced it up with Serrano chiles and added lots of greens at the end.

SERVES 4

2 tablespoons soy sauce

2 tablespoons dry sherry

3 teaspoons toasted sesame oil

2 teaspoons light brown sugar

1¼ pounds skinless, boneless chicken breasts, cut into 3 x 1-inch pieces

3 tablespoons peanut oil

4 scallions, white and green parts chopped separately

2 teaspoons chopped seeded Serrano chile

1 pound greens, such as baby spinach or baby kale

Kosher salt and freshly ground black pepper

½ cup roughly chopped toasted cashews or peanuts

In a medium bowl, whisk together 1 tablespoon of the soy sauce, 1 tablespoon of the sherry, 1 teaspoon of the sesame oil, and 1 teaspoon of the sugar. Add the chicken, turn to coat in the marinade, and let it sit unrefrigerated for 20 to 30 minutes.

In a small bowl, whisk together the remaining soy sauce, sherry, sesame oil, and sugar and set aside.

In a wok or a large heavy skillet, heat 2 tablespoons of the peanut oil over high heat. Add the white parts of the scallions and the chile and stir-fry until fragrant, about 30 seconds. Add the chicken and stir-fry until just cooked through, about 3 minutes. Transfer the chicken mixture to a medium bowl and set aside.

Add the remaining 1 tablespoon peanut oil to the wok and heat over high heat. Add the greens in large handfuls, stirring each batch until it wilts, about 4 minutes, depending on the greens you're using. Return the chicken to the wok, add the reserved soy sauce mixture, and stir-fry until just heated through, about 1 minute. Season with salt and pepper. Transfer to a warm serving bowl. Sprinkle with cashews and the green parts of the scallions and serve.

Lemony Cornish Hens

Although roasted chicken is the gold standard in many Jewish homes for Friday night dinner, we think Cornish hens are a festive option at your Shabbat table. Even if you're too polite to lick your fingers at the table, someone else might do so while eating these delicious hens. (Just let them. And don't cringe when they want to nibble on the bones.) The marinade can be prepared in advance.

NOTE: *You can use this marinade and technique for 3-pound chickens cut in eighths as well. Just increase the cooking time.*

SERVES 4 TO 8

Preheat the broiler on high for 15 minutes.

In a medium bowl, combine the ¼ cup of olive oil with the lemon juice, vinegar, garlic, and oregano. Season with salt and pepper and whisk. (If not using immediately, cover and refrigerate. Whisk, or shake vigorously in a tightly closed container, before using.)

Place the hens, skin side up, in roasting pans or shallow baking dishes that will fit into your broiler. Rub with the remaining olive oil. Working in 2 batches if necessary, broil the hens about 3 inches from the heat source, turning once, until their skin is golden brown, 7 to 10 minutes per side. Adjust the distance between the hens and the heat source if necessary to prevent burning.

Preheat the oven to 350°F.

When the hens are cool enough to handle, cut each half into 2 parts. Discard any fat that may have accumulated in the pans and arrange the hens in the pans so the pieces don't overlap. Pour the lemon sauce over the hens and turn a few times to coat, finishing skin side up. Bake the hens for 10 to 15 minutes more, until juices run clear.

Transfer the hens to a warm plate. Pour the juices from the pans into a heavy medium saucepan. Add the stock and cook over high heat until reduced by a third, about 5 minutes. Stir in the parsley. Spoon some of the sauce over the hens and pass the remaining sauce.

¼ cup plus 1 tablespoon extra-virgin olive oil

1 cup lemon juice

1½ teaspoons red wine vinegar

1 garlic clove, chopped (about 1 teaspoon)

¼ teaspoon dried oregano or ½ teaspoon fresh oregano

Kosher salt and freshly ground black pepper

4 Cornish hens, cut in half, backbone removed

¼ cup chicken stock

¼ cup chopped fresh flat-leaf parsley

Chicken Bouillabaisse

We've adapted this from Jacques Pépin's chicken bouillabaisse in *Fast Food My Way*. Chef Pépin is a longtime friend of JCC Manhattan, serving as a judge in April 2011 for the Annual Man-O-Manischewitz Cookoff. Bouillabaisse is a hearty stew, and this version proves you don't need shellfish to make it. We serve it with a dollop of *rouille*, a delicious garlic-heavy Provençal condiment. You can also add sweet or spicy peppers to it to get more punch, and spread the rouille on crusty baguette slices you then float in each serving. Or serve the stew with Two-Grain Saffron Couscous (page 150) and pass the rouille alongside.

In a large bowl, combine the onion, celery, carrot, oil, garlic, zest, saffron, fennel seeds, herbes de Provence, salt, and pepper. Add the chicken and mix to coat the chicken well. Cover with a lid or plastic wrap and refrigerate until ready to proceed. (This can be done up to a half-day ahead.)

Transfer the contents of the bowl to a medium heavy enamel or stainless steel pot and add the tomatoes, stock, wine, Pernod, if using, and potatoes. Cover and bring to a boil over high heat, then reduce the heat to low and simmer gently for 25 minutes, checking twice to ensure all the chicken is submerged. Add the sausage and simmer until the sausage is cooked through and the chicken and vegetables are fork-tender, about 5 minutes.

To make the rouille, combine half a potato from the soup, ¼ cup liquid and vegetables from the soup, the garlic, paprika, and cayenne in a food processor and process for 10 seconds. Add the egg yolk, if using. With the processor running slowly, add the oil in a slow, steady stream, processing until the oil is incorporated and the mixture is thick and creamy. Adjust the seasoning with the salt and lemon juice if necessary.

Transfer the bouillabaisse to warm soup plates. Top each with a spoonful of the rouille, sprinkle with the fresh herbs, and serve.

½ cup coarsely chopped onion (from 1 small onion)

¼ cup coarsely chopped celery

¼ cup coarsely chopped carrot

1 tablespoon extra-virgin olive oil

1 tablespoon coarsely chopped garlic

1 teaspoon grated lemon zest

½ teaspoon saffron threads

¼ teaspoon fennel seeds, crushed

¼ teaspoon herbes de Provence

¾ teaspoon kosher salt

½ teaspoon freshly ground black pepper

4 skinless chicken leg and thigh pieces (about 2 pounds), any fat removed

1 cup canned diced tomatoes

1 cup chicken stock

½ cup dry white wine

2 teaspoons Pernod or Ricard (optional)

5 small Yukon Gold potatoes (about ¾ pound), peeled and halved

8 ounces chicken-apple sausage, cut into 4 equal pieces

1 tablespoon chopped fresh tarragon, chives, or parsley, or a combination, for garnish

Rouille

1 large garlic clove, roughly chopped

¼ teaspoon sweet or smoked paprika

⅛ teaspoon cayenne

1 large egg yolk (optional)

½ cup extra-virgin olive oil

Dash of kosher salt, if needed

Lemon juice (optional)

Great Roast Chicken

We couldn't leave this recipe out of our cookbook. It's adapted from the well-regarded *Zuni Café Cookbook* by the late Judy Rodgers. The original recipe is three-plus pages in length and includes a fantastic amount of detail—it's a great read. We simplified her version, but kept the chicken-drying technique (over 1 to 3 days) that makes the result perfect. This is, by far, the best way to achieve the most tender and moist roasted bird. (**NOTE:** *Our recipe uses a kosher chicken, which is pre-salted. Rodgers's guideline is to use ¾ teaspoon of salt per pound of chicken when the bird has not been pre-salted.*)

This is a good dish for hosting a crowd because the prep work is done days in advance. You only need to increase the number of chickens and the ingredients proportionally. This dish has become so beloved in our families that even as our children begin to fly the coop (pun intended), this is one recipe that always goes with them.

SERVES 2 TO 4

One to 3 days before serving, remove any excess fat from the chicken, rinse, and pat dry inside and out. Starting at the cavity, slide a finger under the skin of each of the breasts, making 2 pockets. Create two more pockets under the skin at the thickest section of each thigh. Using a finger, push two herb sprigs into each of the 4 pockets.

Season the outside of the chicken with salt and pepper. Sprinkle a little of the salt inside the cavity. Leave uncovered and refrigerate for at least 1 day or up to 3.

Bring the chicken to room temperature. Position a rack in the center of the oven and preheat it to 475°F.

Preheat a shallow roasting pan or heavy ovenproof skillet barely larger than the chicken over medium-high heat. Dry the chicken and set it breast side up in the pan.

Transfer the pan or skillet to the center rack of the oven and roast the chicken until it starts to brown, about 20 minutes. If the chicken hasn't browned, increase the temperature by 25 degrees and continue to roast until the skin is browned and blistered.

Roast another 10 minutes and turn the bird over. Continue to roast another 15 minutes, then turn the chicken back over to let the breast skin crisp, 5 to 10 minutes, until the juices run clear. Lift the chicken from the roasting pan and set on a cutting board or plate. Let rest for 10 minutes.

Cut the chicken into serving pieces, arrange on a warm platter, and serve. If you want to make a sauce to serve with the chicken, tilt the roasting pan and skim off the last of the fat. Place over medium-low heat, add any juice that has collected under the chicken, and bring to a simmer. Stir and scrape to soften any hard drippings and transfer to a gravy boat.

1 (2½-to-3-pound) chicken

8 (2-inch-long) sprigs fresh thyme, marjoram, rosemary, sage, or a combination

¾ teaspoon kosher salt

¾ teaspoon freshly cracked black pepper

INGREDIENTS FOR A FULL LIFE

Walk into the gym at JCC Manhattan any morning and you will see an odd sight: three-year-olds running relay races with a rubber chicken. No one knows exactly how it started but it's a beloved tradition. What makes it so much fun? Partly, it's because it's just ridiculous watching small children grabbing for the rubber chicken. But something deeper is going on. Children learn patience as they wait their turn to run. They develop confidence as they realize that each week they are running a little faster. They connect to one another and learn about interdependence and teamwork. Finally, they learn to support one another even in the face of "defeat."

Walk into the gym at the Marcus Jewish Community Center of Atlanta, and you'll see people in their 80s and beyond playing pickleball—the fast-growing sport for older adults that is a mixture of badminton, tennis, and Ping Pong. You will notice Sid Cojac right away. No spring chicken, Sid recently celebrated his 100th birthday, but he literally bounds into the gym with his racket, ready for action. Sid's 94-year-old girlfriend knows that it is the many hours that Sid spends at the Marcus JCC with his friends that keeps him going. And it's not just pickleball. Sid lunches at the JCC surrounded by adults who have just come from a class or the pool. After lunch, many of them go to Talking Heads, an education group with different speakers each week.

Whether you are three or ninety, the ingredients for a full life are not very different: constant growth, physical activity, lots of support, and much laughter—all found at JCCs around the country.

Citrus and Balsamic–Glazed Turkey Breast

This recipe relieves you of any turkey timing and carving anxieties left over from Thanksgiving. It makes a delicious alternative to the standard Friday night roasted chicken dinner, plus it's an easy way to serve a crowd. It uses a boneless turkey breast, which cooks much more quickly than a whole bird. It also slices beautifully and the leftovers are great in sandwiches.

SERVES 8 TO 10

Position a rack in the center of the oven and preheat it to 500°F.

Rub the breast with 2 tablespoons of the olive oil and sprinkle with 1 teaspoon salt and ½ teaspoon pepper. Transfer the breast to a baking dish or roasting pan. Scatter the onions and lemon slices around the breast. Roast for 15 minutes. Reduce the heat to 325°F and continue to roast until the juices run clear and a meat thermometer inserted in the thickest part registers 160°F, about 1½ hours.

Meanwhile, make the glaze: In a medium saucepan, heat the remaining 1 tablespoon olive oil over medium heat. Add the shallot and sauté until softened, 2 to 3 minutes. Add the orange juice, balsamic vinegar, honey, and rosemary and bring to a boil. Reduce the heat and simmer until reduced by about half, about 10 minutes. Whisk in the cornstarch, stirring to avoid lumps. Remove from the heat and cool. During the last 30 minutes of cooking, brush the turkey with enough glaze to coat it.

When the turkey is done, transfer it to a board to rest. Scrape the drippings into the remaining glaze and add the wine and stock. Bring the mixture to a boil and cook until the liquid is reduced by half, about 5 minutes. Season with salt and pepper. Pour the liquid into a gravy separator or spoon off any fat that has collected on the top. Remove the strings, slice the turkey, and serve with the gravy.

1 (4-to-5-pound) boneless turkey breast, skin on and tied

3 tablespoons extra-virgin olive oil

1 teaspoon kosher salt, plus more for seasoning

½ teaspoon freshly gound black pepper, plus more for seasoning

1½ pounds cipollini onions or small shallots

1 Meyer lemon, clementine, or small orange, sliced thin and seeded

1 shallot, finely chopped (about 1 tablespoon)

¾ cup orange juice

¼ cup good-quality balsamic vinegar

3 tablespoons honey

4 sprigs fresh rosemary

½ teaspoon cornstarch, arrowroot, or potato starch

⅔ cup dry white wine

⅔ cup chicken stock

Braised Duck Legs

This is the perfect make-ahead dinner for a cold winter night, when we crave rich meats cooked in wine. Here, the duck is braised with madeira and red wine, vegetables, and herbs, then crisped in a hot oven—delicious! Serve with Garlic Mashed Potatoes (page 280) or wide noodles.

At least 1 hour or up to 3 hours in advance, sprinkle the duck with the thyme leaves. Season with salt and pepper. Set aside.

Heat a very large, deep heavy sauté pan or Dutch oven over high heat until very hot. Add the oil, swirl to coat the pan, and wait 1 minute to ensure that the oil is very hot as well. Then, working in batches if necessary, place the duck legs in the pan, skin side down. Don't crowd the pan. Cook until the skin is just past golden, 8 to 12 minutes. Turn the legs, reduce the heat to medium, and cook just to sear, 2 minutes more. Transfer the legs, skin side up, to a plate and set aside.

Remove all but 1 tablespoon of the fat from the pan (save or discard the rest of the fat). Add the onion, garlic, carrots, celery, thyme sprigs, bay leaf, and sage leaves. Season with pepper and sauté until the vegetables have browned, about 10 minutes. Stir in the tomato paste and add the madeira and red wine. Increase the heat to high, bring the liquid to a boil, and cook until the liquid is reduced by half, 6 to 8 minutes. Add the stock, reduce the heat, and simmer until slightly reduced, about 10 minutes.

Preheat the oven to 350°F.

Gently place the duck legs skin side up on top of the vegetables and broth in the pan. Don't crowd the pan and make sure no liquid or vegetables are on top of the duck. Cover the pan tightly with heavy-duty foil and a tight-fitting lid. Transfer to the oven and braise until the duck is very tender, but not yet falling off the bone, about 2 hours.

Increase the oven heat to 400°F. Carefully transfer the duck pieces, skin side up, to a baking sheet. Return to the oven and bake until the skin is crisp, 10 to 15 minutes. Meanwhile, spoon off as much fat as possible from the sauce (keep or discard), and cook over high heat until the sauce is further thickened and hot, about 5 minutes.

To serve, spoon the sauce with vegetables onto a warm platter, top with the crisped duck, and sprinkle with the parsley. Serve with the additional sauce passed separately.

4 large duck legs with thighs (8 to 10 ounces each), excess fat removed

½ tablespoon fresh thyme leaves, plus 6 (2-inch) sprigs

Kosher salt and freshly ground black pepper

2 tablespoons extra-virgin olive oil

1 large red onion, chopped (about 1 cup)

1 garlic clove, chopped (about 1 teaspoon)

2 medium carrots, peeled, diced (about 1 cup)

1 large celery stalk, diced (about ½ cup)

4 (2-inch) fresh thyme sprigs

1 bay leaf

3 fresh sage leaves

1 tablespoon tomato paste

1¾ cups madeira or marsala wine

¼ cup dry red wine

3 cups duck or chicken stock, plus more as needed

2 teaspoons chopped fresh flat-leaf parsley, for garnish

Many people shy away from cooking duck because of the cost and the fat. We suggest buying a whole duck, which is more economical. Have your butcher divide it into quarters. Use the leg-thighs for this; save the breasts to make Duck Breasts with Apples and Maple Cider Sauce (page 204); and use the wings to make your own duck stock. In this recipe, most of the fat is rendered off during the cooking process. In the Old World, when our forebears were forced to be resourceful, rendered duck fat or, more commonly chicken fat, was used in cooking and was also enjoyed as a spread on a hearty piece of rye or pumpernickel. Use the duck fat collected from this dish to enrich a stew or to make sublime and decadent roasted or fried potatoes. Strain the excess duck fat and pour it into freezable containers or ice cube trays. Store in the freezer for up to one year. You can use it to replace any solid or liquid fat in equal proportion.

Duck Breasts with Apples and Maple Cider Sauce

When prepping this recipe, the scent of maple syrup cooking will warm your soul as it fills your kitchen. If you're concerned about the breasts' layer of fat, which is mostly rendered during the cooking process, buy kosher duck breasts, which are remarkably lean. If you don't have the time to grill the apples, you can serve the duck with apple sauce.

4 boned duck breasts, 6 to 8 ounces each

Kosher salt

½ tablespoon freshly ground black pepper, plus more to taste

1 tablespoon olive oil, plus more for the grill pan

2 garlic cloves, finely chopped (about 2 teaspoons)

2½ cups apple cider

½ cup dry white wine

3 tablespoons pure dark maple syrup (Grade B)

2 tablespoons lemon juice

5 cloves

1 (½-inch) piece cinnamon stick or ⅛ teaspoon ground cinnamon

2 teaspoons arrowroot, corn starch, or potato starch

3 tablespoons chicken stock

3 tablespoons Dijon mustard

2 teaspoons fresh thyme leaves or ½ teaspoon dried thyme

2 large Granny Smith apples, peeled, cored, cut into ½-inch slices, and tossed with 1 tablespoon lemon juice

2 tablespoons chopped fresh flat-leaf parsley

SERVES 4

At least 30 minutes before cooking, remove the breasts from the refrigerator. Remove any excess fat and score the skin lightly with a very sharp knife. Season with salt and ¼ teaspoon pepper.

In a heavy saucepan, heat the olive oil over medium heat. Add the garlic and sauté until it has begun to give off its aroma, about 3 minutes. Add the cider, wine, maple syrup, lemon juice, cloves, and cinnamon. Increase the heat to medium and bring the mixture to a boil. Reduce the heat immediately to low and simmer gently until slightly reduced, about 20 minutes.

Meanwhile, in a small bowl, combine the arrowroot and stock and whisk to blend. Whisk the mixture into the sauce and continue simmering until the sauce is clear and slightly thickened, 1 to 2 minutes. Season with salt and pepper. Transfer 6 tablespoons of the sauce to a small bowl and keep the remaining sauce warm until serving.

Add the mustard, thyme, and ¼ teaspoon pepper to the sauce in the bowl and combine. Brush this mixture on the breasts.

Lightly oil a grill pan or a large heavy skillet. Warm the pan over medium-low heat and add the apple slices in a single layer. Grill, turning once gently, until the slices are lightly browned. With a spatula carefully transfer the slices to a plate and set aside.

Turn the heat under the grill pan or skillet to medium-high. Sear the duck breasts, skin side down, until the skin is crisp, 8 to 10 minutes, making sure not to cook all the way through. Turn the breasts and continue to cook to medium-rare, 2 to 3 minutes (the breasts will be springy to the touch). Before you remove the duck from the grill, brown its edges, about 30 seconds each. Transfer the breasts onto a rack to drain any fat and allow them to rest for 5 minutes.

Slice the breasts on the diagonal and transfer to a platter or plates. Surround with the apple slices, garnish with the parsley, and serve with the remaining sauce.

There's a wonderful story about mothers-in-law who couldn't agree on anything. One swore by frying in duck fat, the other in chicken fat. One Chanukah there was a storm and they had to cook together. There wasn't enough of either fat to make the latkes, so in the end they made the latkes with both in the same pan. The result was delicious, so they realized that collaboration was far better than going it alone. This story exemplifies our philosophy: The sum is greater than the parts, and honor everyone's traditions.

MEAT

Prime Rib Bones with Roasted Potatoes 209

Summer Grilled Rib Eye Steaks with Chimichurri 210

Thai Grilled Beef Salad 213

Cajun Barbecue Brisket 214

Meatballs 217

Pot-au-Feu 218

Braised Veal Stew with Butternut Squash 220

Pan Roasted Veal with Sage 221

Iraqi Lamb Burgers with Mint Pesto 222

Rack of Lamb 224

Moroccan Lamb Tagine 227

Prime Rib Bones with Roasted Potatoes

Tasty, crispy, caramelized, and finger-licking good, we love rib bones. This recipe is not for the dainty, but if you're that person who eyes the rib roast hungrily and loves a garlicky bone, you'll adore these prime rib bones: They are the 6-inch-long bones that are left over when the butcher shells out the rib eye from a standing rib roast. There is still plenty of meat on them. We like serving the ribs with roasted potatoes. For super crispy potatoes, an English trick is to parboil the potatoes for 7 to 10 minutes, drain them, then roast them. They won't need to roast for as long. Our Braised Red Cabbage with Caraway Seeds (page 265) rounds out this recipe.

SERVES 6 TO 8

In a small bowl, combine the garlic, mustard, paprika, wine, and salt and mix well. Rub the mixture over the bones, transfer to a large resealable bag or any container with a lid, and add the rosemary. Marinate overnight in the refrigerator or on the counter for about 2 hours.

Preheat the oven to 400°F.

Place a large rack on a baking sheet or baking pan and transfer the bones to the rack, meat side down. Roast until the meat is crispy on the edges and well browned, about 1 hour.

Meanwhile, prepare the potatoes to roast with the meat. In a baking dish or pan that will fit the potatoes in a single layer, combine the potatoes, olive oil, sea salt, and rosemary, and toss. Spread the potatoes out and roast. After 30 minutes, add the onions and shake the pan to distribute the onions and turn the potatoes. Roast, shaking occasionally, until the potatoes are golden brown and soft, 25 to 30 minutes more. Season with the pepper and shake the potatoes to coat.

Sprinkle the potatoes with the parsley and serve with the ribs.

6 garlic cloves, finely chopped (about 2 tablespoons)

6 tablespoons Dijon mustard

1 tablespoon sweet or hot paprika

1 cup dry red wine

½ teaspoon kosher salt

5 to 6 pounds prime rib bones

2 (4-inch) fresh rosemary sprigs

Potatoes

3 pounds new (small) potatoes, such as red, purple, or Yukon Gold

3 tablespoons extra-virgin olive oil

2 teaspoons sea salt

6 (2-inch) fresh rosemary sprigs

3 small red onions, halved and thinly sliced (about 1½ cups)

Freshly ground black pepper

Chopped fresh flat-leaf parsley, for garnish

Summer Grilled Rib Eye Steaks with Chimichurri

The aroma of barbecue or outdoor grilling in the summer is intoxicating. When you have excellent-quality beef like rib eye steaks, a roaring flame, and an appetite, you need little else. We love a good Argentinean chimichurri sauce with our grilled meats. Use half of the sauce to serve alongside the meat; then, as a great side, toss the rest with bulgur or another grain, chopped cucumbers, and tomatoes for a delicious tabbouleh. The sauce will keep in the refrigerator for up to a week.

SERVES 6 TO 8

Chimichurri

¼ cup red wine vinegar

3 medium shallots, finely chopped (about 3 tablespoons)

6 to 8 garlic cloves, finely chopped (2 to 3 tablespoons)

1 jalapeño pepper, seeded and minced

1 teaspoon kosher salt, plus more for seasoning

3 cups packed fresh flat-leaf parsley leaves, finely chopped

1 tablespoon chopped fresh oregano leaves

¾ cup extra-virgin olive oil
Freshly ground black pepper

Steaks

6 (1½-inch-thick) rib eye steaks

4 garlic cloves, pressed (about 4 teaspoons)

2 tablespoons extra-virgin olive oil
Kosher salt and freshly ground black pepper

To make the chimichurri, combine the vinegar, shallots, garlic, jalapeño, and salt in a medium bowl. Allow to stand for 15 minutes.

In another medium bowl, combine the parsley and oregano. Using a fork, whisk in the olive oil gradually. Alternatively, pulse the parsley in a food processor, adding the oil gradually with the machine running. Then stir in the oregano.

Just before serving, combine the parsley-oregano oil with the vinegar-onion mixture and stir with a fork to blend. Adjust the seasoning with salt and black pepper.

To grill the steaks, rub them with the garlic and olive oil, cover, and refrigerate for 1 hour.

Preheat the grill at least 20 minutes before you're ready to grill.

Season the steaks with salt and pepper. Grill, turning once, 5 to 7 minutes per side for medium rare (or to an internal temperature 130 to 135°F), or to the degree of doneness you prefer. Let the steaks rest for 5 to 10 minutes. (The meat continues to cook a little more during this time.) Slice and serve with the sauce.

Thai Grilled Beef Salad

When a cousin from Chiang Mai came to visit at the time of one of our daughters' bat mitzvahs, he made this delicious version of Thai beef salad for Sunday brunch. We've included it here because everyone can use a delicious go-to main course salad. With layers of flavor, a light touch of beef, and loads of greens, the salad adds up to a meal that reflects today's trend in reversing the ratio of meat to vegetables. Serve with rice and pickled carrots (page 68).

SERVES 4

In a medium bowl, combine 1 tablespoon of the lime juice, the soy sauce, oil, brown sugar, if using, garlic, ginger, and red curry paste. Pour half the mixture into a resealable bag or glass dish, and reserve the rest in the refrigerator. Rinse the meat, pat dry, and add to the bag or dish. Add the remaining 2 tablespoons lime juice and seal the bag tightly or cover the dish. Allow the meat to marinate in the refrigerator, turning occasionally, at least 4 hours or overnight.

Preheat an outdoor grill or grill pan. Remove the steak from the marinade (discard the marinade). Grill the steak until medium rare, turning once, about 5 minutes per side for London broil, 3 minutes per side for skirt steak. Let the steak rest for 10 minutes then slice it thinly against the grain.

In a salad bowl, combine the beef, lettuce, cilantro, basil, cucumber, and two-thirds of the shallots. Add the reserved marinade and toss. Divide the salad among 6 plates. Garnish with the remaining shallots, add sliced chiles, if using, and serve.

3 tablespoons lime juice

3 tablespoons low-sodium soy sauce

3 tablespoons safflower oil

1 tablespoon brown sugar (optional)

1 garlic clove, minced (about 1 teaspoon)

1½ teaspoons minced fresh ginger

1¼ teaspoons red curry paste or chili-garlic sauce

1 pound London broil (1 to 1½ inches thick), or skirt steak (½ inch thick)

½ head red-leaf lettuce or about 6 cups mixed greens, torn

½ cup cilantro leaves

1 cup fresh basil leaves, torn

1 medium cucumber, peeled, halved, seeded, and sliced into half moons

4 medium shallots, thinly sliced (about ¼ cup)

2 small Thai chiles, seeded and sliced (optional)

Cajun Barbecue Brisket

When you host a hungry team of teenagers, starving after a game or meet, quinoa isn't going to cut it. We created this Cajun spiced barbecue brisket to rival any smokehouse version. It's tender, flavorful, and certainly well spiced. Though it takes some time and effort, it's well worth it. And it's so much tastier than takeout. We like to cook it a day before we serve it. Since the meat needs to marinate overnight, you may want to start two days in advance. Reheat it in its sauce.

SERVES 8 TO 10

Dry Rub and Brisket

- 2½ tablespoons dark brown sugar
- 2 tablespoons paprika, preferably smoked
- 1 tablespoon garlic powder
- 2 teaspoons dry mustard
- 2 teaspoons onion powder
- 1½ teaspoons dried basil
- 1 teaspoon ground bay leaves
- ¾ teaspoon ground coriander
- ¾ teaspoon ground savory
- ¾ teaspoon dried thyme
- ⅛ teaspoon ground cumin or chili powder
- ½ to 1 teaspoon kosher salt
- 1½ teaspoons freshly ground black pepper
- 1 (5-pound) "second cut" brisket, deckle, or French roast, trimmed of excess fat

The Mop

- 4 cups beef or chicken stock
- 2 bay leaves
- 1 teaspoon dried oregano
- 2 tablespoons olive or grapeseed oil
- 2 to 3 medium onions, chopped (about 2½ cups)
- 1 celery stalk, chopped
- ½ red or green bell pepper, cored, seeded, and chopped (about ½ cup)
- 1 small head garlic, cloves separated and minced
- ½ teaspoon dry mustard
- ½ teaspoon kosher salt
- ½ teaspoon freshly ground black pepper
- ½ teaspoon freshly ground white pepper
- ¼ teaspoon cayenne
  Finely grated zest and juice of 2 lemons
- 2 tablespoons white wine vinegar
- 1 (12-ounce) bottle natural smoky barbecue sauce, or Homemade Barbecue Sauce (see box)

- 1 tablespoon olive oil
- 8 medium carrots, peeled, trimmed, and halved lengthwise

HOMEMADE BARBECUE SAUCE

You can substitute the following mixture for the bottled barbecue sauce: In a medium bowl, combine 1½ cups ketchup, 1 tablespoon molasses or honey, ½ teaspoon dry mustard, and 1 teaspoon natural liquid smoke. After you add it to the "mop"—the traditional sauce applied to meat during smoking—the mixture will cook and reduce to become a true barbecue sauce.

The day before you cook the brisket, combine all the dry rub ingredients in a small bowl. Reserve 2 tablespoons for the mop. Rub the remaining dry rub all over the brisket. Put in a resealable plastic bag or a covered container and refrigerate overnight.

Bring the brisket to room temperature.

To make the mop, combine the stock, bay leaves, and oregano in a medium saucepan and bring to a slow simmer over medium heat. Meanwhile, heat the oil in a large skillet over medium heat. Add the onions, celery, bell pepper, garlic, mustard, salt, black and white peppers, cayenne, and the reserved 2 tablespoons dry rub and sauté until the vegetables have softened and the mixture is fragrant, 5 to 7 minutes. Transfer the mixture to the stock in the saucepan. Add the lemon zest and juice, vinegar, and barbecue sauce and simmer until reduced by one-quarter, 30 to 45 minutes.

Preheat the oven to 350°F.

In a large Dutch oven or other heavy pot with a tight-fitting lid, heat the olive oil. Add the brisket and brown, turning once, 3 to 5 minutes per side. (The spices will char a little.) Add the mop and carrots, cover, and braise in the oven until the brisket is tender when pierced with the tip of a sharp-pointed knife, about 1½ hours. Let the brisket sit for 20 minutes then transfer to a cutting board. Set the pot with the mop and carrots aside.

Slice the brisket thinly across the grain, return it to the pot, maintaining its original shape. (You can make the brisket through this point and then refrigerate until the next day.) Cover and return to the oven (still at 350°F), and braise, basting occasionally, until very tender, about 1 hour. Serve.

SHARING STORIES ACROSS THE GENERATIONS

Gathered around the table in the synagogue kitchen, ninety-three-year-old Leon tried to explain to a group of ten-year-olds that cooking was much more complicated when he was their age. "To make chopped liver, first we had to kill the chicken," he related.

The children's eyes widened as they listened to history firsthand. They were gathered in one of the classes from the Jewish Journey Project, an alternative after-school Jewish education program for third-to seventh-graders, conceived by JCC Manhattan. JJP, in conjunction with local synagogues, offers hands-on experiential classes in subjects such as film or cooking, and outreach programs to make Jewish education more relevant to today's youth. In this particular class, children cook with seniors from DOROT (an Upper West Side organization that serves older adults) while sharing stories and memories.

Leon reminds the children that there was no supermarket, no real recipes, and not very much money back in Poland when he was a child. "We gathered the coins we had and went to the farmer and got what he had and came home and cooked it." He goes on to explain that none of the families in his village had ovens in their homes. The women would assemble their Shabbat stews from meat, barley, potatoes, and whatever else they had, and they would bring their stews (called *cholent*) to the communal bakery, which kept its ovens on all night. Shabbat afternoon, the women would stop at the bakery to pick up their *cholent* for Shabbat lunch. As the community of women came together they would laugh as they tried to identify which of the identical pots belonged to each family.

For Leon, *cholent* is a metaphor for the Jewish people, all of whom come from different places and perspectives but become so much better and richer when "stewed" together over time. For the children enrolled in the JJP program, who have never heard of a dish that takes twenty-four hours to cook, it's an eye-opening experience and a meaningful way to learn their cultural history.

So much good happens in these JJP afternoon sessions. The children get a sense of a world that textbooks can never describe, and the seniors become teachers, grandparents, and friends to the children. Everyone learns about Jewish traditions, history, and classic Jewish food.

Meatballs

It's not easy to make light, delicious, authentic-tasting meatballs without adding milk. These dairy-free meatballs (which work in a kosher kitchen) are so good, though, that any Italian *nonna* would approve. Serve them over pasta with additional chopped parsley sprinkled on top, or over Sautéed Greens with Shallots (page 281) or Lemon-Thyme Zucchini "Spaghettini" (page 253).

SERVES 6 TO 8

Heat the 2 teaspoons olive oil in a large skillet over medium-low heat. Add the onion and garlic and sauté until translucent, 2 to 3 minutes. Remove the pan from the heat, stir in the parsley, and set aside to cool.

In a large bowl, combine the turkey and beef and mix with your hands. Add the onion mixture and mix into the meats.

In a small bowl, combine the challah with the stock and allow the bread to soften, about 5 minutes. Add the egg, salt, and pepper to the bread mixture, then stir into the meat mixture. Using your hands, mix until the bread has broken down thoroughly and combined with the meat. Let sit for 20 minutes.

Form the mixture into meatballs, using ¼ cup for each. If using bread crumbs, place in a large shallow dish and roll the balls in the crumbs to coat completely. (Breading the meatballs before browning ensures a crustier, classic meatball. You can brown them without the crumbs for a more tender result.) Transfer the coated meatballs to a second plate.

Line a plate with paper towels. In a 12- or 14-inch skillet, heat the ½ cup olive oil over medium heat. Working in batches, brown the meatballs, turning as necessary, 2 to 3 minutes. Do not allow the meatballs to cook through. Place the browned meatballs on the prepared plate.

Wipe out the pan and add the marinara. Return the meatballs to the pan, cover, and simmer over low heat until the meatballs are cooked through, about 1 hour.

½ cup plus 2 teaspoon extra-virgin olive oil

½ small onion, minced (about ¼ cup)

2 garlic cloves, minced (about 2 teaspoons)

½ cup packed fresh flat-leaf parsley leaves, minced (about ¼ cup)

1 pound ground dark-meat turkey

1 pound ground lean beef

2 (½-inch-thick) slices challah

¼ cup chicken or vegetable stock

1 extra-large egg, beaten

¼ teaspoon kosher salt

⅛ teaspoon freshly ground black pepper

1 cup bread crumbs (optional)

3 cups marinara sauce (homemade or store-bought)

Pot-au-Feu

Pot-au-feu (a meal of boiled meat and vegetables) is a traditional Alsatian dish that was made often by the large Jewish community that has lived in Alsace for over 1,000 years. As the author Joan Nathan has explained, the Shabbat pot was commonly hung over the fireplace to simmer all night as the fire died down and turned into embers. The next day, the stew would be complete and ready to eat. Considered a French classic today, modern versions, such as ours, start a day in advance, but don't need to be simmered through the night.

Traditionally this dish is served as two courses. Start with the broth garnished with some chopped herbs. But leave a bit of the broth behind in the pot to keep the meat and the vegetables warm and moist. For a more informal dinner, we like to serve the broth in a mug, which can accompany the main course. Condiments are an important part of this dish, making for a very social gathering. Try: Parsley Oil (page 88); coarse-grain mustard and gherkin pickles; Apple Beet Horseradish Relish (page 83); sriracha or hot sauce.

Trim the short ribs of excess fat, leaving silverskin intact and the meat attached to the bones. Place in a heavy stockpot or enamel Dutch oven. Add the stock or cold water to cover the ribs by 1 to 2 inches. Bring to a simmer and skim the bits of foam and scum as they are released.

Meanwhile, tie the juniper, cloves, peppercorns, bay leaves, and thyme sprigs in a cheesecloth bundle. Add the cheesecloth bundle, yellow onions, and garlic to the pot and stir. Cook, uncovered, at a gentle but steady simmer, skimming occasionally, for about an hour.

Add the leeks, cipollini onions, celery root, parsnip, carrots, and potatoes. Add more stock or water if needed, so the meat and vegetables are just covered by liquid. Bring to a gentle boil, then reduce the heat to a simmer. Taste for seasoning and add salt and pepper if necessary. Simmer until the meat is yielding but not soft, about another hour. The vegetables should be just fork-tender. If they are done before the meat, remove them with tongs, so they do not overcook, and set aside.

When the meat is done, allow the stew to cool in the broth for at least 1 hour. Remove cheesecloth bundle and discard. Remove the vegetables and refrigerate separately. Keep the meat and broth in the pot and refrigerate overnight (for a clearer broth you can strain it before refrigerating).

The next day, remove the congealed fat from the top of the broth and meat, and discard. Gently reheat the broth together with the meat and vegetables over low to medium-low heat. This could take as long as 45 minutes. Taste for seasoning and add salt and pepper if necessary.

To serve the broth as your first course, ladle it into individual soup bowls. Serve garnished with a sprinkle of minced parsley. Remember to reserve some of the broth to keep the meat moist in the pot. Meanwhile, leave the meat and vegetables in the covered pot and keep warm over a very gentle heat.

To serve the main course, lift the meat from the pot and thickly slice across the grain. Arrange on individual deep plates, surround with vegetables, and add a splash of broth.

5 pounds short ribs, cut across the bone into 3-inch-thick slabs (about three 6-inch pieces)

2 quarts chicken stock or water

1 tablespoon juniper berries, roughly crushed

4 whole cloves

¼ teaspoon black peppercorns

2 bay leaves

6 (2-inch) sprigs fresh thyme, plus more for garnish (optional)

2 small yellow onions, halved

4 to 6 garlic cloves, peeled

2 medium leeks, white and light green parts only, quartered lengthwise

½ pound cipollini onions or small shallots, peeled

1 small celery root (about 8 ounces), peeled and cut into 6 chunks

1 medium parsnip, peeled and cut into 6 chunks

2 medium carrots, peeled and cut into 6 chunks

1 pound fingerling potatoes or Red Bliss new potatoes

Salt and freshly ground black pepper

2 tablespoons minced fresh flat-leaf parsley, for garnish

Braised Veal Stew with Butternut Squash

This recipe comes from the Jewish community of Venice, Italy, and was adapted from Joyce Goldstein's *Cucina Ebraica*. Warm, hearty, and comforting, you can make the stew the day before and reheat it before serving. Marsala and butternut squash lend a sweet note to the dish, balancing the piney aroma of the rosemary. The recipe doubles easily.

SERVES 4 TO 6

4 tablespoons extra-virgin olive oil

1 butternut squash (about 1½ pounds), halved, seeds and fibers removed, peeled, and cut into ½-inch cubes

3 medium carrots, peeled and roughly chopped (about ½ cup)

2 medium onions, chopped (about 1½ cups)

2 garlic cloves, minced (about 2 teaspoons)

1 tablespoon chopped fresh rosemary

2 pounds veal shoulder, trimmed and cut into 1½-inch cubes

Kosher salt

1 cup marsala or other sweet wine

1½ cups chicken or vegetable stock, plus more if needed

Freshly ground black pepper

In a large Dutch oven or heavy-bottomed pan with a tight lid, heat 1 tablespoon of the olive oil over medium-high heat. Add the squash and carrots and cook, stirring occasionally, until the squash starts to brown, 8 to 10 minutes. Transfer the mixture to a plate and set aside.

In the same pan, warm 2 tablespoons of the olive oil over low heat. Add the onions, garlic, and rosemary and sauté until tender and translucent, about 8 minutes. Transfer the mixture to a plate and set aside.

Warm the remaining 1 tablespoon olive oil in the same pan over high heat. Pat the meat dry and, working in batches, add to the very hot pot and brown on all sides, about 5 minutes per side. Sprinkle with salt, add the wine, and let it bubble up.

Add the squash, onions, and the stock to cover and bring to a boil. Cover, reduce the heat to low, and simmer gently until the meat is tender, 1 to 1¼ hours. If the stew begins to dry out, you can add additional stock. Adjust the seasoning with salt and pepper and serve.

Pan Roasted Veal with Sage

In memory of Marcella Hazan, who sadly passed away in 2013 and is rightly credited with bringing classic Italian cooking to America, we're including our adaptation of her roasted veal. Jewish American cooks adopted her as our *nonna* because her husband, Victor, was proudly Italian, Jewish, and American. Marcella's recipes teach us that high-quality ingredients cooked in the simplest ways can result in the most delicious meals. Traditionally, Italian households didn't have an oven and therefore many of their classic dishes are cooked stovetop, as here. If you are very lucky, there will be some leftovers, which will make the most amazing sandwiches. One idea: Stack slices of the veal with our Caramelized Saffron Onions (page 244), tomatoes, and arugula on whole-wheat bread or our Rye Bread (page 39), and schmear with a mustard mayonnaise.

NOTE: *This recipe doubles very well. Make sure to get two equal-size roasts and not one large piece.*

SERVES 4 TO 5

Pat the roast dry with paper towels. Tuck the garlic slices into the roast wherever you can find an opening. Tuck 4 sage leaves under the string. Season with the pepper.

In an enamel pot or heavy-bottomed saucepan into which the meat just fits, heat 2 tablespoons of the olive oil over medium-high heat. Add the meat and sear on all sides until golden brown, about 15 minutes. Don't worry if the sage leaves darken. Season with the salt and transfer the meat to a large plate.

Add the remaining 1 tablespoon olive oil to the pan and heat over medium heat. Add the shallots and sauté until they begin to color, about 5 minutes. Add the remaining 2 sage leaves, the rosemary sprigs, bay leaf, and wine and bring to a boil.

Return the meat to the pan. Reduce the heat to a very slow simmer and add the carrots. Set the cover slightly askew and braise, turning the meat from time to time, until the roast is fork-tender, about 1 hour and 15 minutes. If the pan seems dry while the meat is cooking, add 1 to 2 tablespoons of water.

Transfer the meat to a cutting board and let it rest at least 10 minutes. There should be some pan sauce; if there isn't, add ¼ to ⅓ cup water, deglaze the pan over high heat, and reduce until thick. Discard the rosemary sprigs and bay leaf. Cut the roast into slices about ⅛ inch thick and place on a platter with the carrots alongside. Drizzle the pan sauce over the veal, garnish with parsley, and pass additional sauce to serve.

1 (2½-to-3-pound) tightly rolled and tied veal shoulder roast, no more than 3 inches in diameter

3 medium garlic cloves, thinly sliced

6 fresh sage leaves

About ¼ teaspoon freshly ground black pepper

3 tablespoons extra-virgin olive oil

1 teaspoon kosher salt

4 medium shallots, finely chopped (about ¼ cup)

4 fresh rosemary sprigs

1 bay leaf

1⅓ cups dry white wine

6 ounces baby carrots

Chopped fresh flat-leaf parsley or tarragon, for garnish

We like to serve this veal garnished with fried sage leaves for an extra flourish: Heat ¼ inch of olive oil in a small skillet over medium-high heat. Slip 12 sage leaves into the oil and fry until crispy, 3 to 4 minutes. If your do this ahead of time, you can use the oil to brown the roast.

Iraqi Lamb Burgers with Mint Pesto

As the three of us have Ashkenazi backgrounds, we find it exciting to draw upon Sephardic food traditions and flavors in our cooking. A burger infused with Middle Eastern spices—mint, cinnamon, and allspice—and with added pine nuts is a nice break from a traditional American hamburger. We serve the burgers on toasted pita bread with our wonderful mint pesto and Caramelized Saffron Onions (page 244), which amplifies the regional flavor profile. The pesto lasts in an airtight container, refrigerated, for up to 2 weeks.

To make the pesto, combine all the ingredients in a food processor and purée. Transfer to a small bowl and set aside.

In a small pan over medium-low heat, toast the pine nuts, watching carefully and stirring, until lightly colored, about 3 minutes. Transfer to a bowl.

To make the burgers, preheat the broiler or lightly oil a grill pan. In a medium bowl, combine the pine nuts, lamb, parsley, mint, onion, salt, allspice, and cinnamon. Knead well by hand, squeezing the meat through your fingers. Add the ice water and continue mixing by hand. Add the bread crumbs and knead well again until the meat is very soft and all the ingredients are well blended, about 3 minutes.

Shape the meat into six 2½-inch patties by rolling it between your palms into 1-to-1½-inch-diameter balls and then flattening them.

Transfer the patties to a broiling pan and broil, turning once, until brown and cooked through, 2 to 4 minutes per side. Alternatively, grill over high heat for 2 to 4 minutes per side. Remove from the heat and set on a serving plate.

Before serving, warm the pitas in foil in a 300°F oven for a few minutes. Serve the burgers with the pita, mint pesto, and saffron caramelized onions.

Mint Pesto

3 cups packed fresh mint leaves

1¼ cups olive oil

1 to 2 teaspoons honey

4 garlic cloves, peeled

1 teaspoon kosher salt

½ teaspoon crushed red pepper flakes (optional)

Burgers

6 tablespoons pine nuts

2 pounds ground lamb

½ cup finely chopped fresh flat-leaf parsley

½ cup finely chopped fresh mint leaves

1 medium onion, finely chopped (about ½ cup)

2 to 3 teaspoons kosher salt

1½ teaspoons ground allspice

1 teaspoon ground cinnamon

½ cup ice water

2 tablespoons bread crumbs or matzah meal

6 pita breads

STUFFED CABBAGE

You can use the lamb mixture to make delicious Sephardic-flavored stuffed cabbage: Core a large savoy or green cabbage and steam it over boiling water until whole leaves can be peeled off the cabbage head. If you find that you can only peel off a few at a time, return the cabbage to the steamer for a few more minutes until the leaves are tender enough to remove without tearing. You should get about 12 large leaves. Slice the remaining inner leaves, which are too small to stuff, very thinly. Scatter half of these sliced leaves in the bottom of a medium pot. With a knife, score the ribs on the leaves you will stuff so that the leaf is pliable. Place about ¼ cup of the lamb mixture on the stem end of a leaf and begin to roll, tucking the sides in as you enclose the filling. Arrange the rolls tightly in the pot and add the rest of the sliced cabbage. In a bowl, mix 1 (28-ounce) can of diced tomatoes, 1 cup tomato juice, 3 tablespoons tomato paste, and 2 teaspoons brown sugar (optional). Pour the liquid over the cabbage. Bring to a boil. Reduce to a simmer, cover, and cook for about 1½ hours or until the meat is cooked through. Garnish with chopped mint.

Rack of Lamb

This is a great way to dress up simple broiled lamb chops. For many people, lamb says Passover and this recipe can be a great addition to your holiday repertoire. We've substituted our fresh mint pesto for the traditional mint jelly, but if there's an oddball jar of mint jelly in the back of your refrigerator, feel free to use it.

SERVES 4

2 racks of lamb, 8 chops per rack (about 3½ pounds each, before trimming), trimmed

⅓ cup extra-virgin olive oil

2 tablespoons tomato paste

1 tablespoon lemon juice

8 garlic cloves, pressed (6 to 7 teaspoons)

8 fresh rosemary sprigs, stripped and chopped

¼ teaspoon freshly ground black pepper

mint pesto (page 223) or mint jelly

Wrap the exposed lamb bones with foil to prevent their discoloration while marinating. Place the racks, meat side down, in a 2-inch-deep rectangular dish or platter large enough to hold them. Prop the bones up on the side of the dish.

In a small bowl, combine the olive oil, tomato paste, lemon juice, garlic, rosemary, and pepper and mix well. Rub the meat with this mixture, avoiding the bones. Cover and marinate in the refrigerator at least 3 hours or up to overnight.

One hour before cooking the lamb, remove the racks from the refrigerator and bring to room temperature.

Preheat the broiler to its highest setting.

Place the lamb on a broiling pan, meat side up. Broil 2 to 3 inches from the heat source, turning once, until the meat is seared and has a brown crust, about 5 minutes per side.

Preheat the oven to 450°F. Roast the lamb 10 to 14 minutes depending on desired doneness; 113°F for rare, 118°F for medium, or 124°F for well done. (The meat will continue to cook as it rests.)

Let the lamb rest for 10 minutes. Place the racks on a cutting board. Reserve the pan juices. Cut into single or double chops. Mix the pan juices into the mint pesto or mint jelly, stir, and transfer to a serving bowl. Serve with the lamb.

Moroccan Lamb Tagine

Cooking in a tagine (a conical ceramic cooking vessel) makes meat succulent, tender, and flavorful and is evocative of Morocco. It's a great way to cook lamb shoulder, a very reasonably priced cut that needs to cook for a long time in order to become tender. If you are entertaining, why not make a whole Moroccan feast around this main dish? We serve it with Two-Grain Saffron Couscous (page 150), the Moroccan Chickpeas and the Date Relish from our Moroccan Mezze (page 242), and Moroccan Carrot Slaw (page 135). Don't worry if you haven't got a proper tagine. Any heavy casserole with a tight-fitting lid will do. As the lamb cooks, the aromas will summon everyone into your kitchen. This dish can be easily doubled.

SERVES 4 TO 5

In a large bowl, combine the lamb with the coriander, ground ginger, and saffron, and toss. Refrigerate at least 4 to 8 hours or overnight.

In a large heavy casserole or tagine, heat the 2 tablespoons of olive oil over medium heat. Working in batches, brown the lamb on all sides, 5 to 7 minutes per batch. Transfer to a large plate or bowl and set aside.

In the same pot, combine the onion, garlic, and fresh ginger and cook over low heat, stirring occasionally, until the vegetables have softened, about 5 minutes, adding more oil if needed. Return the meat to the pot. Add the stock, tomato paste, cinnamon, and bay leaf and bring to a boil. Lower the heat to medium, cover, and simmer until the meat is fork-tender, about 1½ hours. Stir the meat occasionally as it cooks, pushing the cinnamon stick under it each time you do.

Meanwhile, preheat the oven to 400°F.

In a small baking dish, toss the shallots with the 1 teaspoon olive oil and salt to taste. Roast until glazed and fork-tender, about 45 minutes.

After simmering the stew for 1½ hours, add the prunes to the casserole and continue to simmer, uncovered, for another 30 minutes. Add the shallots and honey and simmer for 10 minutes, until meat is very tender. Stir in the lemon juice, cilantro, and parsley. Adjust the seasoning with salt and pepper and serve.

2½ pounds boneless lamb shoulder, well trimmed of fat and cut into 2-inch cubes

1 teaspoon ground coriander

1 teaspoon ground ginger

Large pinch saffron threads

2 tablespoons plus 1 teaspoon extra-virgin olive oil

1 large onion, finely chopped (about 1 cup)

1 garlic clove, finely chopped (about 1 teaspoon)

1 teaspoon chopped fresh ginger

1½ cups beef or chicken stock

1 tablespoon tomato paste or sun-dried tomato paste

1 (2-inch) piece cinnamon stick

1 bay leaf

12 shallots, peeled

Kosher salt

1 cup small pitted prunes

1 teaspoon honey

2 tablespoons lemon juice

¼ cup chopped cilantro leaves

¼ cup chopped fresh flat-leaf parsley

Freshly ground black pepper

GRAINS & LEGUMES

Red Quinoa and Black Rice Pilaf

Nowadays it is easy to find red quinoa and black rice in most supermarkets. Along with those darker colors come great health benefits—antioxidants and protein. The chewy texture of both the rice and quinoa make this a satisfying vegetarian dish, particularly if you accompany it with avocado and garnish it with lime slices. This is great for Passover if your custom is to eat rice on the holiday, as the Sephardim do. Or serve it for Passover without the rice, in which case double the amount of quinoa.

SERVES 10 TO 12

1 cup short-grain black rice

4 cups water

2 pints cherry tomatoes

4 tablespoons plus 1 teaspoon extra-virgin olive oil

1 cup red quinoa, rinsed

2 bay leaves

½ teaspoon kosher salt, plus more for seasoning

1 medium red onion, finely chopped (about 1 cup)

2 medium shallots, finely chopped (about 2 tablespoons), or 4 large garlic cloves, minced

1 tablespoon cumin seeds, lightly crushed or coarsely ground

½ cup chopped cilantro

½ cup chopped fresh flat-leaf parsley

¼ cup snipped fresh chives
Freshly ground black pepper

3 tablespoons lemon juice

Preheat the oven to 450°F.

In a small saucepan, combine the rice with 2 cups water and bring to a boil. Cover, reduce the heat to low, and cook until water is absorbed and rice is tender, 25 to 30 minutes.

Meanwhile, in a small bowl, toss the tomatoes with the 1 teaspoon olive oil. Spread on a medium baking pan in a single layer and roast until charred, about 20 minutes.

While the rice and tomatoes are cooking prepare the quinoa. In a medium saucepan, combine the quinoa, remaining 2 cups water, bay leaves, and salt. Bring to a boil, cover, reduce the heat to low, and simmer until the quinoa is tender, about 15 minutes. Drain and return to the pot. Cover and let sit for 15 minutes. Discard the bay leaves, and fluff the quinoa with a fork.

Heat 2 tablespoons of the olive oil in a large skillet over medium heat. Add the onion and cook, stirring occasionally, until soft, about 8 minutes. Add the shallots and cumin and sauté for 2 minutes.

Remove the skillet from the heat, add the rice and quinoa, and mix well. Stir in the charred tomatoes, cilantro, parsley, and chives and season with salt and pepper. Add the remaining 2 tablespoons oil and lemon juice, toss, and serve.

COMMUNITY COOKOFF

For the last few years, the Evelyn Rubenstein Jewish Community Center of Houston, Texas, has been hosting the increasingly popular Kosher Chili Cookoff—so popular it's quickly become the largest kosher event in Houston. This is a big fund-raiser. A time when people come together to give charity, or *tzedakah*, at all levels.

The proceeds from the cookoff are given to many nonprofit organizations in the Houston community. But the event has the added bonus of bringing the entire community together to do something they like to do: eat chili. Everything is bigger in Texas, after all: the flavors, the food, and especially the community gatherings. If one pot of chili is good, then fifty pots of chili are even better.

There are spicy chilis (with hot peppers), super-spicy chilis (with scorching hot peppers), decadent chilis (chocolate is sometimes used), and way-out-there chilis (coffee or jelly chili, anyone?). There may only be one official winner at the end of the day, but whatever side of the debate you're on, you can find a chili just right for you.

The Kosher Chili Cookoff represents the way that the community in Houston has taken the local culture and infused it with Jewish values. JCCs thrive on this kind of melding. We love medleys of flavor, traditions, and backgrounds. Each addition enriches the entire community's experience—and certainly makes everything much more delicious.

Farro with Grilled Onions and Roasted Tomatoes

We love farro—it's healthy *and* delicious. In this recipe the nutty-tasting whole grain is paired with sweet roasted tomatoes and tangy balsamic onions. You can make the dish ahead of time, but if you do, be sure to refrigerate the onions, tomatoes, and farro separately to maintain the best texture.

SERVES 8

Roasted Tomatoes

- 1 pint grape or cherry tomatoes
- 1 tablespoon extra-virgin olive oil
- 2 fresh rosemary sprigs
- 2 fresh thyme sprigs
  Kosher salt and freshly ground black pepper

Grilled Onions

- 2 medium red onions (about 8 ounces each), sliced ½ inch thick
- 2 tablespoons extra-virgin olive oil
  Kosher salt and freshly ground black pepper
- ¼ cup balsamic vinegar

- 1½ cups farro, any type (see box)
- 2 to 3 tablespoons balsamic vinegar
- 1 to 2 tablespoons extra-virgin olive oil
  Kosher salt and freshly ground black pepper
- ½ cup packed fresh basil leaves, cut into thin ribbons

Preheat the oven to 300°F.

To roast the tomatoes, toss them with the olive oil, rosemary, and thyme on a medium baking sheet and season with salt and pepper. Roast until the tomatoes have burst and are beginning to caramelize, 40 to 50 minutes. Strip the crisped leaves from the rosemary stems and reserve. Discard the rosemary stems and the thyme sprigs.

To char the onions, increase the oven temperature to 350°F. Heat a grill pan over high heat or heat an outdoor grill to high. Brush the onions with 1 tablespoon of the olive oil and season with salt and pepper. Grill the onion slices until charred but still firm in the center, turning once with tongs, 3 to 5 minutes per side. Transfer the onions to a medium baking dish and add the remaining 1 tablespoon olive oil and the vinegar. Bake, stirring occasionally, until the onions are tender, 20 to 30 minutes. Let the onions cool in their liquid then remove and chop them coarsely. Reserve the liquid.

Meanwhile, to make the farro, follow the package directions. Drain and transfer to a large bowl.

When ready to serve, add the tomatoes, onions with their liquid, and rosemary leaves to the farro. Stir in the vinegar and olive oil to taste, and season with salt and pepper. Allow the farro to cool to room temperature, stir in the basil, and serve.

FARRO

Farro is a nutritional powerhouse—mineral-rich and high in cholesterol-lowering fiber. It's also high in complex carbs, the kind that breaks down slowly, keeping your energy level stable.

Farro is sold in whole (unpearled), semi-pearled, or pearled versions. Pearling describes how much of the exterior bran is removed, but packages don't always indicate what type of farro they contain. If the package says the farro will cook in less than 15 minutes, it's probably pearled; if it takes around 30 minutes, it's most likely semi-pearled; if 60 to 80 minutes, the farro is whole (or unpearled). Unpearled farro will have the most chew as well as the most fiber.

Wheat Berry and Grape Salad

Wheat berries were among the first of the whole grains that became popular to cook with. Now we also cook with spelt, quinoa, farro, freekeh, and more. All of these can be substituted for wheat berries in this light, summery salad. The grapes add just a hint of sweetness—paired with the salty cheese, the flavors are perfectly balanced.

While the wheat berries take quite a while to cook, you can easily make them a few days ahead of time and store in the refrigerator until you're ready to use. Just remember to bring them to room temperature before you assemble the salad.

SERVES 4

Place the wheat berries in a strainer and rinse thoroughly under cold running water.

In a large pot, bring 8 cups of water to a boil and add the salt. Add the wheat berries and return to a boil. Reduce the heat and simmer until the grains have started to open and are al dente, about 1¾ hours, and drain.

Transfer the wheat berries to a large bowl and toss with the olive oil and lemon juice. Let sit for at least 1 hour or as long as overnight.

Just before serving, add the grapes and romaine to the wheat berries and toss. Add the cheese and chives and stir to combine. Season with salt and pepper and serve.

1 cup wheat berries

1 teaspoon kosher salt, plus more for seasoning

3 tablespoons extra-virgin olive oil

3 tablespoons lemon juice

1 cup seedless red grapes, halved

1 large romaine lettuce, halved lengthwise, then cross-cut into ½-inch slices (about 4 cups)

2½ ounces ricotta salata cheese, shaved with a cheese slicer; or crumbled feta cheese

3 tablespoons fresh chives cut into ¼-inch lengths

Freshly ground black pepper

Bulgur Salad with Pomegranates and Pine Nuts

This colorful salad is based on a great recipe in Claudia Roden's *The Book of Jewish Food*. Nutty, satisfying bulgur is dressed with a mixture that includes pomegranate molasses and "warm" spices. Then we finish it with pine nuts and pomegranate seeds. We like to serve this dish at Rosh Hashanah, when it's traditional to eat pomegranates. The salad is a great accompaniment to grilled meat or fish. It's also a great excuse to find an authentic Middle Eastern grocery store and explore the scents within its aisles.

SERVES 6 TO 8

½ cup pine nuts

1½ cups medium-grain bulgur

3 cups boiling water

½ teaspoon kosher salt, plus more for seasoning

3 tablespoons pomegranate molasses

3 tablespoons tomato paste

2 teaspoons extra-virgin olive oil

Juice of 1 lemon (about 2 tablespoons)

1 teaspoon ground cumin

1 teaspoon ground coriander

½ teaspoon ground allspice

¼ teaspoon Aleppo or cayenne pepper

Freshly ground black pepper

¾ cup chopped fresh flat-leaf parsley

½ cup fresh pomegranate seeds (see page 129)

In a medium skillet, toast the pine nuts over medium-low heat, watching carefully and stirring often, until golden, about 3 minutes. Transfer to a small bowl and set aside.

Place the bulgur in a large bowl and add the boiling water. Add the salt, stir once, and cover the bowl with a plate. Allow the bulgur to absorb the water, about 30 minutes (or follow the package directions). If any water remains after this time, drain it off.

In a small bowl, whisk together the pomegranate molasses, tomato paste, olive oil, lemon juice, cumin, coriander, allspice, and Aleppo pepper. Season with salt and black pepper.

Pour half of the dressing over the bulgur and mix well. Set aside to allow the bulgur to absorb the dressing, at least 10 minutes. Add the pine nuts, parsley, and pomegranate seeds to the bulgur and mix lightly. Add more dressing as desired. Adjust the seasoning and serve.

BULGUR

Particularly common in Middle Eastern cooking, bulgur is a whole-wheat grain that's been cracked and partially precooked. Besides being delicious, it's naturally high in fiber and low in fat. Bulgur is available as medium and coarse grain, as well as fine grain. Each has its own cooking time, so check packages before preparing the grain.

Fava Beans with String Beans and Hazelnuts

Fresh fava beans have such a wonderfully distinct, buttery texture and earthy flavor that it is worth the extra effort to find them. Look for them in markets in the early spring. That said, frozen favas are a good substitution.

SERVES 4 TO 6

1 pound fresh fava beans in their pods or 10 ounces frozen fava beans

½ cup blanched hazelnuts

2 teaspoons extra-virgin olive oil

1 pound string beans, trimmed and left whole

1 tablespoon fresh tarragon leaves

1 tablespoon hazelnut or walnut oil

½ teaspoon coarsely ground fresh black pepper

Kosher salt

Juice of 1 lemon

3 ounces shaved pecorino, Parmesan, or a hard sheep's milk cheese

Prepare fresh fava beans according to the directions below. To prepare frozen fava beans, bring a medium saucepan with water to a boil and add the frozen favas. Cook for 2 to 3 minutes, until al dente, then remove with a slotted spoon and promptly add to an ice bath to stop cooking. When cool, drain, peel off the skins, and set beans aside.

Toast the hazelnuts in a sauté pan over medium heat until lightly toasted, 2 to 3 minutes. Allow to cool slightly and coarsely chop. Set aside.

Heat the olive oil in a large sauté pan over medium-high heat. Add the string beans and sauté until just tender, 3 to 5 minutes. Add the drained fava beans and cook for 2 to 3 more minutes to heat through. The string beans should stay crisp and tender.

Transfer the beans to a serving bowl, stir in the tarragon, and drizzle the nut oil on top. Add the hazelnuts, black pepper, and salt to taste and toss together to coat. Just before serving, add squeezed lemon juice, toss once more, then top with the shaved cheese. Serve immediately or at room temperature.

PREPPING FRESH FAVA BEANS

To shell fresh fava beans, bend the tip of a pod and pull down the seam, unzipping the entire pod to reveal the beans inside. Discard the fuzzy outer pod. Take the shelled beans and pop them in boiling salted water for 1 to 2 minutes to loosen the outer skin. Remove from the boiling water, place the beans into ice water, drain, and peel off the thick outer covering.

Flageolet Beans with Herbs and Tomato

This is one of our recipes that allow the cook's creativity (or pantry supplies) to dictate the final dish. If you don't have dried beans, you can use 4 (15-ounce) cans of white beans, drained and rinsed (then start the recipe with sautéing the garlic). This dish only gets better the next day. To turn this into a light main course, see our variation below.

SERVES 8 TO 10 AS A SIDE

Place the soaked beans in a medium saucepan with the whole garlic cloves, bay leaf, and rosemary. Cover with water by at least 2 inches and bring to a boil. Reduce the heat and simmer partially covered until the beans are tender but not mushy, about 2 hours. Drain the beans and discard the garlic, bay leaf, and rosemary.

Heat the olive oil in a large sauté pan over medium-high heat. Add the chopped garlic and sauté until just beginning to color and release its aroma, 1 to 2 minutes. Add the cooked beans and stir to combine. Break up the whole tomatoes with your hands or with a spoon and add them to the pan (do not add the liquid from the can). Simmer over medium heat for 30 to 45 minutes, until cooked through. Garnish with chopped parsley and serve.

VARIATION

To turn this delicious side dish into a main course: Add lamb or beef sausage. Slice ½ pound sausage and brown for about 12 minutes in the sauté pan before you cook the garlic. Remove the sausage. Add the olive oil and garlic to the pan and cook until the garlic is just beginning to color. Return the sausage to the pan, add the cooked beans and tomatoes, and follow the instructions above.

2 cups (1 pound) dried flageolet or small white beans, soaked (see Soaking Dried Beans, page 241)

2 whole garlic cloves, peeled, lightly smashed, plus 1 tablespoon chopped garlic

1 bay leaf

4 (3-inch) sprigs fresh rosemary

¼ cup extra-virgin olive oil

1 (28-ounce) can whole tomatoes

Chopped fresh flat-leaf parsley, for garnish

Orange-Scented Black Beans
with Crispy Onions

We all save recipes over the years and it's interesting to see which ones we go back to over time. This is based on an old recipe from the *New York Times* that we've updated. For an elegant main course, serve the beans under roasted or pan-seared fish, top with the crispy onions, and garnish with additional orange slices.

To make the beans, char the whole red and poblano peppers over an open flame or in the broiler, turning until the skins are completely black and blistered. Place the peppers in a paper bag, close, and let cool. Remove the skins by rubbing the peppers between 2 paper towels. Seed and dice the peppers. Set aside.

Heat the olive oil in a large saucepan over medium heat. Add the chopped onion and sauté for 5 minutes. Reduce the heat to low, add the garlic and jalapeño, and cook, stirring frequently, for 2 minutes. If using soaked beans, add them with the bay leaf and enough water to cover by 2 to 4 inches. Increase the heat and bring to a boil. Lower the heat and simmer 1 to 1½ hours, until the beans are soft but not mushy. If using canned beans, add them to the onions with the bay leaf, but omit the water, and simmer for 15 minutes.

Stir the orange zest into the beans and continue cooking until the beans are tender but maintain their shape, about 20 minutes more. Discard the bay leaf. Season with salt and pepper and stir in the diced red and poblano peppers.

Meanwhile, make the crispy onions. Place the flour on a plate and add the salt. Heat ½ inch of sunflower oil in a heavy medium skillet over high heat. Add one-third of the onions to the flour mixture and toss lightly to coat. Reduce the heat to medium-high and carefully add just enough of the onions to cover the bottom of the pan. Fry, stirring occasionally with a wooden spoon, until golden and crispy, 5 to 8 minutes. Reduce the heat if the onions appear to be browning too quickly. Transfer the onions to paper towels to drain and season with salt. Repeat with the remaining onions, always being careful not to crowd the pan.

Garnish the beans with the scallions, cilantro, and crispy onions and serve.

Beans

1 red bell pepper

3 or 4 poblano peppers

1 teaspoon extra-virgin olive oil

1 medium onion, chopped (about 1 cup)

1 large garlic clove, minced

1 small jalapeño pepper, seeded, ribs removed, minced

1 cup dried black beans, soaked (see Soaking Dried Beans, below); or 1 (18-ounce) can black beans, drained and rinsed

1 bay leaf

2 teaspoons grated orange zest
   Kosher salt and freshly ground black pepper

Crispy Onions

1½ tablespoons unbleached all-purpose flour

1 teaspoon kosher salt, plus more for seasoning
   Sunflower or grapeseed oil, for frying

2 medium onions, thinly sliced (about 2 cups)

Garnish

3 tablespoons thinly sliced scallions

½ cup chopped cilantro

SOAKING DRIED BEANS

All dried beans must be soaked before cooking. There are a couple of ways to do this. If you have the time, soak the beans overnight in enough water to cover them by 2 to 3 inches. Drain and rinse and follow your recipe for cooking the beans.

If you're pressed for time, or forgot to pre-soak, don't worry. Here is the quick-soak method: In a large pot, combine 1 cup beans with water to cover by 2 to 4 inches. Bring to a boil, reduce the heat, and simmer for 2 minutes. Remove from the heat, cover, and let sit until the beans have softened, about 1 hour. Drain, rinse, and follow your recipe for cooking the beans.

NOTE: *The age of your beans will dictate how long they will need to cook until they are tender. We have made suggestions, but don't be surprised if they need to cook longer for proper texture.*

Moroccan Mezze (Moroccan Chickpeas, Caramelized Saffron Onions, and Date Relish)

Mezze, tapas, whatever you want to call it—people love to make a meal of small plates. In our interpretation, fragrant, stewed chickpeas take center stage: cinnamon, saffron, and turmeric are just some of the typical Moroccan flavorings that make them irresistible; and once the chickpeas have soaked, the dish comes together quickly.

Caramelized saffron onions and date relish pair perfectly with the chickpeas. For a full meal, serve these three dishes with Two-Grain Saffron Couscous (Page 150), harissa for a spicy note, and a bowl of Shredded Beets with Yogurt (page 276) to cool you down. To expand the meal further, add a platter of grilled vegetables finished with a pinch of za'atar.

Moroccan Chickpeas

These chickpeas are infused with lots of wonderful aromatic flavors, including cilantro, ginger, cinnamon, and saffron. As a result, we do not recommend using canned chickpeas here as the pre-cooked canned chickpeas will not absorb all the wonderful flavors of the cooking liquid and will become too mushy.

SERVES 6

- 2 cups dried chickpeas
- 2 carrots, peeled and chopped
- 1 garlic clove, lightly smashed
- 1 small onion, finely chopped (about ½ cup)
- 1 small bunch cilantro, leaves removed and reserved, stems tied into a bundle with kitchen string
- 1 (2-inch) piece fresh ginger, peeled
- 1 (2-inch) piece cinnamon stick
- 1 teaspoon ground turmeric
- ½ teaspoon cayenne
- ¼ to ½ teaspoon smoked or sweet paprika
- Pinch ground saffron
- 2 ripe tomatoes, peeled and chopped; or 3 canned plum tomatoes, chopped
- Kosher salt and freshly ground black pepper

Rinse the chickpeas. Transfer to a medium saucepan and cover with water by 2 to 3 inches. Soak overnight; or bring to a boil, simmer for 2 minutes, turn off the heat, cover, and soak for 1 hour. Drain.

In a medium saucepan, cover the chickpeas with fresh water. Bring to a boil, skim off any foam, and reduce the heat to medium. Add the carrots, garlic, onion, cilantro stems, ginger, cinnamon, turmeric, cayenne, smoked paprika to taste, and saffron. Simmer, partially covered, for 45 minutes. Add more water only if necessary to keep the chickpeas submerged as they cook; do not add more than necessary.

Add the tomatoes and season with salt and pepper. Continue to simmer until the chickpeas are very soft and the broth has thickened slightly, an additional 1 hour. Remove and discard the ginger, cinnamon stick, and cilantro stems.

Adjust the seasoning if necessary, garnish with some of the cilantro leaves, and serve.

recipe continues

Caramelized Saffron Onions

This recipe is a great culinary trick to have up your sleeve. Besides its use here, it can partner with Two-Grain Saffron Couscous (page 150), Iraqi Lamb Burgers (page 222), any grilled meat or fish, and lots of sandwiches. Really, it's great with any meal in need of a flavor boost. The onions keep for weeks when refrigerated.

MAKES ABOUT 1 CUP

- 1 teaspoon saffron threads
- 6 tablespoons extra-virgin olive oil
- 5 medium onions (about 1½ pounds), thinly sliced
- 1 bay leaf
- 1 small crumbled dried red chile
- 1 teaspoon fresh thyme leaves
   Kosher salt and freshly ground black pepper

Using a mortar and pestle pound the saffron into a fine powder.

Heat a large skillet over medium heat for 2 minutes. Add the ground saffron and toast for 20 seconds, watching closely so it doesn't burn. Add the olive oil and heat for 1 minute. Add the onions, bay leaf, chile, and thyme. Season with salt and pepper. Reduce the heat to low and cook, stirring often, until the onions are soft and caramelized, about 30 minutes. Discard the bay leaf. Adjust the seasoning with salt and pepper and serve.

PASTA WITH CARAMELIZED SAFFRON ONIONS

These onions make a fantastic pasta dish. Cook 1 pound radiatore pasta in boiling salted water until al dente, 8 to 10 minutes. Drain and toss with 5 ounces saffron onions (half a recipe, about ½ cup), 6 ounces crumbled feta, 2 tablespoons chopped fresh mint or flat-leaf parsley, and 2 tablespoons Parsley Oil (page 88) or extra-virgin olive oil. Season with a few grinds of black pepper, and *voilà!* Serve warm or at room temperature.

Date Relish

This relish is also delicious alongside roast chicken and it adds a sweet and citrusy note to sandwiches. The relish can be stored in the refrigerator for up to a week.

MAKES 1 CUP

- 10 ounces dates, pitted and sliced ⅓ inch thick (about 1¼ cups)
- ¼ cup extra-virgin olive oil
- ¼ cup coarsely chopped fresh flat-leaf parsley
- 2 tablespoons coarsely chopped cilantro
- 2 teaspoons chopped preserved lemons (optional)
- ½ teaspoon red pepper flakes (optional)
   Kosher salt and freshly ground black pepper
- ¼ cup lemon juice

In a medium bowl, combine the dates, olive oil, parsley, and cilantro. Add the preserved lemons and red pepper flakes, if using. Season with salt and pepper and add the lemon juice just before serving.

White Bean and Turkey Chili

We all need a go-to chili recipe and this one is wonderful. Using turkey lightens the dish and the addition of cocoa powder and molasses gives it depth and a touch of sweetness. This dish also freezes well: A day or two before you want to serve it, defrost the chili in the refrigerator, then heat it in a saucepan over low or medium-low heat (so the beans remain intact) until it begins to bubble.

SERVES 8 TO 10

In a large pot, heat the oil over medium heat. Add the onion and cook, stirring occasionally, until translucent, about 10 minutes. Add the garlic and continue to cook until the garlic is fragrant, about 2 minutes. Add the carrots, celery, peppers, oregano, and cumin and sauté for 4 to 5 more minutes.

Increase the heat to medium high and add the turkey. Sauté until the turkey is no longer pink, 5 to 10 minutes. Break up any chunks with the back of a wooden spoon. Stir in the chili powder, tomato paste, molasses, cocoa powder, salt, cinnamon, and bay leaves. Add the tomatoes, breaking them up as you add them, using your hands or a masher. Stir in 3 cups of beer (or stock) and the mustard, and bring to a boil. Reduce the heat and simmer, uncovered, for 45 minutes, stirring occasionally. If the liquid has cooked out, add another cup of beer (or stock).

Add the beans and simmer until the flavors are blended, about 10 minutes longer. Discard the bay leaves. Serve with accompaniments, if desired.

OPTIONAL ACCOMPANIMENTS

Chopped scallions · Chopped tomato · Chopped jalapeños · Snipped cilantro · Tortilla chips · Cornbread

3	tablespoons olive oil
2	large onions, chopped (about 2 cups)
4	garlic cloves, minced (about 4 teaspoons)
2	medium carrots, peeled and chopped
3	stalks celery, chopped
2	red or yellow bell peppers, seeded and chopped
2	teaspoons dried oregano, or 2 tablespoons chopped fresh oregano
2	teaspoons ground cumin
2	pounds ground dark-meat turkey
5	teaspoons chili powder
2	tablespoons tomato paste
1	tablespoon dark molasses
5	teaspoons cocoa powder
2	teaspoons kosher salt
1	teaspoon ground cinnamon
2	bay leaves
2	(28-ounce) can whole tomatoes
3	to 4 cups dark beer, or beef or chicken stock
½	cup Dijon mustard
2	(15-ounce) cans cannellini beans, rinsed and drained; or 1 cup dried beans, soaked and cooked (see Soaking Dried Beans, page 241)
	Optional accompaniments (see box)

Spicy Lentil Dal

Dal is a delicious, stew-like Indian dish most often made with lentils. Our version combines red and yellow lentils, spices, and a bit of heat to create a fabulous side dish. Leftover dal can be kept in the refrigerator for up to 1 week. Reheat it slowly over low heat, adding water, if necessary, to achieve its proper consistency, which is that of a thick puréed soup.

SERVES 8

1 cup toor dal (split yellow lentils)

1 cup masoor dal (split pink or red lentils)

4½ cups water

1½ teaspoons ground turmeric

1½ teaspoons kosher salt

6 tablespoons safflower or canola oil

1½ teaspoons cumin seeds

1 large onion, halved lengthwise then sliced crosswise into thin half-moons (about 1½ cups)

4 garlic cloves, finely chopped (about 4 teaspoons)

3 small plum tomatoes (8 ounces), chopped

1½ teaspoons ground coriander

1½ teaspoons ground cumin

½ teaspoon cayenne pepper, or to taste

Place the lentils in a sieve and rinse under cold running water. Pick over the lentils, removing any stones or small pebbles. Drain and transfer to a small heavy pan. Add the water and turmeric and bring to a boil. Partially cover, lower the heat, and gently simmer until the lentils are soft and mushy, about 1 hour. Add the salt and stir. Add more salt if necessary, to taste.

Heat the oil in a small skillet over medium heat. Add the cumin seeds and stir for 1 minute, until fragrant. Add the onion and sauté until softened, 6 to 7 minutes. Add the garlic and continue cooking until the onion has browned, 2 to 3 minutes. Stir in the tomatoes, coriander, ground cumin, and cayenne.

Stir the onion mixture into the cooked lentils and serve immediately.

VEGETABLES

Vegetable Prep for Everyday Meals

It can never hurt to have multiple vegetable prep methods up your sleeve. Not every meal needs a complicated vegetable side dish—if you're going all out for your main course, your best option may be to serve something simple as an accompaniment. Here are some useful guidelines you can employ.

BLANCHING: Flash cooking vegetables in a large quantity of lightly salted boiling water is a good way to preserve color, crispness, and flavor. The cooking is stopped with a quick cool down: You can run the drained vegetables under cool water; drop them into an ice bath; or simply lay them out on a kitchen towel to cool off. You can achieve similar results by steaming instead of blanching, but you will need to double the cooking time and cool the vegetables down as directed above.

ROASTING: Roasting vegetables that have been tossed in olive oil in a hot oven is one of our favorite go-to methods. We suggest using a 425°F oven. Make sure the vegetables are uniform in size to ensure even cooking and be sure to enjoy all the browned, caramelized bits. You can line your baking sheet with parchment paper for easier clean up.

SAUTÉING: Cooking and stirring vegetables in a small amount of oil over medium-high to high heat is always easy and the results are delicious. We suggest using olive oil or grapeseed oil, and cutting the vegetables in small pieces or slices so they cook quickly. One exception might be asparagus, which you can sauté as whole spears. We frequently add sliced or chopped garlic as we heat up the oil or during the last 1 or 2 minutes (to prevent burning if we're cooking at high heat).

VEGGIE	BLANCH	ROAST	SAUTÉ	FAVORITE SEASONINGS
Asparagus	2 to 3 minutes	10 to 15 minutes	3 to 5 minutes	Toasted sesame seeds, dill, tarragon, lemon zest
Beans, green or wax	3 minutes		3 to 4 minutes	Sesame seeds, cumin seeds, dill, lemon zest, ginger
Beets		50 to 60 minutes		Thyme, rosemary, garlic, shallots, orange zest, fennel seed, raspberry vinegar
Broccoli (medium florets)	3 minutes	15 to 20 minutes	3 to 4 minutes	Oregano, sesame seeds, ginger
Brussels sprouts (halved)		30 to 40 minutes	20 to 25 minutes	Caraway, mustard seeds, dill, lemon zest
Carrots (whole)		30 to 45 minutes		Thyme, rosemary, curry, dill seeds, poppy seeds, coriander seeds
Carrots (baby)	5 minutes	15 to 20 minutes		Thyme, rosemary, poppy seeds, parsley, dill, cilantro, mint
Carrots (thinly sliced)	2 minutes	8 to 10 minutes	3 to 4 minutes	Parsley, dill, cilantro, mint
Cauliflower (medium florets)	3 to 4 minutes	20 to 30 minutes	3 to 4 minutes	Cilantro, curry, dill seeds, fennel seeds, caraway seeds
Eggplant, ½-inch sliced rounds		30 to 40 minutes		Tahini, za'atar, lemon juice, parsley, yogurt, garlic
Mushrooms		20 to 25 minutes	7 to 10 minutes	Sesame seeds, chives, tarragon, thyme
Onions (½-inch slices)		35 to 45 minutes	10 to 15 minutes	Allspice, balsamic vinegar, thyme, oregano
Peas, shelled or sugar snaps	1 to 2 minutes		2 to 4 minutes	Mint, dill, lemon zest
Peppers, bell, sliced		12 to 15 minutes	4 to 6 minutes	Basil, cumin seeds, fennel seeds
Tomatoes, cherry or grape or halved plum		20 to 25 minutes	3 to 5 minutes	Cumin seeds, basil, cilantro, parsley, mint, fresh oregano, sea salt, garlic, pesto
Zucchini or summer squash (¼-inch disks)		10 to 15 minutes	4 to 6 minutes	Coriander seeds, basil, oregano, chives, dill

Lemon-Thyme Zucchini "Spaghettini"

Zucchini cut into spaghetti-thin strands and combined with lemon and thyme makes a lovely dish that is fabulous with or without the final cheese garnish. For the carb- or gluten-conscious, serve zucchini spaghettini in place of real spaghetti topped with a meat sauce, such as our lamb ragù (page 142).

SERVES 6

In a large skillet, heat 2 tablespoons of the olive oil over medium heat. Add the zucchini and cook, tossing once or twice, until it begins to brighten and soften, 2 to 3 minutes.

Add the thyme. Gradually add 1 tablespoon of water at a time, bringing the liquid back to a simmer before each addition. The water should just cover the bottom of the skillet. Simmer the zucchini until cooked through, 2 to 3 minutes. Toss in the lemon zest and the remaining 1 tablespoon olive oil and season with salt and pepper. Sprinkle with the cheese, if using, and serve.

3 tablespoons extra-virgin olive oil

6 small zucchini (about 3 pounds), julienned

1 teaspoon fresh thyme leaves

3 to 5 tablespoons water

2 teaspoons grated lemon zest
Kosher salt and freshly ground black pepper

2 to 3 tablespoons grated pecorino Romano cheese (optional)

> To achieve perfect strands of zucchini, it's worth having a julienne peeler or a mandolin with a julienne blade attachment. Both are great, inexpensive additions to your kitchen tool drawer.

THE GIVING GARDEN

From the White House's organic garden to the rooftops of Brooklyn, the movement to regain control over our food systems has taken hold. Therefore, it is no surprise that sustainable gardens are springing up at JCCs nationwide. Peek around the back of the building at the Jewish Community Center of Greater Washington, and you will find a special garden.

Everyone at the JCCGW acknowledged that growing fresh fruits and vegetables would be good for the community, and good for teaching Jewish values. As plans were being developed, an opportunity arose for a collaboration with a local chapter of B'nai B'rith Youth Organization (BBYO), a teen youth group that decided it wanted to start a garden for its own social action projects. The youth group needed land, and the JCCGW wanted year-round attention for its garden. It was a perfect match. Luckily for everyone, a longtime JCCGW member and master gardener loaned her expertise to the project.

Now tomatoes, squash, sweet peppers, herbs, and flowers are planted and harvested. As each year passes, more and more groups within the JCC jump in to take responsibility for a part of the garden. While the preschool cultivates the flowers, and the JCC campers care for vegetables during the summer, all the produce from the beds tended by the BBYO group during the school year go straight to a local food bank.

Throughout this cookbook, we celebrate all the sustenance this earth provides by cooking locally, seasonally, and organically whenever we can. Stories like this highlight how JCCs around the country have embraced the movement toward sustainable living.

Braised Roasted Fennel

Braising fennel in milk might sound unusual but it makes the fennel delicately sweet. A final bake under a blanket of Parmesan adds crunch and a touch of caramelization. Cooled to room temperature, the fennel works well as part of a larger spread of vegetable and grain dishes, such as Caponata (page 62), Braised Red Cabbage with Caraway Seeds (page 265), Shredded Beets with Yogurt (page 276), roasted squash and asparagus, bulgur, wheat berries, and more. As many of these are also served at room temperature, a lot of the prep can be done beforehand.

SERVES 6

Preheat the oven to 475°F.

Cut away the fronds and stems from the fennel bulbs (you can keep them for Vegetable Consommé, page 98). Cut away the root end and peel off the outer layer from the bulbs. Quarter the bulbs lengthwise.

Place the fennel, cut side up, in a medium or large saucepan so the pieces fit snugly in one layer. Pour enough milk over the fennel just to cover. Bring to a low boil over medium-high heat. Reduce the heat to medium and simmer until the fennel can be easily pierced with a sharp knife, 15 to 20 minutes. Using a slotted spoon, transfer the fennel to paper towels and pat dry.

Transfer the fennel to a 9 x 12-inch baking dish, cut sides up. Pour the olive oil over the fennel, sprinkle with the Parmesan, and season with salt and pepper. Bake the fennel until the cheese is lightly browned, 20 to 25 minutes. Remove from the oven and serve immediately, or serve at room temperature.

2 medium fennel bulbs (about 2 pounds)

2 to 3 cups low-fat milk, as needed

2 tablespoons extra-virgin olive oil

¼ cup grated Parmesan

Kosher salt and freshly ground black pepper

Roasted Brussels Sprouts with Pomegranate-Citrus Glaze

This tantalizing dish was inspired by a fried version that we love but try to resist because of the amount of oil required. In our easier and lighter recipe, the sprouts are roasted and drizzled with a citrus glaze that contains pomegranate molasses—a widely available syrup that is Turkish in origin. The acidity of the glaze is a perfect counterpart to the crispy, caramelized sprouts.

Reserve any whole leaves that fall off the sprouts as you prepare them and toss them in with the quarters before roasting. The leaves will crisp up beautifully.

SERVES 6 TO 8

2   pounds Brussels sprouts, halved and cored

2   tablespoons extra-virgin olive oil

1   tablespoon orange juice

3   tablespoons lemon juice

2   tablespoons pomegranate molasses

¾   teaspoon fresh thyme leaves

½   to 1 dried chile pepper, seeds removed if less heat is preferred, finely chopped

Seeds from 1 pomegranate

Kosher salt and freshly ground black pepper

Preheat the oven to 500°F.

Line a large baking sheet with parchment paper. Cut the Brussels sprouts in half again. Add the Brussels sprouts, toss with the olive oil, and arrange in a single layer. Roast until brown and crispy, 20 to 30 minutes.

Meanwhile, make the glaze. In a small bowl, combine the orange and lemon juices, pomegranate molasses, thyme, and chile pepper to taste.

Transfer the cooked Brussels sprouts to a large bowl. Drizzle with the glaze a little bit at a time just to coat. Toss with the pomegranate seeds. Season with salt and pepper, taste, and add more glaze if you think it's needed. Serve immediately.

For the brave of heart, and those not counting calories, go ahead and deep-fry the Brussels sprouts in grapeseed oil heated to 375°F, until crispy, 3 to 5 minutes. Drizzle with the glaze and toss to coat. Just make sure to serve them soon after you've taken them out of the fryer, as their crispiness won't last long.

Grilled Cauliflower Steaks

Simple and substantial, this elegant dish is perfect as a vegetarian main course or as a side for any meal. We've treated the cauliflower as though it were a thick cut of meat or fish—searing it and then finishing it in the oven. Once you've tasted roasted cauliflower, you may never go back to boiling it. Serve it right out of the oven or use the sauce below to create an Asian-flavored pairing to serve with rice. Save any extra florets for crudités.

SERVES 4

Preheat the oven to 400°F.

Remove the leaves and trim the stem end of the cauliflower. Place the cauliflower stem side down on a work surface and, using a sharp knife, halve the cauliflower, cutting through the stem end. Cut two or three 1-inch steaks from each half.

Heat a large grill pan over medium-high heat for 5 minutes. Brush it with 1 tablespoon of the olive oil. (If you don't have a large grill pan, grill the cauliflower in batches, using a portion of the oil for each batch.) While the pan is heating, combine the remaining 1 tablespoon olive oil with the sesame oil in a small bowl and brush on the cauliflower steaks. Season with salt and pepper.

Place the slices carefully on the grill pan and sear until browned, turning once with a large spatula, 3 to 5 minutes per side. Place the steaks on a large rimmed baking sheet, transfer to the oven, and bake until the steaks are tender, about 15 minutes.

Meanwhile, to make the sauce, combine the vinegar, sherry, sesame oil, soy sauce, ginger, and pepper flakes in a small bowl.

To serve, transfer the steaks to plates and sprinkle with the chives. Pass the sauce separately for spooning over the steaks.

1 large head yellow, purple, or white cauliflower

2 tablespoons extra-virgin olive oil or grapeseed oil

1 teaspoon toasted sesame oil

Kosher salt and freshly ground black pepper

Sauce

2 tablespoons rice vinegar

1 tablespoon sherry

½ teaspoon toasted sesame oil

½ teaspoon soy sauce

¼ teaspoon grated fresh ginger

Pinch red pepper flakes

3 tablespoons chives cut into ¼-inch lengths, for garnish

Warm Mushroom Sauté

On a family vacation a few years ago, one of our daughters became enchanted by a warm mushroom dish served on a bed of wild greens and garnished with nuts. We were so pleasantly surprised to find a similar recipe from one of our favorite chefs, Suzanne Goin. Here is our rendition of woodsy warm mushrooms partnered with toasted nuts and fresh greens. This dish is wonderful over pasta or polenta (page 155) and the mushrooms alone make a great side dish.

SERVES 4 TO 6

½   cup hazelnuts or walnuts

Vinaigrette

2   medium shallots, finely diced (about 2 tablespoons)

3   tablespoons white balsamic vinegar

Pinch of kosher salt

5   tablespoons extra-virgin olive oil

Mushrooms and Greens

2   tablespoons extra-virgin olive oil

2   tablespoons unsalted butter or additional extra-virgin olive oil

2   pounds fresh wild mushrooms, such as shiitake, chanterelle, oyster, or maitake, stems removed, sliced ¼ inch thick

2   teaspoons fresh thyme leaves, finely chopped

1 ½   teaspoons kosher salt and 2 pinches freshly ground black pepper, plus more for seasoning

¼   cup thinly sliced shallots

2   cups any combination of baby arugula, radicchio, or baby kale

¼   cup roughly chopped fresh tarragon leaves

½   cup roughly chopped fresh flat-leaf parsley leaves

¼   cup thinly sliced fresh chives

Preheat the oven to 375°F.

In a medium skillet over medium-high heat, toast the nuts, stirring occasionally, until golden brown, 5 to 7 minutes. Don't allow them to burn. Let the nuts cool, then chop them coarsely. Set aside.

To make the vinaigrette, in a small bowl combine the finely diced shallots, vinegar, and a pinch of salt. Let the mixture sit for 10 minutes. Whisk in the olive oil and set aside.

To prepare the mushrooms, heat a large skillet over high heat for 2 minutes. Add the olive oil and heat for 1 minute. Add 1 tablespoon of the butter and when it foams, scatter half the mushrooms in the pan. Add 1 teaspoon of the thyme, ¾ teaspoon salt, and a pinch of pepper. Cook the mushrooms, stirring occasionally, until tender and a little crispy, 5 to 8 minutes. Transfer to a plate. Repeat with the remaining butter, thyme, salt, and pepper and the second batch of mushrooms, leaving the mushrooms in the pan.

Add the first batch of mushrooms to the second batch and reheat without further cooking. Add the sliced shallots and stir to warm them as well. Add the greens, herbs, nuts, and vinaigrette to the skillet and toss quickly. Adjust the seasoning with salt and pepper and serve immediately.

Roasted Tzimmes

Remember the super-sweet, gooey carrots always on the buffet tables of your grandmothers' dining rooms? Don't expect that flavor or texture here. Sweet carrots are so evocative of the Jewish holidays that we didn't want to exile them to the history books, but we felt they needed an update. Roasting them allows the natural sugars in the vegetables to caramelize without adding sugar. And instead of prunes and pineapples, we have added dried figs—which are always elegant. With the final addition of za'atar, a Middle Eastern spice mixture, this sweet carrot dish becomes another perfect combination of East meets West—a great mix of Ashkenazi tradition with Middle Eastern flavors.

SERVES 6 TO 8

In a small bowl, combine the figs or raisins and orange juice and let soak for at least 20 minutes or up to 1 hour. Drain and reserve the orange juice.

Preheat the oven to 425°F. Line a baking sheet with parchment paper.

In a large bowl, combine the figs or raisins, carrots, sweet potatoes, and parsnips. Add the olive oil, balsamic vinegar, molasses, za'atar, salt, and pepper to taste and toss to coat.

Spread the mixture on the baking sheet. Roast, tossing occasionally, until the vegetables begin to caramelize, 30 to 40 minutes. Sprinkle 3 tablespoons of the reserved orange juice over the vegetables and toss again. Add more salt to taste and serve.

8 dried figs, cut in eighths or ¾ cup golden raisins

¼ cup orange juice

¾ pound carrots, peeled and cut into 1-inch cubes or 1½-inch-long sticks

¾ pound sweet potatoes, cut into 1-inch cubes or 1½-inch-long sticks

½ pound parsnips, peeled and cut into 1-inch cubes or 1½-inch-long sticks

3 tablespoons extra-virgin olive oil

1 tablespoon balsamic vinegar

1 tablespoon molasses

2 teaspoons za'atar

1 teaspoon kosher salt

Freshly ground black pepper

Celery Root and Potato Purée

Who doesn't love mashed potatoes? This version combines potatoes with celery root, which definitely ups the flavor ante. The dish can be made ahead and reheated over low heat in a heavy-bottomed pot or in a double boiler; add warm milk to the mixture, stirring as it heats.

SERVES 8

3 pounds Yukon Gold or Yellow Finn potatoes, peeled and cut into 1½-inch chunks

Kosher salt

1 medium celery root (about 1 pound), peeled and cut into 1-inch chunks

8 tablespoons (1 stick) unsalted butter

1 cup low-fat milk, or more as needed

Freshly ground black pepper

Splash of white wine vinegar

Place the potatoes in a large pot and cover with cold water. Add a pinch of salt and bring to a boil. Reduce the heat and cook until very tender, about 20 minutes. Drain the potatoes and return to the pot.

Meanwhile, in a medium saucepan, combine the celery root and butter and add enough water to barely cover. Cover the pan and cook over medium heat until the celery root is fork-tender, 20 to 25 minutes. Transfer the celery root and its liquid, if any remains, to the pot with the potatoes.

Using the saucepan from the celery root, warm the milk over low heat. Using a potato masher, work the milk gradually into the potato mixture, mashing until you achieve the consistency you prefer. Add more milk if needed.

Season with salt and pepper and the vinegar. Serve immediately or keep warm in a water bath.

Braised Red Cabbage with Caraway Seeds

This recipe for tart-sweet cabbage with apple is based on an old Viennese family recipe. We've honored the origins of the recipe by using fresh red cabbage instead of the jarred kind. You can cut down on prep time by slicing the cabbage a day ahead and refrigerating it in a plastic bag. But the dish is best made a day in advance so all the flavors have time to marry. In fact, the dish will hold well in a sealed container in the fridge for up to 2 weeks. Serve this alongside the Farmhouse Chicken (page 179) or the Prime Rib Bones with Roasted Potatoes (page 209); or it can make a delicious addition to turkey sandwiches or cheese melts.

SERVES 10

In a large heavy pot, heat the oil or fat over medium heat. Add the onions and caraway seeds and sauté until light golden, 5 to 7 minutes.

Add the cabbage and sauté over medium-low heat until wilted, 7 to 10 minutes. Add the wine, maple syrup, and vinegar and stir. Reduce the heat to low and simmer until the liquid has mostly evaporated, about 15 minutes.

Add the apples, salt, and pepper. Add the lemon juice in small amounts as you continue to cook, until you've reached your preferred level of acidity. Lower the heat, cover, and simmer, stirring occasionally, until the cabbage is cooked through but not mushy, 20 to 30 minutes. Add more lemon juice if needed. Serve or refrigerate for the following day.

2 tablespoons olive oil, chicken fat, or duck fat

3 cups finely chopped onions (about 3 medium onions)

1½ teaspoons caraway seeds

1 head red cabbage (3 pounds), halved, cored, and thinly sliced

1½ cups red wine

2 tablespoons maple syrup

4 teaspoons cider vinegar

2 Granny Smith apples, unpeeled, cored, seeded, and finely chopped or grated

1 well-rounded teaspoon kosher salt

½ teaspoon freshly ground black pepper

Juice of 1 lemon

Savory Butternut Squash Crumble

If you love a crumble and if you love butternut squash, this is your perfect dish. Soft and crunchy textures are combined with sweet and savory flavors to produce a satisfying dish that says "fall harvest" in every bite. We like to serve this for autumnal holidays such as Sukkot and Thanksgiving.

SERVES 8

Roasted Squash

2 medium butternut squash (5 pounds), peeled and cut into 1-inch cubes

2 medium red onions, cut into 1-inch pieces (about 2 cups)

6 tablespoons extra-virgin olive oil

Crumble Topping

1 cup pine nuts

1 cup unbleached all-purpose flour

1 cup medium-grind cornmeal

½ cup grated Parmesan

1 tablespoon chopped fresh flat-leaf parsley

½ teaspoon mustard powder

½ teaspoon freshly ground black pepper

12 tablespoons (1½ sticks) chilled unsalted butter, diced

1 cup vegetable stock

½ cup grated Parmesan

5 tablespoons chopped fresh flat-leaf parsley

2 teaspoons ground coriander

6 to 10 fresh sage leaves, snipped
    Kosher salt and freshly ground black pepper

Preheat the oven to 400°F.

To roast the squash, in a medium bowl, combine the squash, onions, and olive oil and toss to coat. Spread the mixture in a single layer on a baking sheet and roast until the edges of the squash have begun to brown, 25 to 30 minutes.

Meanwhile, prepare the topping: In a medium skillet, toast the pine nuts over medium-low heat, watching closely and stirring often, until golden, about 3 minutes. (Keep a close eye on them, being careful not to let them burn.) Transfer to a small cutting board and coarsely chop.

In a medium bowl, combine the toasted pine nuts, flour, cornmeal, Parmesan, parsley, mustard powder, and pepper and stir to combine. Add the butter and blend with your fingertips until the mixture forms clumps and coarse crumbs. Chill.

To assemble and bake the crumble, reduce the oven temperature to 350°F. Grease a 14-inch oval or rectangular oven-to-table baking dish.

Spoon the roasted squash into a medium bowl. Add the stock, Parmesan, parsley, coriander, and sage and toss. Season with salt and pepper.

Transfer the squash mixture to the baking dish and sprinkle with the topping. Bake until bubbling and golden, about 45 minutes. Serve from the baking dish.

SMASHED PEAS WITH herbs

Sidebar: in the spring and ~~summer~~ this dish is great with fresh mint. During the colder months, try it
with dill, tarragon, or parsley depending on your taste.

2 -10 oz bags of frozen peas

¾ cup vegetable stock

2 t~~~~ olive oil

1 clove of garlic, halved

Salt and pepper to taste

½ cup mint, chiffonade + parsley + any other herbs you have

serves 4-6

1. Defrost peas on countertop for ½ hour. If any ice remains, run under hot water.

~~~~ ~~~~ocessor, reserving 5 oz whole. In a small sauce pan combine stock, olive oil~~~~
~~~~tes. Add stock mixture to peas in food processor and puree until co~~~~
~~~~and pepper.

~~~~hole peas and mint. Mix to combine. Reheat in micro~~~~

~~~~dd a bag of mint tea to the broth and steep~~~~

Smashed Peas with Fresh Mint

Sometimes called mushy peas, smashed peas are an English favorite that often accompanies fish and chips. As their name suggests, the peas are puréed and pretty much served as is. We've brightened up the dish by adding fresh mint, and made the texture more interesting by including whole peas together with the puréed ones. If you like, you can amplify the mint flavor by steeping a bag of mint tea in the stock as it warms. You can also substitute dill, tarragon, or parsley for the mint.

SERVES 6 TO 8

Defrost the peas in the bag for 30 minutes.

In a small saucepan, combine the stock, olive oil, and garlic. Simmer over medium heat until the garlic is cooked through, about 10 minutes.

If the peas in the bag are still icy after 30 minutes, run the bag under hot water. Place the peas in a food processor, reserving 1 cup. Add the stock mixture to the food processor and purée. Season with the salt and pepper. Transfer to a medium bowl, add the whole peas and mint, and combine and serve.

2 (10-ounce) bags frozen peas
¾ cup vegetable stock
2 tablespoons extra-virgin olive oil
1 garlic clove, halved
  Kosher salt and freshly ground black pepper
½ cup fresh mint cut into thin ribbons

Zucchini Eggplant Mina (Savory Layered Pie)

Imagine a vegetarian lasagna made from layered matzah, zucchini, and eggplant. You've imagined *mina*, a delicious dish of Sephardic origin. *Mina* makes a great vegetarian entrée during the week of Passover, but it's also good throughout the year when you want something meatless yet satisfying.

The *mina* can be assembled ahead of time to the point before pouring the egg-tomato "sauce" over the filled matzah layers. The eggplant filling is also great on its own, spread over matzah—you may want to double the filling recipe and keep some in the fridge to have on hand for the week.

SERVES 8

Zucchini Filling

- 3 cups grated zucchini (about 1 pound)
- ¼ teaspoon kosher salt
- ½ cup chopped fresh flat-leaf parsley
- ¼ cup chopped fresh dill
- ¼ cup chopped fresh mint
- 1 bunch of scallions, white and green parts only, very thinly sliced
- 2 extra-large eggs, beaten
- Freshly ground black pepper

Eggplant Filling

- 1 large eggplant (about 1½ pounds), peeled and cut into ½-inch cubes
- Kosher salt
- ⅓ cup extra-virgin olive oil
- 2 to 3 garlic cloves, finely chopped (about 2 to 3 teaspoons)
- 1 large onion, finely chopped
- 2 teaspoons tomato paste
- 4 large tomatoes, peeled, seeded, and chopped; or 8 canned whole plum tomatoes, drained
- ¼ to ½ teaspoon allspice
- Pinch of crushed fennel seeds

To make the zucchini filling, place the zucchini in a colander and toss with ¼ teaspoon salt. Place the colander in the sink and allow the zucchini to drain for 20 minutes. Squeeze the moisture out of the zucchini and transfer to a medium bowl. Add the parsley, dill, mint, scallions, and eggs. Season with pepper and stir to blend. Set aside.

To make the eggplant filling, place the eggplant cubes in a colander and toss with salt. Place the colander in the sink and lay a sheet of parchment or wax paper on top. Weigh the eggplant down with heavy cans and allow it to drain for 30 minutes. Remove the cans and paper and gently rinse the eggplant to remove any bitterness and salt. Dry well with paper towels.

In a large skillet, heat the olive oil over medium heat. Add the garlic and sauté until it begins to soften, about 2 minutes. Add the onion and sauté until soft and translucent, 7 to 8 minutes. Add the eggplant and sauté until soft, 15 to 20 minutes. Add the tomato paste and stir. Add the tomatoes, allspice to taste, and fennel seeds and sauté until the tomatoes fall apart and the mixture thickens, about 5 minutes. Season with salt and pepper. Remove from the heat and cool to room temperature.

Preheat the oven to 350°F. Oil an 8 x 12 x 3-inch baking dish.

To assemble the *mina*, place the matzahs in a deep baking dish. Pour ½ cup of the stock over them and allow the matzahs to soften, about 3 minutes. Take 2 of the matzahs and layer them to fully cover the bottom of the greased dish. Lightly brush olive oil on those matzahs and spread the eggplant filling on top. Lay 2 more soaked matzahs over the eggplant and brush with oil. Spread on the zucchini filling, and top with the 2 remaining matzahs. (You can prepare the dish up to this point 1 day ahead, cover, and refrigerate.)

In a small bowl, combine the remaining ½ cup stock, eggs, tomato sauce, and nutmeg and beat with a fork to blend. Pour over the *mina*. Bake until firm, 45 to 50 minutes. Allow the *mina* to rest for 10 minutes, cut it into squares, and serve.

Freshly ground black pepper

6 matzahs

1 cup vegetable stock

Extra-virgin olive oil, for brushing

3 extra-large eggs, beaten

¾ cup good tomato sauce

¼ teaspoon freshly grated nutmeg

Roasted Sweet Potatoes with Lime and Cilantro

This is Sweet Potatoes 101—with flair. We make this all the time after work because it requires virtually no prep work and the potatoes go well with just about any main dish. Dollop some yogurt on top for added richness and creaminess.

SERVES 4

4 medium sweet potatoes (about 3 pounds), unpeeled, scrubbed

Juice of 2 limes

½ cup packed chopped cilantro

Preheat the oven to 375°F. Cover a standard baking sheet with foil, place the potatoes on it, and roast until they yield to the touch, 1¼ to 1½ hours.

Score the potatoes crosswise and squeeze gently at the ends to open up the potato skin.

Drizzle the potatoes with the lime juice, sprinkle with the cilantro, and serve immediately.

Spring Succotash

Although it is a traditional American dish, succotash has unfortunately gone out of style and is no longer cooked in many households. Most of us don't even know what the word means—we're not sure anyone ever did. We're reviving it here because it's a great vehicle for springtime vegetables and we like to celebrate seasonal cooking. We use corn, of course, but also tomatoes, asparagus, and beans, all stir-fried and graced with chives and fresh basil. We suggest serving it with a simple main dish to allow the variety of vegetables to shine.

SERVES 8

In a large skillet, heat the oil over medium-low heat. Add the shallots and sauté until soft but not brown, 3 to 4 minutes. Stir in the tomatoes and sauté until softened, about 3 minutes. Add the asparagus and corn and sauté until the asparagus is crisp-tender, about 2 minutes. Add the beans, stir to combine, and just heat through, 1 to 2 minutes.

Remove from the heat and stir in the basil, chives, parsley, and thyme. Season with the salt and pepper and serve.

2 tablespoons extra-virgin olive oil or unsalted butter

4 medium shallots, chopped (about ¼ cup)

1 cup (about ½ pint) grape or cherry tomatoes, halved

1 bunch thin asparagus, trimmed, each stalk quartered diagonally

1½ cups fresh corn kernels (about 4 ears corn)

1 cup edamame, lima beans, fava beans, peas, or string beans, blanched or defrosted

¼ cup fresh basil leaves cut into thin ribbons

1 tablespoon fresh chives cut into ¼-inch lengths

1 tablespoon chopped fresh flat-leaf parsley

1 to 2 teaspoons fresh thyme leaves

Kosher salt and freshly ground black pepper

Shredded Beets with Yogurt

The vibrant pink color of this traditional dish may surprise newcomers to Middle Eastern cooking. Throughout the region, there are many versions of this simple dish. Sometimes the beets are puréed, sometimes sliced or cubed, other times, a little tahini is blended in. Here, we grate the beets using the shredding disc of a food processor then fold them into creamy Greek yogurt. Serve as part of a *mezze* (see page 242) or a side dish to fish.

MAKES ABOUT 3 CUPS

4 medium beets (about 2 pounds)
1 tablespoon olive oil
   Kosher salt and freshly ground black pepper
2 garlic cloves, minced (about 2 teaspoons)
2 tablespoons lemon juice
1 cup Greek 0% yogurt, plus more if needed
   Pinch of sugar (optional)

Preheat the oven to 425°F.

Scrub and trim the beets and place in a baking dish. Drizzle with the olive oil and lightly season with salt and pepper. Cover the baking dish tightly with foil and roast the beets for 45 to 60 minutes, until a fork can easily pierce them.

When cool, peel the beets. Using the shredding disc of a food processor, or the large holes on a box grater, coarsely grate the beets.

Place the garlic on a flat surface and sprinkle with salt. Using the back of a large knife, mash the salt into the garlic to form a paste. In a medium bowl, combine the garlic paste and lemon juice and season with salt and pepper. Add the beets and yogurt and blend well. Taste and add additional yogurt if desired. Add the sugar, if using.

Transfer to a serving dish, cover, and refrigerate until well chilled, at least 1 hour, before serving.

Matzah Brei Sri-Lankan Style

In the spring of 2011, JCC Manhattan held a contest for the best recipe using matzah. Many matzah ball and kugel recipes were submitted, all good, but this one for matzah brei with a Sri-Lankan flair won us over. Featuring red peppers and cabbage and flavored with sweet spices and jalapeños, the dish will add variety to your Passover menus.

SERVES 8

Place the matzahs in a medium bowl and cover with cold water, making sure all of them are covered. Set aside to soak for 5 minutes.

Meanwhile, heat the oil in a 14-inch or large nonstick pan over medium-high heat. Add the cumin seeds, and mustard seeds and turmeric, if using. Cook until the spices darken slightly and become fragrant, 3 to 5 minutes. Add the scallion, jalapeños, and curry or basil leaves and sauté until soft but not browned, about 5 minutes. Add the cabbage and sauté until wilted, 5 to 10 minutes. (The cabbage may be sautéed until it is slightly browned to add a caramelized flavor, if you like.) Add the bell pepper and sauté until it begins to soften, about 5 minutes. Season with salt.

Drain the matzahs, squeeze out their liquid, and add to the pan. Let the matzahs rest in the pan undisturbed until they start to dry out, 3 to 5 minutes. Stir-fry until the matzahs begin to crisp and brown, 10 to 15 minutes. Use the back of a wooden spoon to scrape up any crispy bits.

Push the mixture to one side of the skillet. Add a bit of oil to the cleared side and pour in the eggs. Let the egg cook undisturbed for about 1 minute, then mix the eggs until scrambled, about 30 seconds. Stir the scrambled eggs into the other ingredients, garnish with the cilantro, and serve.

3 matzahs, broken into medium-size pieces

3 tablespoons grapeseed or safflower oil, plus more as needed

1 tablespoon crushed cumin seeds

1 tablespoon crushed mustard seeds (optional)

¼ teaspoon turmeric (optional)

2 bunches scallions, white and light green parts, chopped (about 1 cup)

2 jalapeño peppers (about 1½ ounces), seeded and finely chopped

10 to 12 fresh curry or basil leaves

1 pound napa cabbage, shredded (about 6 cups)

1 medium red bell pepper, roughly chopped (about 1 cup)

Kosher salt

4 extra-large eggs, lightly beaten and salted

1 cup chopped cilantro

Garlic Mashed Potatoes

These are the ultimate dairy-free mashed potatoes. They're creamy and garlicky and have a nice color due to the parsley. If you know you'll be serving this to children with a green-food aversion, don't purée the parsley with the garlic, just offer it separately to sprinkle over the finished dish. Another flavor advantage—the garlic is cooked slowly in oil, making it sweet and mellow. This is delicious with any roasted meat, or fish. The dish can also be prepared a day or two ahead, then gently reheated in a double boiler or over a hot water bath.

SERVES 8

3 pounds Yukon Gold or all-purpose potatoes, peeled and cut into 2-inch cubes

½ cup extra-virgin olive oil

14 garlic cloves, peeled

1 cup chicken stock

½ cup packed fresh flat-leaf parsley leaves

Kosher salt and freshly ground black pepper

Place the potatoes in a large saucepan, cover with cold water, and bring to a boil. Reduce the heat to maintain a simmer and cook until the potatoes are tender, 20 to 30 minutes.

Meanwhile, heat the oil over low heat in a small heavy skillet. Add the garlic and cook, stirring occasionally, until the cloves begin to turn a very light gold, about 10 minutes. Watch carefully to avoid burning the garlic and remove the pan from the heat as soon as the cloves begin to color.

When the potatoes are tender, drain and return them to the pot.

Purée the garlic with its cooking oil, the stock, and the parsley in a food processor fitted with a metal blade. (The mixture will be green.) Transfer the purée to the pot with the potatoes and mash together with a hand masher until smooth. Season with salt and pepper. Serve at once or keep the potatoes warm in the pot, covered, over a hot water bath for up to 1 hour.

Sautéed Greens with Shallots

What should you do with all those beautiful greens that can be found at your local farmers' market? Sautéing them is always a great way to go. You can liven this side dish up by throwing in golden raisins or currants, or even some toasted pine nuts if you like.

SERVES 4

Heat the olive oil in a large deep skillet over medium heat. Lower the heat to medium-low and add the shallots and sauté until beginning to brown, 4 to 6 minutes. Add the garlic and continue to cook 1 to 2 minutes. Add the greens, in 2 to 3 batches, and sauté until all the greens have wilted, 5 to 7 minutes. Season with salt and pepper and sauté 2 minutes more, until the greens are tender. Serve immediately or at room temperature.

2 tablespoons extra-virgin olive oil

2 medium shallots, minced (about 2 tablespoons)

1 garlic clove, chopped (about 1 teaspoon)

2 pounds washed and dried greens, such as baby spinach, baby kale, or Swiss chard, tough stems removed

Kosher salt and freshly ground black pepper, or pinch of ground red pepper flakes

DESSERTS

Honey Cake with Grilled Peaches 284

Lemon Layer Cake 287

Lime–Olive Oil Cake with Rhubarb Compote 290

Light and Creamy Cheesecake with Nut Brittle and Blueberries 292

Intensely Chocolate Cupcakes with Chocolate Frosting 295

Chocolate Sour Cream Cake 298

Chocolate Brownie Cookies with Sea Salt 301

Oatmeal–Chocolate Chip Cookies 302

Chocolate Chip–Hazelnut Meringues 305

Cappuccino Thins 306

Ultimate Sugar Cookies 309

Vanilla Crescents with Citrus and Verbena Salad 311

Two Great Dunking Cookies 315

Sour Cherry Pie 317

Pumpkin Rugelach 321

Rustic Apple-Cranberry Pie 322

Summer and Fall Crostatas 324

Roasted Pears with Nutty Crumble Topping 327

Three Sorbets 328

Prosecco-Berry Gelée 330

Goat Milk and Yogurt Panna Cotta with Spiced Fig Compote 331

Honey Cake with Grilled Peaches

You may not think to serve honey cake year-round, but this moist and luscious cake pairs perfectly with our grilled peaches in summer as well as for a Rosh Hashanah dessert. It could easily become your go-to teacake. The cake keeps for days and also freezes well. While you're at it, add vanilla ice cream or whipped cream with a touch of ginger. It's also delicious sliced and toasted as a breakfast treat.

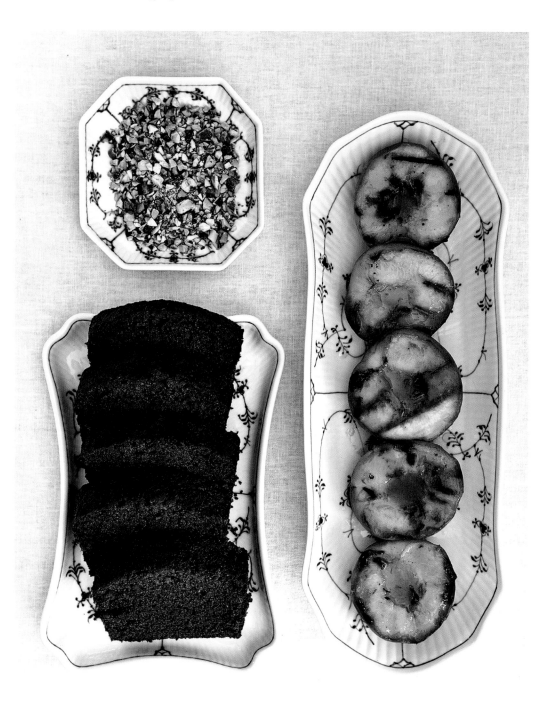

Position a rack in the center of the oven and preheat the oven to 350°F. Oil three 9 x 5-inch loaf pans and line their bottoms with parchment paper.

In a small bowl, combine ¼ cup of the boiling water with the baking soda (to eliminate any bitterness). In the bowl of a standing mixer or with hand beaters and a large bowl, combine the sugar, honey, and oil and beat at medium speed until completely combined, 2 to 3 minutes. Add the eggs, one at a time and beating after each addition. Add the dissolved baking soda and beat until combined. Add the raisins, if using, and stir to incorporate.

In a medium bowl, combine the flour, cinnamon, ginger, salt, and zest and blend with a fork. With the mixer at low speed, gradually add the flour mixture to the honey mixture. When combined, slowly add the remaining 2 cups boiling water. The batter will seem quite thin and a bit runny; this is normal.

Divide the batter among the pans. Bake the cakes on the center rack until a cake tester inserted in the centers comes out clean and the tops are springy to the touch, 45 to 50 minutes. Allow the cakes to cool in their pans for 10 minutes, then transfer to a rack to cool completely. Cut the cakes in ½-inch slices and serve with the grilled peaches.

2¼	cups boiling water
4	teaspoons baking soda
2	cups sugar
2	cups honey
2	cups grapeseed or canola oil
6	extra-large eggs
¾	cup raisins (optional)
4	cups unbleached all-purpose flour
2	teaspoons ground cinnamon
1	teaspoon ground ginger
1	teaspoon kosher salt
1	tablespoon grated lemon zest
	Grilled Peaches with Lemon-Honey Drizzle (recipe follows)

Grilled Peaches with Lemon-Honey Drizzle

Place the peaches in a shallow bowl and brush with the oil, coating them completely. Drizzle 1 tablespoon of the honey on the peaches, sprinkle with the salt, and pour over 1 tablespoon of the lemon juice. Gently move the peaches around to coat them.

Heat a grill pan over medium-high heat. Grill the peaches cut side down until the edges have begun to soften and brown, about 5 minutes. Gently turn the peaches and grill until fork-tender but still firm, about 5 minutes more (the ripeness and size of the peaches may alter the timing). Transfer the peaches to a platter, skin side down.

Make the drizzle: In a small saucepan bring the remaining honey and juice to a gentle simmer over low heat. Stir and simmer to combine, 1 minute more. Drizzle over the peaches, sprinkle with the pistachios, if using, and serve.

SERVES 6 TO 8

4	firm-ripe peaches, unpeeled, halved and stones removed
2	teaspoons grapeseed or light olive oil
2	tablespoons honey
	Pinch of kosher salt
	Juice of 2 small lemons (about 4 tablespoons)
2	tablespoons shelled pistachios, chopped (optional)

A TASTE OF SWEETNESS

The Torah uses the word *devash*—honey—to refer to both date syrup and honey from bees; it's a word for sweetness. And throughout the ages—whether it's honey cake or round challot glistening with honey—Jews everywhere have incorporated honey and other sweet foods into their New Year's celebrations.

Since 2006, the Jewish Community Center of San Francisco's annual community celebration of Rosh Hashanah has included a honey tasting. Each year, the theme is a little different: Once it was local honeys from different San Francisco neighborhoods; another year it was honeys from around the global Diaspora. During the year of the presidential elections, they had red-state honeys and blue-state honeys. One year, the array included unusual honeys like star thistle, chestnut, and Himalayan wildflower, as well as natural sweeteners from barley malt, dates, and agave.

"This one is *neem* honey," a JCC staff member told two young girls. "It comes from a tree in India, part of the mahogany family. And *this* one isn't honey, but a nectar that comes from the sap of coconut flowers, that is similar to the date syrup used in biblical times." The two girls then joined a tradition stretching back to ancient Israel of marking Rosh Hashanah by celebrating the sweetness of a new year with sweet delicacies.

For some, the honey brings back a flood of memories. Tasting the chestnut honey, one man reminisced about the last time he had tasted that flavor: forty years earlier, as a child. After a nutritional support program for seniors, a woman stopped by the table. She tasted the honey, closed her eyes, and recited her mother's apple-honey cake recipe from memory.

The JCCSF's Chief Jewish Officer noted that one honeybee makes $\frac{1}{12}$ teaspoon of honey over its lifetime and that a single jar of honey is the life's work of hundreds of bees. Honey, as is cooking, is an extravagant gift.

Lemon Layer Cake

This is a lemon cake times three. Not only does it boast a superior lemon-flavored cake, but it's filled with Meyer lemon–laced curd, then finished with a creamy lemon frosting. But it is not only for those obsessed with lemon flavor: Our kids adore it. And, by the way, it's gluten-free. In fact, it's been requested so regularly that we figured out other ways to enjoy it (see the variations on page 288).

By the way, don't be thrown by the use of xanthan gum, which is available in many supermarkets and baking-goods stores. It's a natural emulsifier that ensures volume in this gluten-free cake. Can't get Meyer lemons? The regular kind also work beautifully. But buy organic lemons, if available, as this recipe uses a lot of zest. You will need to zest and squeeze three or four lemons—remember to zest them before juicing.

The layers can be made (but not halved) a day ahead. Cool them completely, wrap with plastic wrap, and keep at room temperature. The curd can be prepared and chilled up to 3 days in advance. The frosting can also be made a day ahead and refrigerated. (Remember to bring it to room temperature before spreading.)

MAKES 8 TO 10 SERVINGS

To make the cake layers, position a rack in the middle of the oven and preheat the oven to 350°F. Brush two 9-inch round cake pans with oil. Line the bottom of each pan with a round of parchment paper, then oil the paper.

In a medium bowl, whisk together the brown rice flour, potato starch, and tapioca flour. Measure 2½ cups of this mixture into a second medium bowl. (Save or discard the remaining mixture.) Add the baking powder, xanthan gum, and salt and mix well.

In another medium bowl, mix together the milk, oil, vanilla, and lemon zest.

In the bowl of an electric mixer, combine the sugar and eggs and beat at medium speed until just combined, about 1 minute. Reduce the speed to low and add the flour and milk mixtures alternately in 3 batches, beginning and ending with the flour mixture. Mix until just combined.

Divide the batter evenly between the pans and smooth the tops with a spatula. Bake until a wooden pick or skewer inserted in the center of each layer comes out clean, 35 to 40 minutes. Cool the layers in their pans on racks for at least 10 minutes. Run a thin knife around the edge of one cake layer, place a rack over the pan, and invert the cake onto the rack. Repeat with the second layer and second rack. Peel off the paper and cool the layers completely. Re-invert so the layers are right side up.

recipe continues

Cake

- 2 cups brown rice flour
- ⅔ cup potato starch
- ⅓ cup tapioca flour
- 1 tablespoon baking powder
- 1 teaspoon xanthan gum
- ½ teaspoon kosher salt
- 1 cup low-fat milk
- 1 cup grapeseed oil
- 1 teaspoon pure vanilla extract
- 1 tablespoon finely grated lemon zest
- 2 cups sugar
- 4 extra-large eggs

ingredients continue

Lemon Curd

6 extra-large egg yolks

1 extra-large egg

½ cup plus 4 tablespoons sugar

Finely grated zest of 1 lemon

½ cup Meyer or regular lemon juice (from 3 to 4 lemons)

Pinch of kosher salt

8 tablespoons (1 stick) unsalted butter, at room temperature, cut into 16 pieces

Frosting

1 cup (2 sticks) unsalted butter, softened

3½ cups confectioners' sugar

2 teaspoons finely grated lemon zest (from 1 to 2 lemons)

¼ cup Meyer or regular lemon juice

Meanwhile, make the lemon curd. In a medium bowl, whisk together the egg yolks, whole egg, and sugar. Add the lemon zest, lemon juice, and salt. Fill a medium saucepan with 2 inches of water and bring to a simmer over medium heat. Place the bowl over the saucepan and whisk briskly until the mixture has doubled in volume and holds the lines made by the whisk, 7 to 10 minutes.

Fill a large bowl with ice and add enough water to make an ice bath. Place the bowl with the curd mixture in the ice bath and let cool, stirring occasionally, until the mixture is just warm to the touch. Be careful not to get any water in the curd. Add the butter gradually, mixing until it's completely combined. Chill the curd until ready to use.

To make the frosting, beat the butter with an electric mixer at high speed until light and fluffy, about 2 minutes. Reduce the speed to low and add the confectioners' sugar, lemon zest, and lemon juice. Mix until creamy and smooth, 3 to 5 minutes.

To assemble the cake, using a long serrated knife, halve each of the cooled cake layers horizontally. Divide the curd into thirds. Place the first cake layer on a cake plate, cut side down, and spread with a portion of curd. Repeat with the other 2 layers. The last layer will get the lemon frosting. Frost the top and sides or just the top of the cake.

CUPCAKE VARIATIONS

The cake components are very versatile. The cake batter can be used to make 12 large or 18 regular-size cupcakes. Bake them at 350°F for 25 to 30 minutes. Scoop out their centers with a spoon, fill them with the curd, and frost. Or frost the cupcakes with a thin layer of raspberry jam. Or top with a layer of curd or frosting and add a fresh raspberry to each cupcake.

TART AND TRIFLE VARIATIONS

The curd also makes a great tart filling. Just pour it into a partially baked sweet pastry shell or Our Pie Crust (page 318). Bake at 350°F until the curd is firm and the crust is golden brown, 10 to 15 minutes. Or layer the curd with pound cake, berries, and whipped cream to make a delicious trifle.

Lime–Olive Oil Cake
with Rhubarb Compote

Ten years ago American cooks wouldn't have baked a cake made with olive oil or chamomile tea, two of the key ingredients in this recipe. Serve the cake for Chanukah when it's traditional to prepare foods made with oil—and throughout the rest of the year as well. We like to pair it with rhubarb compote, but you can also try it with a scoop of sorbet (page 328) and berries.

Preheat the oven to 350°F. Brush olive oil on the bottom and sides of an 8-inch tart pan with a removable bottom or an 8-inch cake pan. Line the pan with a round of parchment paper, and brush with more oil. Dust the sides and bottom of the pan lightly with cornmeal.

In a large bowl, whisk together the olive oil, eggs, sugar, and tea until smooth. Add the cornmeal, flour, baking powder, salt, and lime zest and juice. Stir gently to combine.

Pour the batter into the pan. Bake until the cake begins to pull away from the pan sides and a cake tester inserted into the center comes out clean, 30 to 35 minutes. Cool the cake in the pan on a rack for 20 minutes.

If using a tart pan, remove the metal ring. If using a cake pan, run a knife along the inside of the pan to loosen the cake. Set the cake on a platter, dust with confectioners' sugar, and garnish with additional lime zest. Serve with the compote.

½ cup extra-virgin olive oil, plus more for the pan

¾ cup fine yellow cornmeal, plus more for the pan

2 extra-large eggs

1 cup sugar

½ cup extra-strong chamomile tea (use 4 teabags in 1 cup hot water)

1 cup unbleached all-purpose flour

2 teaspoons baking powder

1 teaspoon kosher salt

Finely grated zest of 2 limes, plus additional for garnish

1 tablespoon lime juice

Confectioners' sugar, for dusting

Rhubarb Compote (recipe follows)

Rhubarb Compote

When available, choose rhubarb with the darkest red stalks, which become a pretty rosy pink color when cooked.

In a medium saucepan, combine the rhubarb with the water, sugar, and cinnamon, if using. Bring to a simmer over medium-low heat. Cook until the rhubarb is fork-tender and becoming sauce-like, 15 to 20 minutes. For a thinner consistency, add more water and stir to combine. Discard the cinnamon stick. Serve warm or at room temperature. Leftovers keep well in the refrigerator for up to a month.

SERVES 8

2½ pounds deep red, tender rhubarb, washed, trimmed, and cut into 1½-inch pieces

½ cup water

¾ cup sugar

1 (2-inch) piece cinnamon stick (optional)

Light and Creamy Cheesecake with Nut Brittle and Blueberries

New Yorkers have lots of opinions about cheesecake—not surprisingly, as it is a hometown favorite. This version made it into the book because it combines low-fat farmer cheese and goat cheese to lighten up the classic recipe, which relies heavily on rich cream cheese and sour cream or whipping cream. The result is a light and tangy cake that we surround with a crunchy, nutty, caramel brittle.

Cheesecake is the main dessert made for Shavuot (the Jewish holiday that celebrates the giving of the Torah to the Israelites at Mount Sinai), when it is customary to eat dairy foods. While there are many reasons for this tradition, one of the most compelling is the reference to the description of the Land of Israel as a "land flowing in milk and honey."

The cake and brittle can be prepared a few days ahead. The cake will keep in the refrigerator for up to a week (do not freeze it), and the brittle should be kept tightly covered at room temperature. Remember to bring the cake to room temperature, which takes at least 1 hour, before serving. For a version with a more traditional crust, see the variation at the end of the recipe.

SERVES 10

- 1 pound low-fat farmer cheese
- ¾ cup (5 ounces) cream cheese, at room temperature
- 1 log (11 ounces) Montrachet goat cheese, at room temperature
- Grated zest of 1 lemon
- ¼ cup lemon juice
- ¾ cup sugar
- 1 teaspoon pure vanilla extract
- Pinch of kosher salt
- 6 extra-large egg whites (about 1 cup)
- ¼ cup low-fat plain yogurt or mascarpone
- Nut Brittle (recipe follows)
- ½ pint fresh blueberries, blackberries, or raspberries

Position a rack in the bottom third of the oven, and preheat the oven to 350°F. Grease an 8-inch springform pan and wrap the exterior with foil up the sides to make it watertight.

In a food processor, purée the farmer cheese, scraping down the sides of the bowl 2 or 3 times. Add the cream cheese and goat cheese and purée until smooth. Add the lemon zest, lemon juice, sugar, vanilla, and salt and combine. Add the egg whites and continue to process the mixture until smooth. Pour the cheese mixture into the pan and tap it a few times on the counter to knock out any bubbles.

Set the springform pan in a roasting pan or other ovenproof pan with 2-inch sides. Add 1 inch of boiling water to the roasting pan. Carefully transfer the roasting pan to the lower third of the oven and bake until the cake is set and its edges are beginning to color, about 1 hour. Remove the cake from the water bath and allow to cool in the springform pan to room temperature. Chill for at least 2 hours before serving. Run a thin knife around the sides of the pan then open the hinge and release the sides. Remove the pan ring, leaving the cake on the pan bottom.

Spread the yogurt or mascarpone over the top and sides of the cake. Gently pat the brittle up the sides and gingerly press to help crumbs adhere to the cake. Serve with the berries.

recipe continues

4 ounces graham crackers or gluten-free oat biscuits

¼ cup packed brown sugar

4 tablespoon (½ stick) chilled unsalted butter

Combine the crackers, sugar, and butter in a food processor and process into fine crumbs. Press into the bottom of the springform pan. Pour batter on top and follow baking directions above.

Nut Brittle

Our brittle was inspired by the New York City restaurant Chanterelle's astounding peanut brittle. It's great sprinkled on almost anything—ice cream, sorbets, chocolate cake. You can't go wrong.

Preheat the oven to 350°F. Line a baking sheet with parchment paper. If using organic sugar, pulse-chop the sugar in a food processor fitted with a metal blade for 8 to 10 seconds to get the finer texture you will need for this recipe.

In a small heavy saucepan, combine the sugar, cream of tartar, and water and bring to a rapid boil over high heat. Reduce the heat to medium and continue to cook (do not stir) until the caramel turns a golden brown color and smells like burnt sugar, 5 to 7 minutes. Pour the mixture onto the baking sheet and cool.

Break the brittle into pieces. Transfer to a food processor and pulse to grind to the consistency of sugar. Transfer to a medium mixing bowl, add the hazelnuts and ginger, if using, and mix to combine.

Re-line the baking sheet with parchment paper and spread the caramel-nut mixture over it in an even layer. Bake until the caramel has melted again and begins to bubble, about 5 minutes.

Remove from the oven and sprinkle with the salt. Allow to cool. Break into oat-size crumbs.

MAKES ABOUT 1 CUP

½ cup sugar
Pinch cream of tartar

2 tablespoons plus 2 teaspoons water

¼ cup finely ground blanched hazelnuts

¼ teaspoon ground ginger (optional)

⅛ teaspoon finely ground sea salt

Intensely Chocolate Cupcakes with Chocolate Frosting

This recipe has been passed around our neighborhood and circle of friends for years and we're still making it—it's that good. Moist with a great crumble, the super-chocolatey cupcakes are also incredibly versatile (see the Layer Cake Fillings box on page 297). We also provide an all-chocolate frosting that adds a perfect intensity and richness to these lovely cakes.

MAKES 18 CUPCAKES, TWO 9-INCH ROUND CAKES,
OR ONE 10-INCH TUBE CAKE

Preheat the oven to 350°F. Place 18 liners in 2 muffin tins (you can half-fill any empty cups with water), line two 9-inch round baking pans with parchment paper, or grease one 10-inch tube pan.

Place the chocolate in the top of a double boiler, or in a glass bowl. Melt over simmering water, or in the microwave in 30-second bursts, stirring in between. (Stop when the chocolate is two-thirds melted; it will continue to melt off the heat.) Allow the chocolate to cool.

Sift together the flour, sugar, cocoa, baking powder, baking soda, and salt into a large bowl. Add the room-temperature water, oil, eggs, and vanilla and mix to combine. Add the melted chocolate and mix to combine. Stir in the boiling water. Spoon the batter into the prepared muffin tins, filling the liners two-thirds full, or scrape the batter into the round cake pans or the tube pan.

Bake, turning the pan(s) halfway through, until a tester or toothpick inserted into the center of the cupcakes or cake(s) comes out clean, 15 to 20 minutes for cupcakes, 20 to 25 minutes for round pans, and 35 to 40 minutes for the tube pan. Transfer the pan(s) to a rack and allow to cool completely before frosting.

Frost the cupcakes or cakes immediately after making the frosting.

3 ounces semisweet chocolate, chopped

1¾ cups unbleached all-purpose flour

1½ cups sugar

¾ cup Dutch-processed cocoa powder

1½ teaspoons baking powder

1½ teaspoons baking soda

1 teaspoon kosher salt

1 cup room-temperature water

½ cup grapeseed or canola oil

2 extra-large eggs, beaten

2 teaspoons pure vanilla extract

1 cup boiling water

Chocolate Frosting (recipe follows)

recipe continues

Chocolate Frosting

The technique for making this frosting is so crazy, it's amazing it works. But it really does. The idea for making it came from an article in the *New York Times* that suggested making a rich mousse by beating melted chocolate and water over ice until the mixture thickened but was still light and airy. We decided to adopt the method to make an incredibly easy frosting prepared with nothing but chocolate and water.

A few things to know: The recipe won't work with milk chocolate or with dark chocolate that has less than 54% cacao. Also, if you beat the chocolate too long it will revert to its hard state. If that happens, the good news is that you can set it over a double boiler, melt it, and start again.

Fill a large bowl with ice and about 2 inches of cold water to make an ice bath.

In a small heavy saucepan, combine the chocolates and 1 cup water and heat over medium heat to melt the chocolates. Whisk to incorporate the water and ensure that the mixture is smooth, about 5 minutes.

Pour the melted chocolate into a small bowl and immediately transfer it to the ice bath. Begin to whisk vigorously, making sure not to allow any ice water to get into the mixing bowl. Beat until thick and mousse-like, 5 to 7 minutes. (It will seem as if nothing is happening for the first few minutes but continue to whisk until you reach the desired consistency.) Immediately remove the frosting from the ice bath and frost the cupcakes or cake. If you leave the frosting to sit it will continue to harden.

MAKES ENOUGH TO FROST 18 CUPCAKES, TWO 9-INCH CAKES, OR ONE 10-INCH TUBE CAKE

12 ounces 54% cacao bittersweet chocolate, chopped

4 ounces 70% cacao bittersweet chocolate, chopped

1 cup water

LAYER CAKE FILLINGS

Here's a delicious filling for a two-layer cake: Chop ¾ cup dried cherries and mix them with ⅛ teaspoon cinnamon and ¼ cup melted and strained apricot preserves. You could also top the cake with a traditional buttercream mocha frosting, a sprinkling of confectioners' sugar, or vanilla sugar.

Chocolate Sour Cream Cake

Chocolate cake falls into two camps: moist and gooey or dense, yet crumbly. But why choose? We give you recipes for both. This cake, which falls into the second camp, is deliciously light; it doesn't scream rich or decadent. For your gooey fix, go to our Intensely Chocolate Cupcakes (page 295).

MAKES 1 BUNDT-SIZE CAKE OR TWO 9-INCH CAKES FOR LAYERING

4½ ounces unsweetened chocolate, chopped

10 tablespoons (1¼ sticks) unsalted butter, 2 of the tablespoons melted, for the pan

1 cup packed dark brown sugar

1 cup sugar

2 extra-large eggs

1½ teaspoons pure vanilla extract

Pinch of ground cinnamon (optional)

1 cup (8 ounces) sour cream

1 teaspoon baking soda

½ cup warm water

2 cups unbleached all-purpose flour

½ to ¾ cup bittersweet chocolate chips (optional)

½ pint heavy cream, whipped

1 pint raspberries

Place the chocolate in the top of a double boiler, or in a glass bowl. Melt over simmering water, or in the microwave in 30-second bursts, stirring in between. (Stop when the chocolate is two-thirds melted; it will continue to melt.) Allow the chocolate to cool.

Preheat the oven to 350°F. Brush a Bundt pan or two 9-inch round cake pans with the melted butter. If using the round pans, also line with parchment paper. (NOTE: *We like to chill the greased Bundt pan before adding the batter. We find this helps ensure that the cake will not stick.*)

In the bowl of a standing mixer, cream the sugars and 8 tablespoons butter on medium speed until well combined and fluffy, 3 to 4 minutes. Beat in the eggs one at a time. Reduce the speed to low, add the melted chocolate, vanilla, and cinnamon, if using, and mix thoroughly. Add the sour cream and continue to mix until it's just incorporated.

In a small bowl, dissolve the baking soda in the water to eliminate any bitterness. Add the flour and baking soda mixture to the batter in two parts. Mix until just combined. Fold in the chocolate chips, if using.

Pour the batter into the pan(s). Bake until the cake is springy to the touch and a tester inserted into the cake comes out clean, 45 to 50 minutes for the Bundt pan, 25 to 30 minutes for round pans. Allow the cake(s) to cool in the pan(s) on a rack for 15 minutes. Turn out from the pan(s) and set onto a serving dish (or fill and frost the layers with additional whipped cream). Serve with the raspberries and whipped cream.

Chocolate Brownie Cookies with Sea Salt

For one of us growing up in a Belgian Jewish household, dessert always meant chocolate. This cookie is definitely for chocolate lovers. The sea salt adds a depth of flavor that makes the cookies a bit more grown-up and the recipe can work with margarine as well as butter. For a cakier cookie, double the amount of flour. Please note that the batter must rest in the refrigerator for at least 2 hours before baking. Or it can be made further ahead and stored in the refrigerator for up to 1 day.

MAKES ABOUT SIXTEEN 2½–INCH COOKIES

Combine the chocolate and butter in the top of a double boiler or glass bowl. Melt over simmering water, stirring, for 5 to 7 minutes. Stir once to make sure the butter and chocolate are melted. Remove from the heat.

In the bowl of a standing mixer or with a handheld mixer and large bowl, beat the eggs and sugar at medium-high speed until pale and creamy, about 4 minutes. Add the vanilla and kosher salt and beat 1 minute more.

With a rubber spatula, fold in the chocolate mixture. Fold in the flour and baking powder. Fold in the chocolate chips (or nuts) and apricots, if using Refrigerate for at least 2 hours.

Preheat the oven to 350°F. Line two baking sheets with parchment paper.

Scoop out the cookie batter by the tablespoon, depending on how large a cookie you want. Roll the batter in your palms to form a loosely rounded shape. (The batter can be very sticky—this is normal.) Transfer the balls to the baking sheets, press down to flatten slightly, and sprinkle with the sea salt. Bake, rotating the pan halfway through, until the cookies are glossy at their centers and the edges are firm, 12 to 15 minutes. Allow the cookies to cool on the pan for about 5 minutes and then transfer to a rack to cool completely. Store in an airtight container.

- 16 ounces 70% cacao bittersweet chocolate, chopped
- 4 tablespoons (½ stick) unsalted butter or margarine, cut in 4 slices
- 4 extra-large eggs, at room temperature
- 1½ cups sugar
- 1 teaspoon pure vanilla extract
- ¼ teaspoon kosher salt
- ½ cup unbleached all-purpose flour
- ½ teaspoon baking powder
- 8 ounces semisweet chocolate chips, or chopped pecans or walnuts
- 2 tablespoons diced dried apricot (optional)
- Sea salt flakes, for sprinkling

Oatmeal–Chocolate Chip Cookies

If you love chocolate chip cookies as much as we do, you're always on the prowl for another great variation. In line with our attempts to use whole grains whenever we can, we were thrilled to discover the technique of adding ground rolled oats and white whole-wheat flour to a cookie dough. Crisp, but full-bodied, these cookies are as wholesome as a chocolate chip cookie can be. Please note, we leave the dough in the refrigerator overnight or for a minimum of 2 hours. This improves the flavor and texture considerably.

NOTE: *This recipe yields a large amount of dough. We like to reserve half of it and roll it into logs, freeze, and have them ready to bake at any time. Soften frozen logs long enough to slice before baking.*

MAKES THIRTY-SIX 3-INCH COOKIES

¾ cup pecans

¾ cup walnuts

¾ cup rolled oats

Pinch of cinnamon (optional)

1½ cups white whole-wheat flour

1 teaspoon baking soda

½ teaspoon kosher salt

12 tablespoons (1½ sticks) unsalted butter, at room temperature

1¼ cups packed dark brown sugar

2 extra-large eggs

¾ teaspoon pure vanilla extract

3 cups semisweet or bittersweet chocolate chips or any combination of the two

In a medium skillet, toast the pecans and walnuts over medium heat, shaking the pan occasionally, until lightly browned, 3 to 4 minutes. Transfer to a board. When cool, chop and set aside.

Using a food processor or powerful blender, process the oats until ground into a fine powder. Add the cinnamon, if using, and pulse 3 more times. In a large bowl, combine the oats, flour, baking soda, and salt.

In a standing mixer, or hand mixer and large bowl, beat the butter at medium speed until creamy. Add the brown sugar and continue beating until light and fluffy, about 4 minutes, occasionally scraping the sides of the bowl. Continue beating and add the eggs, one at a time. When the eggs are incorporated, add the vanilla. Reduce the speed to low. In 2 additions, stir in the flour mixture until just combined. Fold in the toasted nuts and chocolate chips with a wooden spoon as the batter is very thick.

Refrigerate the dough for at least 2 hours or overnight.

Preheat the oven to 350°F. Line a large baking sheet with parchment paper.

Drop 2-tablespoon portions of batter onto the baking sheet, leaving 1 inch between the cookies. Bake until lightly browned, 12 to 15 minutes. Allow to cool and store in an airtight container.

Chocolate Chip–Hazelnut Meringues

We think the chocolate and hazelnut combination creates a perfectly balanced meringue cookie, but feel free to play around with the ratio of chips to nuts, depending on your audience. These light and airy meringues are a great vehicle for many other flavor combinations, so you can experiment with different ingredients to suit your taste. Some options include: pumpkin pie spices with coarsely chopped pumpkin seeds; roughly chopped pistachios, dried cherries, and a pinch of ground cinnamon; chopped walnuts and dry unsweetened coconut with lime zest. The meringues are best baked on low humidity days or they will be gummy.

MAKES ABOUT 30 COOKIES

Preheat the oven to 300°F. Line two baking sheets with parchment paper. If using organic sugar, pulse-chop the sugar in a food processor fitted with a metal blade for 8 to 10 seconds to get the finer texture you need for this recipe.

In a medium skillet, toast the hazelnuts over medium heat, stirring often, until golden, about 10 minutes. Transfer to a cutting board and chop the nuts roughly.

Using a standing mixer and a very clean bowl, beat the egg whites to soft peaks. Add the vanilla, cream of tartar, and salt. Gradually add the sugar, beating continuously, until the whites form stiff, glossy peaks. (**NOTE**: *For the most stable foam, start beating the egg whites slowly and gradually increase the speed. When you need to check the consistency, turn the mixer off quickly and turn it back to speed quickly to minimize any deflating.*) Fold in the nuts and chocolate chips.

Scoop up a heaping teaspoon of the mixture and, with a second spoon, push gently onto the baking sheet. With the back of the spoon, press down lightly on the top of the meringue; as you lift the spoon away a soft peak will form. Repeat with the remaining meringue mixture. Bake until the meringues are dry on the edges but still soft in the center, about 25 minutes. (If you prefer a drier, harder meringue, continue baking 5 to 10 minutes more.) The meringues shouldn't brown; watch them carefully. Allow to cool and store in an airtight container.

¾ cup sugar

⅔ cup blanched hazelnuts

2 extra-large egg whites, at room temperature

¼ teaspoon pure vanilla extract

⅛ teaspoon cream of tartar

⅛ teaspoon kosher salt

⅔ cup bittersweet or semisweet chocolate chips

Cappuccino Thins

The dough for these cookies is easy to make using a food processor. It will keep in the fridge for up to 4 days or in the freezer for a couple of months. The recipe has a large yield, so you can use as much dough as you want and freeze the rest for another day. Be sure to remove the cookies promptly from the oven as they can overbake very easily.

Coffee and chocolate flavors pair famously with ice cream. Use these cookies for a decidedly sophisticated version of an ice cream sandwich, loved by everyone.

MAKES 24 LARGE COOKIES (FOR ICE CREAM SANDWICHES) OR 6 DOZEN 1½-INCH COOKIES

3 ounces semisweet baking chocolate, broken into pieces

½ cup plus 2 tablespoons sugar

½ cup packed light brown sugar

1 extra-large egg

1 tablespoon finely ground espresso

1 tablespoon Dutch-process cocoa powder

½ teaspoon ground cinnamon

½ teaspoon kosher salt

2 cups unbleached all-purpose flour

1 teaspoon baking powder

1 cup (2 sticks) cold unsalted butter, cut into 16 tablespoon-size pieces

2 pints ice cream of your choice, softened

In a food processor, pulse-chop the chocolate until it has the texture of coarse meal. Transfer to a small bowl and set aside.

In the processor, combine the sugars, egg, espresso, cocoa, cinnamon, and salt and process to combine well, 1 minute. Add the flour and baking powder and pulse to combine. Add the chocolate and butter and pulse until just combined. Don't overprocess; the dough should appear marbled.

Divide the dough into 2 parts for sandwich cookies or 4 parts for smaller cookies. Using your hands, roll each part into a log, 2½ inches in diameter for large cookies, 1½ inches in diameter for small. Wrap in parchment and chill the dough for 2 hours.

Preheat the oven to 350°F. Line 2 baking sheets with parchment paper.

Slice the logs ¼ inch thick for large cookies, slightly less than ¼ inch thick for small. (Each large log yields about 12 to 14 cookies, each 1½-inch-diameter log about 18 cookies.) Working in batches, place the cookies ½ inch apart on the sheets. Bake until the edges begin to brown and center is still soft, 8 to 10 minutes for large cookies, 6 to 8 minutes for small. Transfer to racks to cool.

To make ice cream sandwiches, scoop softened ice cream of your choice and place atop one large cookie. Place the second cookie on top and press down gently. Wrap individual sandwiches in parchment or wax paper. Store in the freezer until ready to serve.

VARIATION

Wary of too much caffeine? You can omit the ground espresso and replace it with an additional tablespoon of cocoa, making it a chocolate thin instead. Looking to make a dairy-free alternative? Replace the butter with margarine, and use soy ice cream if you're making sandwiches.

Ultimate Sugar Cookies

These are the best sugar cookies ever. The dough is very easy to make and makes a large quantity, so we always keep a couple of logs in the freezer to have freshly baked cookies on hand for any occasion. It is also a perfect dough to roll out and cut with cookie cutters. Serve them plain or sprinkle with cinnamon sugar or confectioners' sugar, or decorate with icing. The dough also makes great Linzer cookies or sandwich cookies made with dulce de leche or Nutella (see variations).

MAKES FORTY 3-INCH CUT-OUT COOKIES OR 8 DOZEN
1½-INCH COOKIES

In a standing mixer, cream the butter and sugar on high speed until light in color and fluffy, about 4 minutes. Add the vanilla and egg and beat to combine.

Reduce the speed to low. Place the flour and baking powder in a sifter and sift into the bowl. Mix until totally combined.

Preheat the oven to 400°F. Line 2 cookie sheets with parchment paper.

To make cookie-cutter cookies: Divide the dough in half and roll each half between 2 sheets of parchment paper to a ¼-inch thickness. Chill for at least 20 minutes. Cut out the desired shapes (baking time is based on a 3-inch cookie; baking time will decrease for a smaller cookie) and gently lift the cookies with a spatula onto the sheets, spacing the cookies at least 1 inch apart. (If the dough gets sticky or too soft to work with, return it to the refrigerator to chill again.)

For sliced and sandwich cookies: Turn the dough onto a board and divide into 4 parts. Form into logs with a diameter of about 1½ inches. Wrap the logs in parchment paper and chill for at least 20 minutes or longer, or freeze them for future use. (If you froze the logs, allow them to soften slightly before slicing.) Slice into ¼-inch-thick cookies, then gently lift the cookies with a spatula onto the baking sheets.

Bake until the cookie edges are golden and the centers are firm, 8 to 12 minutes. Using a spatula, loosen the cookies from the pan when partially cooled and continue cooling on a rack. Store in an airtight container.

1 cup (2 sticks) unsalted butter, at room temperature

1 cup sugar

1 teaspoon pure vanilla extract

1 extra-large egg

3 cups unbleached all-purpose flour

2 teaspoons baking powder

recipe continues

VARIATIONS

For Linzer cookies: Roll each log in ¼ cup finely chopped toasted almonds. Cut ⅛-inch slices from the logs. If desired, cut a small circle out of the center of half the cookies. Bake until the edges are golden and centers are firm, 8 to 10 minutes. Loosen the cookies from the pan when partially cooled and continue cooling on a rack. When almost completely cooled, invert 1 cookie, spread its underside (now facing you) with raspberry jam and top with another cookie to create a sandwich. Sprinkle with confectioners' sugar.

For dulce de leche or Nutella sandwich cookies: Cut ⅛-inch slices from the logs. Bake until the edges are golden and centers are firm, 8 to 10 minutes. Loosen the cookies from the pan when partially cooled and continue cooling on a rack. When completely cooled, invert 1 cookie, spread its underside (now facing you) with dulce de leche (recipe follows) or Nutella and top with a second cookie to create a sandwich.

Dulce de Leche

This caramel sauce makes a great filling for a sandwich cookie, but is also delicious as a topping for waffles or drizzled over ice cream or apple pie. There are several ways to make dulce de leche, but this is one of the easiest and least messy. If you let the dulce de leche cool thoroughly it gets nice and thick and becomes perfect for spreading. Store it in a glass jar or plastic container in the fridge for up to two weeks. Before using, bring to room temperature or warm in a water bath.

1 can (14 ounces) sweetened condensed milk

Kosher salt

Preheat the oven to 425°F. Pour the milk into a ceramic or glass baking dish that holds at least 1 quart. (It's best if the dish is at least 2 to 3 inches deep.) Sprinkle with the salt and cover tightly with aluminum foil.

Place the baking dish in a larger shallow baking dish. Pour water into the larger dish to reach roughly three-fourths of the milk depth. (**HINT:** Place the pan on the oven rack before you fill it with water.) Bake until the milk has a beautiful golden color, 60 to 90 minutes. Check every 30 minutes to make sure that the water has not evaporated and replenish if necessary. Remove from the oven and whisk to remove any lumps. Cool before using.

MAKES 1½ CUPS

Vanilla Crescents with Citrus and Verbena Salad

Vienna is famous for its coffeehouses and pastries. Among its most famous cookies are *vanillekipferl*, vanilla crescents. Nutty, crumbly, light, and addictive, they are cookie heaven. Our recipe is an updated version of the classic brought to us via a Viennese mother-in-law. We pair the cookies with a verbena-flavored citrus salad, a refreshing accompaniment. You can make the cookie dough a day ahead and keep it in the fridge. In fact, doing this allows the dough to rest and develop a more distinct flavor, and it will be easier to shape into crescents.

NOTE: *The vanilla sugar needs to be made at least 2 days in advance, but this recipe makes more than you need for the cookies and it can be stored as long as regular sugar—and has just as many uses. Sprinkle over pancakes or muffins, put a pinch in whipped cream, or stir into hot chocolate. Keep it as a staple among your baking products. If you don't have superfine sugar on hand, you can process sugar in a food processor fitted with a metal blade to achieve a finer texture.*

MAKES 6 DOZEN COOKIES

At least 2 days ahead, make the vanilla sugar: Put the sugar in an airtight container, bury the vanilla bean in it, close, and store at room temperature. Shake the container every few days to distribute the vanilla flavor.

To make the cookies, in a large bowl, combine the flours and salt and mix. Add the ground nuts and mix thoroughly.

In the bowl of a food processor fitted with a metal blade, combine the butter and confectioners' sugar and pulse until light and fluffy. Add the flour and nuts and pulse until the ingredients are fully combined. Then pulse until the dough just starts to come together, 5 or 6 times. Do not overwork the dough. Wrap the dough in plastic wrap or parchment paper and refrigerate for at least 1 hour or overnight.

Preheat the oven to 350°F. Line two baking sheets with parchment paper. Remove the dough from the refrigerator and allow to soften, about 20 minutes.

Divide the dough into three equal pieces. With your hands, roll the dough into logs 1½ to 2 inches in diameter. Cut the logs into ¼-inch slices, then roll the dough between your palms back and forth two times to form a small sausage shape that is slightly thicker in the middle. Bend into crescents and place on the lined baking sheet. Bake, in batches, until the bottoms of the crescents are just golden, 10 to 12 minutes. Place the cookies on wire racks to cool slightly, 5 to 10 minutes.

Vanilla Sugar

2 cups superfine sugar

1 whole vanilla bean, sliced open lengthwise

Cookies

1 cup white whole-wheat flour

2½ cups unbleached all-purpose flour

½ teaspoon kosher salt

2½ cups ground hazelnuts

2¼ cup ground almonds

12 tablespoons (1½ sticks) unsalted butter, softened

½ cup plus 1 teaspoon confectioners' sugar

Citrus Verbena Salad (recipe follows)

recipe continues

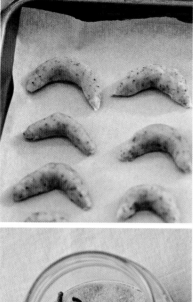

Spread half the vanilla sugar on a tray. Very carefully, remove the still-warm crescents from the racks and roll in the vanilla sugar. (Save excess sugar for next time.) Serve with the citrus salad, and store leftovers in airtight containers.

VARIATION

This dough can make a delicious shortbread-style finger cookie (see photo page 283). Prepare the dough as directed on page 311. Line a 15 x 10-inch jelly roll pan with parchment paper. Place the dough into the pan and spread it evenly, using your fingers to get the dough into the corners. Place another piece of parchment paper over the dough and use a small rolling pin or a can to smooth down the top and fill in the edges. Refrigerate until firm, at least 2 hours or overnight. Preheat the oven to 325°F. Before you bake the cookies, make shallow cuts in the dough with a knife to outline the cookies, measuring roughly 1 inch by 3 inches. Bake 25 minutes, until a tester comes out clean. Remove from the oven and while the cookies are still warm and while still in the pan, re-score the shallow cuts and sprinkle with the vanilla sugar. Allow to cool completely. Cut along the lines again and remove from the pan.

GROUND NUTS

Many specialty stores sell pre-ground nuts. This can be a big time-saver, but be aware that ground nuts can go rancid much more quickly than whole nuts. Store nuts in the refrigerator or freezer to prolong shelf life. If you cannot find pre-ground nuts, you can grind them in a food processor fitted with a metal blade. When grinding, the nuts can quickly turn into a paste. We suggest tossing the nuts with up to 1 tablespoon flour from your recipe before you start grinding them, to avoid ending up with nut butter.

Citrus Verbena Salad

This salad may be made ahead and stored in the refrigerator for up to 3 days. Don't add the herbs, coriander, or nuts until serving.

Cut the fruits into *supremes* (see page 115). Transfer the *supremes* to a large bowl. Squeeze the juice from the fruit membranes into a small saucepan. Stir in the honey. Simmer over medium heat until reduced by one-third. Allow to cool slightly. Add coriander if desired. Pour over the *supremes*.

Right before serving, stack, roll, and cut the verbena or mint into thin ribbons. Toss with the citrus, sprinkle with pistachios (if using), and serve.

SERVES 4 TO 5

2 pink grapefruits

1 white grapefruit or pomelo

2 navel oranges

2 blood oranges

2 teaspoons honey

Pinch of ground coriander (optional)

10 fresh lemon verbena leaves or mint leaves

¼ cup roasted shelled pistachios, chopped (optional)

Two Great Dunking Cookies

Known as biscotti to some and *mandelbread* to others, we love these cookies no matter what they are called! Most baking authorities distinguish between the two on the basis of fat content. Mandelbread usually contains a bit more fat, making it slightly softer. But technically they're both biscotti because they're both baked twice (*biscotti* means "twice baked"). Dunked in cappuccino or in a *glezel tei* (Yiddish for a glass of tea) we know you'll enjoy them.

Pistachio Anise Biscotti

This recipe can easily be doubled. If anise is not to your taste, use 2 teaspoons lemon zest instead of the anise seed. These keep for a week in an airtight tin, or frozen for a month.

MAKES 24 BISCOTTI

1   cup shelled pistachios
8   tablespoons (1 stick) unsalted butter or margarine, at room temperature
½   cup plus 2 tablespoons sugar
2   extra-large eggs
2   tablespoons crushed anise seed
4   teaspoons pure vanilla extract
3   cups unbleached all-purpose flour
¼   cup cornmeal
1½ teaspoons baking powder
    Pinch of kosher salt

Preheat the oven to 350°F. Line a baking sheet with parchment paper.

In a small skillet, toast the pistachios over low heat, stirring, until lightly toasted, about 3 minutes. When cool, chop them.

In a food processor or standing mixer, cream the butter and sugar until light and fluffy. Add the eggs, anise seed, and vanilla and pulse or beat to combine.

In a medium bowl, combine the flour, cornmeal, baking powder, and salt and mix well. Add to the butter mixture and pulse or mix to just combine.

Transfer the dough onto the baking sheet and use your hands to work the pistachios into the dough. Mold the dough into 2 equal logs with your hands (about 4 x 15 inches) and arrange 3 inches apart on the baking sheet. Bake until golden brown and firm but still soft in the middle, about 30 minutes.

Remove the logs from the oven and cool on the sheet on a rack until you can handle them. Reduce the oven temperature to 325°F.

Using a serrated knife, cut each log into ¼-inch slices on the diagonal. Place the slices, cut side down, on the sheet. Return to the oven and bake until crisp and golden, 10 to 15 minutes. Cool on a rack and store in an airtight container.

Coconut Mandelbread

Current thought holds that coconut oil is good for you. Since we grew up thinking it would contribute to heart disease, we're thrilled to know that it can raise your HDL ("good") cholesterol levels. We're also happy to use it instead of butter or margarine for our mandelbread.

We're providing a basic recipe, but please feel free to be creative by including nuts, dried fruits, seeds, or chocolate. You can freeze the mandelbread in an airtight container or freeze the loaf before baking it. These cookies are fabulous paired with mango and pineapple fruit salad.

recipe continues

½ cup pecans or mini chocolate chips

2½ cups unbleached all-purpose flour

1½ teaspoons baking powder

Pinch of kosher salt

4 ounces solid coconut oil, unsalted butter, or margarine, at room temperature

¾ cup sugar

2 extra-large eggs

2 teaspoons pure vanilla extract

⅓ cup shredded unsweetened coconut

Mango and Pineapple Fruit Salad (recipe follows)

Preheat the oven to 350°F. Line a baking sheet with parchment paper.

In a small skillet, toast the pecans over low heat, stirring occasionally, until golden, about 3 minutes. Transfer to a cutting board and chop fine when cool. If using chocolate chips, set them aside.

Sift the flour, baking powder, and salt into a medium bowl.

In a food processor or standing mixer, combine the solid coconut oil and sugar and cream until light and fluffy, about 2 minutes. Add the eggs and beat. Add the vanilla and mix. Add the flour mixture gradually and mix to combine. Remove the dough and place it on the parchment paper on the baking sheet. Add the nuts (or chocolate chips) and coconut and work into the dough by hand.

Mold the dough into 2 equal logs with your hands (about 3 x 15 inches) and place them 3 inches apart on the baking sheet. Bake until the logs are slightly brown, about 30 minutes. Remove the logs from the oven and allow to cool slightly until you can handle them. Reduce the oven temperature to 325°F.

Using a serrated knife cut the logs into ½-inch slices on the diagonal. Place the slices, cut sides down, on the baking sheet. Bake, turning once, until crisp and golden, 10 to 15 minutes. Cool on a rack.

Serve with Mango and Pineapple Fruit Salad.

Mango and Pineapple Fruit Salad

We believe the secret to a great fruit salad is taking the time to consistently dice all the fruit into small (¼-inch) pieces. The pomegranate seeds add a great textural crunch. You'll make this again and again, changing the fruits as the seasons and availability allow. Cut each of the fruits up and, if not serving immediately, store in separate containers until ready to serve.

In a serving bowl, combine the mangoes and pineapple. In a large bowl, combine the pears and/or apples with the orange juice. Add to the mango and pineapple with the pomegranate seeds or blueberries. Gently mix to combine. Garnish with mint and serve.

SERVES 6 TO 8

2 mangoes, pitted, peeled, and cut into small dice

1 pineapple, peeled, cored, and cut into small dice

3 firm Anjou pears or apples (or a combination), peeled, cored, and cut into small pieces

Juice of 1 orange

1 cup pomegranate seeds (see page 129) or 1 pint small blueberries

Mint leaves, for garnish

Sour Cherry Pie

Growing up, sour cherry pie was a special treat in some of our homes. In the '50s the only sour cherries available came in a jar. It was nearly impossible to find fresh sour cherries, until the proliferation of farmers' markets that we are now blessed with in New York City and around the country. Truth be told, the pie is still great made with jarred sour cherries, but, when time allows, making it with fresh sour cherries can't be beat. These cherries are only available for a short time in June and July. If you grab them, invest a few dollars in a cherry-pitter. It's worth the time it will save you. Serve the pie with ice cream or whipped cream.

Because the season for sour cherries is so short, we have also provided you a wonderful blueberry pie variation.

MAKES ONE 9-INCH DOUBLE-CRUST PIE

Preheat the oven to 400° F.

Prepare Our Pie Crust. Partially blind bake the bottom crust (see Blind Baking box, page 318) and reserve top crust for lattice.

Place the cherries in a large bowl, add the tapioca flour and sugar, and toss carefully until well combined. Add the lemon zest and juice. Lower the oven temperature to 375°F.

Fill the partially baked crust with the cherry mixture.

In a small bowl, combine the cream and egg yolk and mix well.

Cut the remaining rolled out dough round into ¾-inch-wide strips. Place the longest strip at the center of the pie, draping it over the edges slightly. Place the next largest strip perpendicular to the first one, crossing the pie at the center. Place the remaining strips in decreasing size order, alternating direction, over and under one another to weave a lattice pattern. Crimp the ends of the strips to the bottom crust. Brush the lattice with the cream mixture.

Bake the pie on a baking sheet until the top crust is golden and the fruit is bubbling, 50 to 60 minutes. If the crust edges seem to be getting too brown, loosely tent them with foil. Transfer the pie carefully to a rack and cool for at least 2 hours to ensure the filling sets.

VARIATION

You can substitute blueberries for the cherries and you'll get a fabulous result. If you do, use the same ingredient amounts for the filling, but increase the tapioca to 3 to 4 tablespoons (the tapioca amount is dependent on how firm you like your filling, as blueberries give off a lot of liquid).

Our Pie Crust (recipe follows)

6 cups sour cherries (about 2 pounds), fresh or frozen, pitted

2 to 3 tablespoons tapioca flour, depending on how firm you like your filling

1 cup superfine sugar, or to taste

Grated zest of 1 lemon (about 1½ teaspoons)

1 tablespoon lemon juice

1 tablespoon heavy cream or whole milk

1 extra-large egg yolk

recipe continues

Our Pie Crust

A generation ago, most home bakers would have used vegetable shortening and bleached all-purpose flour to make this crust. In trying to avoid trans fats we replaced the shortening with butter. We think we've improved the flavor as well. We've also switched to pastry flour, which ensures a flaky crust, and added a bit of whole-wheat flour.

In the bowl of a food processor fitted with a metal blade, combine the flours, sugar, and salt and pulse until combined. Add the butter and pulse until the mixture resembles a coarse meal. Add the water 1 tablespoon at a time, pulsing until the dough forms a ball. Be careful not to overwork the dough at this point.

Divide the dough into 2 balls, one just slightly larger than the other. Handling the dough as little as possible, as too much reduces flakiness, form the dough into 2 flat discs. Wrap each in plastic wrap and refrigerate for at least 1 hour.

Place the larger disc between 2 pieces of parchment paper, or lightly flour a work surface and a rolling pin. Working from the center outward, roll out to form a 12-inch circle. (To ensure that the dough isn't sticking to your work surface, carefully lift it a few times as you roll.) If you have an extra-large dough spatula, use it to loosen the dough and transfer to a 9-inch pie plate, or move it by hand. Gently fit into the dish. Trim the edges with a sharp knife, as needed. Refrigerate for 15 to 30 minutes to chill and rest the dough.

Fully blind bake the bottom crust for a no-bake filling (see box); partially blind bake for a fruit filling.

To prepare the top crust for a lattice pie see the description on page 317.

MAKES 1 DOUBLE CRUST FOR A 9-INCH PIE

2 cups pastry flour

½ cup whole-wheat pastry flour

1 tablespoon sugar

1 teaspoon kosher salt

1 cup (2 sticks) chilled unsalted butter, cut into ¼-inch cubes

6 to 8 tablespoons cold water, as needed

BLIND BAKING

Some pie or tart recipes call for you to bake the crust "blind," which means to partially or fully bake the crust before filling it. This is meant to ensure that your pie crust won't be soggy.

To partially blind bake a pie shell, fit the rolled-out dough round into a pie plate and chill. Then cover the dough with foil or parchment paper, weigh it down with dried beans or ceramic pie weights, and bake for about 20 minutes at 400°F. Carefully remove the paper and weights and prick the crust with a fork. Return the crust to the oven for an additional 5 to 10 minutes, until the bottom of the crust is lightly golden. Remove and cool completely, before proceeding with the filling.

If using a no-bake filling such as a lemon curd, after removing the pie weights return to the oven and bake an additional 15 to 20 minutes until golden brown all over. If you are making a single-crust pie, freeze the second disk of dough for use at another time. The dough can be kept in the freezer for up to 4 months.

Pumpkin Rugelach

In 2013, in a very rare lunar and solar calendar alignment, Chanukah coincided with Thanksgiving and was unofficially dubbed "Thanksgivukkah." Home cooks and chefs looked for ways to blend the flavors and foods of both traditions. These pumpkin rugelach were created with that idea in mind. We fell in love with them and continue to make them, even knowing that the two holidays will never coincide again in our lifetimes. The sweet and spicy pumpkin is the perfect tasty filling for the rich and delicate dough. The dough can be schmeared with other fillings such as cinnamon sugar and raisins, apricot jam and chopped almonds, walnuts, or mini chocolate chips.

Watch how quickly these disappear from your kitchen, but if you do have any left over, they freeze well.

MAKES ABOUT SIXTY-FOUR 2-INCH RUGELACH

To make the dough, place the flour, butter, cream cheese, and sour cream in a food processor fitted with a metal blade or the bowl of a standing mixer. Pulse or blend on medium speed to combine. Sprinkle the sugar over the dough and pulse or blend until the ingredients are well distributed.

Transfer the dough to a board. It will be very sticky. Divide the dough into 4 equal balls and flatten with your hands. Wrap with plastic wrap and refrigerate for at least 2 hours. The longer you wait, the easier the dough will be to handle.

To make the filling, mix the pumpkin purée and cider in a saucepan over medium-low heat. Add the sugar, cinnamon, nutmeg, allspice, lemon zest, if using, and salt, and stir until combined. The mixture will be a dark caramel color. Raise the heat to medium-high and bring the mixture to a boil. Lower the temperature and simmer for 30 minutes, stirring occasionally to keep the mix from burning on the edges. The filling should be thick yet spreadable.

If using currants, soak them in the hot water for 10 to 15 minutes. Drain.

Preheat the oven to 375°F. Line a baking sheet with lightly floured parchment paper.

Remove the dough from the refrigerator and let it soften for 5 to 10 minutes, until it is soft enough to roll. Roll out one ball of the dough to a 9-inch circle between two pieces of parchment paper. Chill in the refrigerator for 15 minutes. Remove the top piece of parchment paper. Spread ¼ cup of the filling evenly over the dough, leaving a ¼-inch border without filling. If using currants, sprinkle them around the edge of the filling. Slice the circle into 16 wedges. Pull the first wedge out of the circle and roll from the widest part to the narrowest. Place on the prepared baking tray. Repeat with the rest of the wedges, placing the rugelach about 1 inch apart. Continue with the remaining dough portions and filling.

Bake until the rugelach are golden brown, 20 to 25 minutes. Cool and dust with confectioners' sugar before serving.

Dough

2 cups unbleached all-purpose flour

1 cup (2 sticks) unsalted butter

½ pound plus 2 tablespoons cream cheese

1 tablespoon sour cream

2 tablespoons sugar

Filling

15 ounces canned or fresh pumpkin purée

½ cup apple cider or apple juice

1 cup sugar

1 teaspoon ground cinnamon

½ teaspoon freshly grated nutmeg

½ teaspoon allspice

½ teaspoon grated lemon zest (optional)

Pinch of kosher salt

½ cup dried currants (optional)

1 cup hot water (optional)

Confectioners' sugar, for dusting

Rustic Apple-Cranberry Pie

This mountain of a pie, as delicious as it is beautiful, is a dramatic version of good-old American apple pie—and why not have a new variation in your repertoire? While apples are available all year long, make sure you bake this pie at least once during the fall or at Rosh Hashanah, when apples fill the markets and the varieties seem endless. The partial whole-wheat crust can be prepared ahead of time and refrigerated a few days or frozen for 2 weeks. Defrost it overnight in the refrigerator. Serve the pie with ice cream or fresh whipped cream. If whipping your own cream, add a splash of vanilla and a touch of honey before it is completely whipped.

SERVES 8 TO 10

Crust

- 1½ cups whole-wheat pastry flour
- 1½ cups unbleached all-purpose flour
- 1 tablespoon sugar
- 1 teaspoon kosher salt
- 1 cup (2 sticks) frozen unsalted butter, cut into many small pieces
- ¾ to 1 cup ice water, as needed

Apple Filling

- 3½ pounds assorted apples (preferably local), peeled, cored, and sliced in ¼-inch pieces
- ¼ cup plus 1 teaspoon unbleached all-purpose flour
- 1½ teaspoons ground cinnamon
- 2 cups fresh or frozen cranberries
- ¾ cup sugar, plus 2 teaspoons to sprinkle on top
- Pinch of kosher salt

To make the crust, combine the flours, sugar, and salt in a food processor and pulse. Add the butter and, with a spoon, coat each piece with flour. Pulse to create coarse meal. Pulsing, slowly drizzle in ¾ cup of the ice water, until the dough is moistened and begins to form a single mass. Drizzle more ice water if needed. Stop pulsing just before the dough forms a ball. Transfer this crumbly mixture onto a large piece of parchment paper and, using your hands, gently squeeze the dough to form a ball. Divide the dough in half and roll one half into a 13-inch round between parchment paper. Drape over a 9-inch pie dish, then gently fit it into the dish. Roll out the remaining dough to a 13-inch round. Chill both parts of the dough for 30 minutes.

Preheat the oven to 400°F. Line a baking sheet with foil.

To make the filling, in a large bowl, combine the apples, ¼ cup flour, and 1 teaspoon cinnamon and toss. In a medium bowl, combine the cranberries with ¼ cup of the sugar and the 1 teaspoon flour. Add ½ cup of the sugar and the salt to the apple mixture and toss. Add the sugared cranberries and mix.

Pile the apple-cranberry mixture into the middle of the pie dish. Go slowly and pile up gently; it will seem as if there's too much of the apple mixture, but the amount is correct.

Cover with the remaining dough. Trim excess dough and pinch the edges together. Using a serrated knife, cut ten to twelve 1-inch slits into the top crust to let the steam out as the pie is baking. Generously sprinkle with the 2 teaspoons sugar and remaining ½ teaspoon cinnamon. Place the pie on the baking sheet and bake until the crust is golden and the filling is bubbling, 65 to 75 minutes. Transfer to a rack to cool. Serve warm or at room temperature.

APPLE VARIETIES

With so many apple varieties available, how do you choose? For the best filling, a trio combining tart, sweet, and softer apples is a winning combination. Here are some of our favorite varieties to bake with:

CORTLAND: creamy, sweet, tart

EMPIRE: crisp, creamy

GOLDEN DELICIOUS: soft-textured

GRANNY SMITH: hearty, crisp, tart

HONEYCRISP: crisp, juicy, mild sweet flavor

MACOUN: crisp, moist, sweet with a hint of berry

MUTSU: firm, crisp, juicy, slightly spicy

CRISPIN: firm, not overly sweet

Summer and Fall Crostatas

These seasonal free-form tarts are a perfect marriage of buttery crust, sweet honey, luscious fruit, and a hint of pepper. In the summer, use any stone fruit and berries; in the fall, try apples or pears with a bit of dried fruit plumped in madeira, sherry, or dry port. We're excited to report that you can use frozen organic peach slices for the summer filling and the result is still sublime. Don't defrost the slices, just toss them with sugar and flour while still frozen. Serve them with vanilla- and honey-flavored whipped cream or Pear Sorbet (page 328).

For the crust, in the bowl of a food processor fitted with a metal blade, combine the flours, sugar, and salt and pulse to combine. Add the butter or solid coconut oil and, with a spoon, coat each piece with the flour mixture. Pulse to create coarse meal, 15 to 20 times. Add the lemon juice and drizzle in 3 tablespoons water. Pulse until the dough comes together, 12 to 15 times. Do not overwork. Transfer this crumbly mixture onto a large piece of parchment paper and press the mixture into a ball with your hands. Knead in the remaining 1 tablespoon water, if necessary, to bring the dough together.

Preheat the oven to 400°F.

Shape the dough into a flat disk with your hands, place between 2 sheets of parchment, and roll to make a 14-inch circle. Transfer the dough, still on the bottom parchment, onto a baking sheet and chill.

If making the fall filling: In a small saucepan, warm the madeira over low heat. Transfer to a small bowl, add the dried cherries, and allow them to plump, about 15 minutes. Core and cut the pears into ¾-inch cubes, transfer to a medium bowl, and toss with the lemon juice. Add the flour and sugar to the pears and toss to combine.

If making the summer filling: Combine the fresh or frozen peaches with the flour and sugar.

For both fillings: Spread the honey on the crust 3 inches from the edge. Sprinkle the honey with the black pepper. Arrange the pears or peaches on the dough, covering the honey portion only. Drain the cherries and sprinkle all around the pears, or toss the blackberries about the peaches. With your hands, carefully fold the 3-inch border of dough over the fruit, overlapping it as necessary. (The dough needs to be cold when it goes into the oven, so work quickly, or re-chill before baking.)

Bake for 35 minutes, turning the sheet a few times. Reduce the temperature to 350°F and bake until the crust is golden and the fruit is fork-tender, 10 to 15 minutes more. Transfer the crostata to a rack. Allow it to cool for at least 20 minutes. Cut the crostata into quarters and each quarter into thirds and serve.

We often freeze fruit when it is in its peak season. Berries can be frozen in a single layer on a tray. Once frozen solid, transfer to any kind of container and return to the freezer. The same can be done to stone fruit that has been blanched, peeled, and sliced or halved.

Crust

3 tablespoons semolina flour

2¼ cups unbleached all-purpose flour

¼ cup sugar

1 teaspoon kosher salt

1 cup (2 sticks) chilled unsalted butter or solid coconut oil, cut into tablespoon-size pieces

1 tablespoon lemon juice

3 to 4 tablespoons ice water

Fall Filling

¼ cup madeira, sherry, or dry port

¼ cup dried cherries

3 pears, such as red, Bosc, or Anjou, or a combination

2 teaspoons lemon juice

2 teaspoons unbleached all-purpose flour

1 tablespoon sugar

Summer Filling

3 firm peaches (about 1¼ pounds), peeled, halved, pitted, and sliced ¼ inch thick; or 20 ounces frozen peach slices

2 teaspoons unbleached all-purpose flour

1 tablespoon sugar

½ pint blackberries

1 tablespoon honey

½ teaspoon freshly ground black pepper

Roasted Pears with Nutty Crumble Topping

This is an updated and more elegant version of a pear crumble. Roasted pears, which hold their shape beautifully, are topped with a nutty, crunchy mix that is somewhere between a yummy granola and a light crumb. Feel free to experiment with the ratio of seeds to nuts. The crumble works equally well with apples or peaches.

SERVES 8

Preheat the oven to 375°F; position a rack in the top third of the oven and another in the bottom third. Line a baking sheet with parchment paper.

Place the pears on the sheet, cut side up, and brush with the butter. Roast on the upper rack until the pears are soft and easily breakable with a dessert spoon, 30 to 45 minutes. Cool on the sheet.

Meanwhile, line another baking sheet with parchment paper. In a medium bowl, combine the pecans, almonds, pumpkin seeds, brown sugar, oats, olive oil, and salt and mix. Spread on the baking sheet. Bake on the lower rack, stirring occasionally, until the crumble is fragrant and golden, 12 to 15 minutes. Mix in the sesame seeds, if using, and cool.

In a small bowl, combine the mascarpone and honey. For a smoother, thinner consistency, add the milk, stirring it in 1 teaspoon at a time.

Divide the mascarpone among serving plates. Top with pear halves, sprinkle the pears and mascarpone with the crumble, and serve.

4 firm-ripe Bartlett pears, unpeeled, halved and cored

4 tablespoons (½ stick) unsalted butter, melted

½ cup pecan halves, roughly chopped

¼ cup raw almonds, roughly chopped

¼ cup pumpkin seeds

¼ cup packed dark brown sugar

¼ cup rolled oats

2 tablespoons light olive oil

¼ teaspoon kosher salt

2 tablespoons sesame seeds (optional)

1 cup mascarpone

4 teaspoons honey

2 teaspoons low-fat milk (optional)

Three Sorbets

Do you ever open your refrigerator only to be greeted by the sight of too much overripe fruit? Maybe you have a bunch of limes that are no longer green; excess grapefruits from that Florida gift box; pears that are beginning to bruise; or berries about to grow beards. If so, make sorbet! It is easier to prepare than ice cream and, obviously, dairy free. While best made using an ice cream maker, the following recipes can be easily prepared using old-fashioned ice-cube trays or ice pop molds.

You'll need to chill the sorbet mixture thoroughly in the refrigerator (1 to 2 hours, or overnight) before using the ice cream maker and then store the sorbet at least 1 hour in the freezer before serving.

Grapefruit Sorbet

MAKES ABOUT 1 QUART

1⅓ cups rosé wine or water
1 cup sugar
2½ cups freshly squeezed pink grapefruit juice
2 teaspoons grated lime zest

In a medium saucepan, combine the rosé and sugar. Simmer over medium-low heat, stirring frequently, until the sugar has dissolved, 3 to 4 minutes. Cool.

Stir in the grapefruit juice and lime zest. Chill the mixture thoroughly in the refrigerator.

Transfer the mixture to a chilled ice cream maker and process according to the manufacturer's directions. Transfer to a container and freeze again for at least 1 hour before serving.

Pear Sorbet

MAKES ABOUT 1 QUART

2½ pounds ripe pears
1 lemon, halved
1¼ cups water, plus more if needed
¾ cup sugar
1 tablespoon lemon juice

Peel, halve, and core the pears, reserving the peels and cores. As you work, rub the pear flesh with half the lemon to prevent browning. Transfer the pears to a large glass bowl.

In a medium saucepan, combine the peels, half of the cores, the water, and sugar. Simmer over low heat, dissolving the sugar to make a syrup, about 10 minutes. Strain the syrup through a mesh sieve into a medium bowl. (You should have about 1¼ cups syrup.)

Place the pears in the same saucepan, pour the syrup over them, and cover. Cook over medium-high heat until pears are tender when poked with a paring knife, 10 to 15 minutes. If the liquid begins to boil off, add up to ½ cup water.

Let the mixture cool and transfer to a blender. Add the lemon juice and purée until smooth. Chill the mixture thoroughly in the refrigerator.

Transfer the mixture to a chilled ice cream maker and process according to the manufacturer's directions. Transfer to a container and freeze again for at least 1 hour before serving.

Herbed Citrus Sorbet

MAKES ABOUT 1 QUART

1⅓ cups water

1 cup sugar

3 2-inch sprigs mint or tarragon, or 10 small basil leaves

2 teaspoons grated lime zest

1 tablespoon grated Meyer lemon zest or regular lemon zest

¾ cup orange juice

¾ cup lime juice

1 cup Meyer lemon juice, regular lemon juice, or blood orange juice

In a medium saucepan, combine the water and sugar. Simmer over medium-low heat, stirring frequently, until the sugar has dissolved, 3 to 4 minutes. Remove from heat, add the herbs, and allow the mixture to steep for at least 30 minutes.

Add the zests and juices and stir to combine. Chill the mixture thoroughly in the refrigerator. Remove the herbs.

Transfer the mixture to a chilled ice cream maker and process according to the manufacturer's directions. Transfer to a container and freeze again for at least 1 hour before serving.

VARIATION

Once you're an adept sorbet maker, you'll want to expand your repertoire. Here's a recipe for berry sorbet or ice pops: You'll need 4 cups of any berries (fresh or frozen), 1 cup water, ⅔ cup sugar, and 1 tablespoon lemon juice. Combine in a food processor or blender and purée. Pass through a sieve to remove seeds. Freeze, using pop molds if you like, or follow instructions to process with your ice cream maker.

Prosecco-Berry Gelée

A glass of fine prosecco is a lovely prelude to a summer meal. Transformed into a sophisticated gelée, it's a great ending, too. Orange-flower water, a flavoring extract, adds a delicate floral essence to the dish. It is available in the cocktail mixers or baking section of upscale supermarkets, liquor stores, and Middle Eastern markets. The gelée requires at least 3 hours to firm up, but it can be made up to 2 days ahead of time. Serve with Ultimate Sugar Cookies (page 309) or Two Great Dunking Cookies (page 315).

SERVES 8

7 cups mixed berries (2¼ pounds)
¾ cup sugar
1 tablespoon lemon juice
1½ cups prosecco or champagne (make cocktails with the rest!)
1 tablespoon unflavored powdered gelatin or agar-agar powder
½ teaspoon orange-flower water (optional)

Place the berries in an 8-cup oval or rectangular ceramic or glass dish. Sprinkle ¼ cup of the sugar and the lemon juice over the berries. Set aside for 20 minutes on the countertop, then toss gently and set aside.

Pour ½ cup of the prosecco into a small bowl. Sprinkle the gelatin over the prosecco and let stand until the gelatin has begun to break down, about 5 minutes.

In a small saucepan, combine the remaining prosecco with the remaining sugar and boil, stirring, until the sugar is dissolved, 3 to 4 minutes. Remove from the heat, stir in the gelatin mixture, and continue to stir until dissolved. If the gelatin has not dissolved completely, place the saucepan over medium heat and stir until it is completely dissolved. (Different gelling agents work slightly differently. Consult package directions.)

Add the orange-flower water, if using, and stir to combine. Pour over the berries and pop any bubbles that form on the surface by gently tapping the side of the dish with a rubber spatula.

Cover with taut plastic wrap so that the wrap doesn't touch the mixture. Chill until firm, about 3 hours. Spoon into individual glasses and serve.

Goat Milk and Yogurt Panna Cotta with Spiced Fig Compote

Once again, today's newest food trends harken back to our Old World forebearers. Goat products—milk, cheese, yogurt, and even meat—are found in specialty markets today. How far we've come from the time when the only reference to goat's milk we knew was in the Isaac Bashevis Singer folk story "Zlateh the Goat."

Panna cotta is a classic European eggless custard. It needs to chill for at least 3 hours before serving, but is even better if made 2 days ahead. It keeps for a week if refrigerated. Creamy and lightly tart, we've partnered the custard with a spiced fig compote to create a balanced flavor profile. An alternative way to dress up the panna cotta if you don't want to make the compote is to line the ramekins with a caramel sauce (see Caramel Sauce box, page 333). In the summer, we like to serve the panna cotta with a simple sauce of fresh blueberries simmered with a little bit of sugar for 15 minutes.

This is lovely with a crumbly cookie passed alongside. See our Cappuccino Thins (page 306) or Vanilla Crescents (page 311).

SERVES 12

Pour 1 cup of the milk in a medium saucepan, sprinkle with the gelatin, and allow the mixture to stand for 5 minutes.

In the meantime, in a medium bowl, whisk together the remaining ½ cup milk, yogurt, and heavy cream and whisk until smooth. Oil twelve 3½-inch ramekins or glass jars. (If using caramel, pour it into unoiled ramekins or jars to coat the bottoms.)

Gently heat the gelatin mixture over low heat, stirring until the gelatin completely dissolves, 3 to 4 minutes. Remove from the heat and stir in the honey and vanilla. Add this to the cold yogurt mixture. Whisk until fully combined.

Pour or ladle ½ cup of the mixture into each prepared ramekin. Place the ramekins on a tray and refrigerate, uncovered, until firm, about 1 hour. Once firm, cover and return to the refrigerator for 2 more hours.

Remove from the refrigerator 30 minutes before serving. Run a thin knife blade around the inside of each ramekin. Top with a small dessert plate, invert the ramekin and plate, and wait until the panna cotta drops onto the plate. If it doesn't release, dip the ramekin into warm water, being careful not to get the custard wet. Repeat with the remaining ramekins. Spoon the fig compote around the panna cotta and serve.

- 1½ cups goat milk or low-fat milk
- 2½ teaspoons powdered gelatin or agar-agar powder
- 2¼ cups Greek yogurt
- 1 cup heavy cream (or a combination of cream and additional milk)
- Grapeseed oil to coat the ramekins or jars
- ½ cup honey
- ½ teaspoon pure vanilla extract
- Spiced Fig Compote (recipe follows)

recipe continues

CARAMEL SAUCE

To make caramel for lining the ramekins, combine 1 cup sugar, 1 cup water, and a pinch of salt in a saucepan and bring to a boil over low heat, stirring to dissolve the sugar, 3 to 4 minutes. Stop stirring, increase the heat, and watch the mixture carefully. When the sugar syrup has turned medium amber or just a touch beyond, about 5 minutes, remove it from the heat and carefully pour a little bit in each unoiled ramekin, swirling to coat the bottoms with caramel, then set aside. It will harden as it sits. Proceed to fill the ramekins as the recipe directs.

Spiced Fig Compote

This is also delicious spooned over ice cream or served with our Pistachio Anise Biscotti (page 315) or Coconut Mandelbread (page 315).

In a medium saucepan, heat the water and sugar over medium heat until the sugar dissolves and the mixture boils, about 3 minutes. Add the port, lemon slices, cinnamon, star anise, peppercorns, and vanilla bean. Reduce the heat to low and simmer about 20 minutes to develop the flavors.

Add all the dried figs, cover, and simmer until the figs are soft enough to cut with the side of a spoon, 30 to 40 minutes. Reduce the heat to the lowest setting. If using fresh figs, add them now and simmer to soften and warm through, 3 to 5 minutes.

Allow to cool, then refrigerate until ready to use. Discard the lemon, cinnamon stick, star anise, peppercorns, and vanilla bean before serving.

SERVES 12

1¼	cups water
¾	cup sugar
2½	cups port
½	lemon, thinly sliced
1	(3-inch) piece cinnamon stick
1	star anise
5	black peppercorns
1	vanilla bean, split lengthwise
12	dried plump black Mission figs, halved, hard stems removed
12	fresh black figs or 12 additional dried plump black Mission figs, halved, hard stems removed

APPENDIX A: RECIPE CHART: DAIRY, MEAT, OR PAREVE

CHAPTER	DAIRY	MEAT	PAREVE
BREADS	Chocolate Crumb Babka Light and Easy Cornbread Swedish Cardamom Ring Lemon Scones Bubbe's Hungarian Sweet Cheese Hamantaschen		Weekly Challah Queen Esther's Crown Purim Bread Fig and Fennel Bread Grilled Rosemary Flatbread Rye Bread Morning Glory Muffins with Oat Flax Topping Homemade Pretzels
STARTERS	Buckwheat Buttermilk Blinis 21st Century Whitefish Salad Summer and Winter Vegetable Tarts Yogurt Sauce Two Ways Homemade Ricotta Potato and Zucchini Egg Tart (Feinkochen)		Truffle Popcorn Roasted Delicata Squash Rings Crostini with Three Toppings Pickled String Beans and Baby Carrots Pickled Grapes with Rosemary Savory Plum-Tomato Jam Latkes Four Ways Black Bean Cakes with Tomato Salsa Salmon-Halibut Gefilte Fish with Apple Beet Horseradish Relish
SOUPS	Stracciatella Vegetarian Russian Borscht Tomato Soup with Gougères	Vietnamese Rice-Noodle Soup with Beef Chicken Soup with Cilantro Matzah Balls	Yellow Cauliflower Soup with Parsley Oil Kasha and Mushroom Kreplach with Vegetable Consommé Red Lentil Soup with Lime Fish Soup with Fennel and Saffron Wild Mushroom Barley Soup
SALADS	Fennel, Green Apple, and Pecorino Salad Kale, Farro, and Carrot Salad Cold Minted Pea Salad	Tahini-Dressed Chicken Salad with Arugula	Orange, Frisée, and Radish Salad Roasted Red Pepper, Tomato, and Parsley Salad Plum and Spinach Salad Summer Corn, Cucumber, and Tomato Salad Karpas Salad Syrian Potato Salad (Salata Batata) Moroccan Carrot Slaw

CHAPTER	DAIRY	MEAT	PAREVE
PASTA, POLENTA & RISOTTO	Whole-Wheat Pasta with Caramelized Red Peppers Summer Pappardelle with Corn and Tomatoes Risotto with Salmon, Leeks, and Peas Barley Risotto with Zucchini Israeli Couscous Risotto Polenta with Winter Greens	Papardelle with Lamb Ragù Egg Noodles with Savoy Cabbage and Sausage	Gemelli with Mushroom Bolognese Spaghettini with Garlic and Oil Nokedli (Hungarian Spaetzle) Two-Grain Saffron Couscous Buckwheat Noodles with Grilled Hen-of-the-Woods Mushrooms
FISH	Turkish Roasted Whole Fish Simple Sole with Tartar Sauce		Fish Tacos with Orange Chipotle Sauce and Jicama-Grapefruit Slaw Grilled Halibut Kebabs with Marcona Almond Sauce Steamed Salmon on Chard Leaves Pan-Seared Branzini Simple Sole with Roasted Red Pepper Sauce Simple Sole with Yuzu Sauce Lemon Cardamom Halibut Red Snapper Layered with Tomatoes and Pickled Jalapeños
POULTRY		Farmhouse Chicken Grilled Chicken Paillards for Four Seasons Roasted Chicken Paprikash Green Masala Chicken Chicken and Apple Round "Sausages" Spicy Chicken Stir-Fry with Greens and Cashews Lemony Cornish Hens Chicken Bouillabaisse Great Roast Chicken Citrus and Balsamic–Glazed Turkey Breast Duck Breasts with Apples and Maple Cider Sauce Braised Duck Legs	

CHAPTER	DAIRY	MEAT	PAREVE
MEAT		Prime Rib Bones with Roasted Potatoes Summer Grilled Rib Eye Steaks with Chimichurri Thai Grilled Beef Salad Cajun Barbecue Brisket Meatballs Pot-au-Feu Braised Veal Stew with Butternut Squash Pan Roasted Veal with Sage Iraqi Lamb Burgers with Mint Pesto Rack of Lamb Moroccan Lamb Tagine	
GRAINS & LEGUMES	Wheat Berry and Grape Salad Fava Beans with String Beans and Hazelnuts	White Bean and Turkey Chili	Red Quinoa and Black Rice Pilaf Farro with Grilled Onions and Roasted Tomatoes Bulgur Salad with Pomegranates and Pine Nuts Orange-Scented Black Beans with Crispy Onions Flageolet Beans with Herbs and Tomato Moroccan Mezze (Moroccan Chickpeas, Caramelized Saffron Onions, and Date Relish) Spicy Lentil Dal
VEGETABLES	Lemon-Thyme Zucchini "Spaghettini" Braised Roasted Fennel Warm Mushroom Sauté Celery Root and Potato Purée Savory Butternut Squash Crumble Shredded Beets with Yogurt	Garlic Mashed Potatoes	Roasted Brussels Sprouts with Pomegranate-Citrus Glaze Grilled Cauliflower Steaks Roasted Tzimmes Braised Red Cabbage with Caraway Seeds Smashed Peas with Fresh Mint Zucchini Eggplant Mina (Savory Layered Pie) Roasted Sweet Potatoes with Lime and Cilantro Spring Succotash Matzah Brei Sri-Lankan Style Sautéed Greens with Shallots

CHAPTER	DAIRY	MEAT	PAREVE
DESSERTS	Lemon Layer Cake Light and Creamy Cheesecake with Nut Brittle and Blueberries Chocolate Sour Cream Cake Chocolate Brownie Cookies with Sea Salt Oatmeal–Chocolate Chip Cookies Cappuccino Thins Ultimate Sugar Cookies Vanilla Crescents with Citrus and Verbena Salad Pumpkin Rugelach Sour Cherry Pie Rustic Apple-Cranberry Pie Our Pie Crust Summer and Fall Crostatas Roasted Pears with Nutty Crumble Topping Goat Milk and Yogurt Panna Cotta with Spiced Fig Compote		Honey Cake with Grilled Peaches Lime–Olive Oil Cake with Rhubarb Compote Intensely Chocolate Cupcakes with Chocolate Frosting Chocolate Chip–Hazelnut Meringues Citrus and Verbena Salad Pistachio Anise Biscotti Coconut Mandlebread Mango and Pineapple Fruit Salad Three Sorbets Prosecco-Berry Gelée

Shabbat

MEAT DINNER

Weekly Challah

Red Lentil Soup with Lime

Rack of Lamb

Farro with Grilled Onions and
Roasted Tomatoes

Fava Beans with String Beans and
Hazelnuts (use olive oil instead
of butter)

Herbed Citrus Sorbet

Pistachio Anise Biscotti or
Coconut Mandelbread

Berries

MEAT DINNER

Weekly Challah

Simple green salad with herbs
and dressing from Plum and
Spinach Salad (page 119)

Lemony Cornish Hens

Braised Veal Stew with Butternut
Squash

Grilled zucchini

Flageolet Beans with Herbs and
Tomato

Chocolate Chip–Hazelnut
Meringues

Mango and Pineapple Fruit Salad

DAIRY DINNER

Weekly Challah

Kasha and Mushroom Kreplach
with Vegetable Consommé or
Vegetarian Russian Borscht

Simple Sole with Tartar Sauce

Summer or Winter Vegetable Tart

Roasted Tzimmes

Sautéed broccoli with garlic and
olive oil

Sour Cherry or Blueberry Pie

DAIRY DINNER

Weekly Challah

Gemelli with Mushroom
Bolognese

Pan-Seared Branzini

Braised Roasted Fennel

Sautéed Greens with Shallots

Chocolate Sour Cream Cake with
berries

Rosh Hashanah

Weekly Challah: Round Challah
with Honey Bowl

Orange, Frisée, and Radish Salad

Salmon-Halibut Gefilte Fish or
Fish Soup with Fennel and
Saffron

Duck Breasts with Apples and
Maple Cider Sauce

Bulgur Salad with Pomegranates
and Pine Nuts

Honey Cake with Grilled Peaches

Sukkot

MEAT DINNER

Crostini with Three Toppings:
Caponata, Mushroom
Chopped "Liver," White Bean
Purée

Pickled String Beans and Baby
Carrots

Cajun Barbecue Brisket

Roasted Delicata Squash Rings

Roasted Red Pepper, Tomato, and
Parsley Salad

Chocolate Brownie Cookies with
Sea Salt

DAIRY DINNER

Plum and Spinach Salad

Savory Butternut Squash Crumble

Grilled Halibut Kebabs with
Marcona Almond Sauce

Moroccan Carrot Slaw

Two Great Dunking Cookies

LUNCH

Yellow Cauliflower Soup with
Parsley Oil

Tahini-Dressed Chicken Salad
with Arugula

Fall Crostata or Three Sorbets

Thanksgiving

TRADITIONAL DINNER

Rye Bread

Karpas Salad

Citrus and Balsamic–Glazed
Turkey Breast

Farro with Grilled Onions and
Roasted Tomatoes

Roasted Sweet Potatoes with Lime
and Cilantro

Celery Root and Potato Purée

Rustic Apple-Cranberry Pie

Chocolate Chip–Hazelnut
Meringues

Spiced Fig Compote

Pear Sorbet

Citrus and Verbena Salad

VEGETARIAN DINNER

Fig and Fennel Bread

Savory Plum-Tomato Jam

Yellow Cauliflower Soup with
Parsley Oil or Wild Mushroom
Barley Soup

Fennel, Green Apple, and
　　Pecorino Salad or Kale, Farro,
　　and Carrot Salad

Savory Butternut Squash Crumble

Roasted Brussels Sprouts with
　　Pomegranate-Citrus Glaze

Grilled Cauliflower Steaks

Ultimate Sugar Cookies

Rustic Apple-Cranberry Pie

Pumpkin Rugelach

Chanukah

DAIRY DINNER

Latkes Four Ways

Crostini with White Bean Purée

21st-Century Whitefish Salad

Simple Sole with Three Sauces

Braised Roasted Fennel

Ultimate Sugar Cookies

Lemon Layer Cake

MEAT DINNER

Pickled Grapes with Rosemary

Latkes Four Ways

Crostini with Caponata

Prime Rib Bones with Roasted
　　Potatoes

Sautéed Greens with Shallots

Warm Mushroom Sauté (use olive
　　oil instead of butter)

Lime–Olive Oil Cake with
　　Rhubarb Compote

Tu B'Shevat Seder

DAIRY DINNER

Wild Mushroom Barley Soup or
　　Red Lentil Soup with Lime

Wheat Berry and Grape Salad

Israeli Couscous Risotto

Goat Milk and Yogurt Panna
　　Cotta with Spiced Fig
　　Compote

Vanilla Crescents with Citrus and
　　Verbena Salad

Passover

With eight days of special holiday
cooking to do, there are a number
of menus you could create. See
Appendix C for a complete list of
Passover-friendly recipes in this
book.

Shavuot

DAIRY DINNER

Homemade Ricotta

Tomato Soup with Gougères

Pan-Seared Branzini

Barley Risotto with Zucchini

Light and Creamy Cheesecake
　　with Nut Brittle and
　　Blueberries

Pumpkin Rugelach

APPENDIX C: RECIPES THAT ARE KOSHER FOR PASSOVER

These recipes are all appropriate for Passover according to our tradition—Ashkenazi.
Feel free to make other recipes from our book, according to your traditions.

Starters

21st-Century Whitefish Salad

Roasted Delicata Squash Rings

Yogurt Sauce Two Ways

Homemade Ricotta

Savory Plum-Tomato Jam

Latkes Four Ways

Potato and Zucchini Egg Tart
(Feinkochen)

Salmon-Halibut Gefilte Fish with
Apple Beet Horseradish Relish

Soups

Yellow Cauliflower Soup with
Parsley Oil

Stracciatella

Vegetarian Russian Borscht

Cilantro Matzah Balls with
Vegetable Consommé or
Chicken Soup

Tomato Soup (*skip the gougères!*)

Chicken Soup

Fish Soup with Fennel and Saffron

Salads

Orange, Frisée, and Radish Salad

Roasted Red Pepper, Tomato, and
Parsley Salad

Fennel, Green Apple, and
Pecorino Salad

Karpas Salad

Syrian Potato Salad (Salata
Batata)

Fish

Grilled Halibut Kebabs with
Marcona Almond Sauce

Turkish Roasted Whole Fish

Pan-Seared Branzini

Lemon Cardamom Halibut

Red Snapper Layered with
Tomatoes and Pickled
Jalapeños

Simple Sole with Roasted Red
Pepper Sauce

Poultry

Roasted Chicken Paprikash

Green Masala Chicken

Chicken and Apple Round
"Sausages"

Lemony Cornish Hens

Chicken Bouillabaisse

Great Roast Chicken

Citrus and Balsamic–Glazed
Turkey Breast

Duck Breasts with Apples and
Maple Cider Sauce

Meat

Summer Grilled Rib Eye Steaks
with Chimichurri

Pot-au-Feu

Braised Veal Stew with Butternut
Squash

Pan Roasted Veal with Sage

Rack of Lamb

Moroccan Lamb Tagine

Iraqi Lamb Burgers with Mint
Pesto

Vegetables

Lemon-Thyme Zucchini
"Spaghettini"

Roasted Tzimmes

Roasted Brussels Sprouts with
Pomegranate-Citrus Glaze

Braised Roasted Fennel

Warm Mushroom Sauté

Celery Root and Potato Purée

Braised Red Cabbage with
Caraway Seeds

Zucchini Eggplant Mina (Savory
Layered Pie)

Roasted Sweet Potatoes with Lime
and Cilantro

Shredded Beets with Yogurt

Matzah Brei Sri-Lankan Style

Garlic Mashed Potatoes

Desserts

Light and Creamy Cheesecake
with Nut Brittle and
Blueberries

Chocolate Chip–Hazelnut
Meringues

Three Sorbets

Prosecco-Berry Gelée

Goat Milk and Yogurt Panna
Cotta with Spiced Fig
Compote

METRIC CONVERSION CHART

Use these charts as a guideline. In the U.S., recipe ingredient lists are usually based on volume, rather than weight. Baking recipes (breads, muffins, cakes) do require precision, so exact conversions are necessary.

U.S. TO METRIC CONVERSION, VOLUME (LIQUID)	
U.S.	METRIC
¼ teaspoon	1 milliliter
½ teaspoon	2 milliliters
1 teaspoon	5 milliliters
1 fluid ounce (2 tablespoons)	30 milliliters
2 fluid ounces (¼ cup)	60 milliliters
8 fluid ounces (1 cup)	240 milliliters
16 fluid ounces (1 pint)	480 milliliters
32 fluid ounces (1 quart)	950 milliliters (0.95 liter)
128 fluid ounces (1 gallon)	3.75 liters

U.S. TO METRIC CONVERSION, FLOUR	
U.S.	METRIC
¼ cup	30 grams
½ cup	60 grams
¾ cup	90 grams
1 cup	120 grams

U.S. TO METRIC CONVERSION, TEMPERATURE	
DEGREES FAHRENHEIT	DEGREES CELSIUS
325	163
350	177
375	191
400	204
425	218
450	232
475	246

ACKNOWLEDGMENTS

When three authors pen a cookbook, the acknowledgments could go on forever. In no special order we extend our deepest thanks to the community that was created around this book:

Sara Weiss, our editor, who brought fresh eyes to this project at a much-needed time.

Gail Solomon, our creative director, who translated our concept for this book into a visual symphony. Her never-ending creativity, design talent, sense of style, and unflagging spirit made this book as beautiful as it is.

John Tavares, our gifted photographer, who had the intuitive eye that captured the natural beauty of our ingredients, techniques, and finished dishes.

Andrew Jarvis, our early and consistent publishing consultant, whose wisdom guided us through a few tough patches.

Friends and family: Marti Meyerson, Rachel Ringler, Ulrika Citron, Barbara Applbaum, Linda Sterling, Dorian Goldman, Nick Bunzl, Lydia Schmelzer, Forest Sonnenfeldt, Alexandra Bunzl, Isaac Sonnenfeldt, Natasha Bunzl, Joya Sonnenfeldt, and Alan Divack, all of whom contributed recipes, tested recipes, and consumed a few extra calories together with us.

Our indispensable helping hands: Maria Gjela, Barbara Debique, Alicia Echeverria, Anna Walkiewicz, and Ella Jankowska many thanks for the hours of kitchen prep, testing, and tasting.

Untold amounts of thanks are due to the staff of JCC Manhattan who guided us through the publishing process, particularly thanks to Elana Parker. We would also like to thank Joan Linder and Erica Werber. But it was the JCC's executive director, Rabbi Joy Levitt, who against all odds supported our voices and vision for this book.

Thanks to Jennifer Goren and the chefs and culinary instructors from the Patti Gelman Culinary Arts Center of JCC Manhattan: Kim Pistone, Adeena Sussman, John Scoff, Jennifer Abadi, Lauren Costello, Sherri Maxman.

We want to acknowledge the work being done in the Marti Ann Meyerson Center for Health and Wellness and the Michelle C. Feig Nutrition Program, both of which embody JCC Manhattan's commitment to healthy living.

We also want to thank the many people who have been incredible resources to us: Menachem Schmelzer, Debbie Haramati, Adam Kaye, Marisol Marquez, Chris Peña, Andrea Pitchford, Paul Whitman, Steve Niederman, Israel Brown, Dorian Mecir, Teresa Lundahl, Andre Blais, Paul Warner, Glenn Turner, Sherrie Nickol, and Arthur Boehm.

Finally, in loving admiration for the women who bequeathed their love of cooking and their recipes to us: Frieda Rotmil, Pauline Rotmil, Ruth Schmelzer, Regina Fisher, Joyce Goldman, Else Bunzl, and Mona Bernstein.

Recipe for a Community Center

INGREDIENTS

VISION	as much as you can get
FUNDS	as my grandmother would say, as much as you need
COMMUNITY PARTNERS	large pluralistic selection
PERSISTENCE	tons
PASSION	never too much
ENERGY	add at the right time
FORTITUDE	lots
HUMOR	wherever you can find
PATIENCE	unending amounts
JEWISH VALUES	to drizzle amply throughout

DIRECTIONS

Measure who is hungry in the community for a new kind of Jewish Community Center. Gather visionary people willing to work. Schedule many meetings, probably at inconvenient times. Add to mix as many friends and connections as will fit around table—use larger space as necessary. Knead ingredients into a strong rising idea. Hire fantastic executive director with boundless energy. Proof concept by sprinkling with new ideas, a little honey, and a lot of luck. Wait for bubbles, confirming it's alive. Meanwhile, as idea rises, in separate bowl, combine: energetic staff, exciting programming, committed, generous board members, and set aside. Work in additional ingredients: brilliant architect, construction crew, patient neighborhood. Watch carefully. Glaze with inspiration, innovation, values, and culture that span the generations. Share immediately.

— Excerpt from Katja Goldman's speech given at JCC Manhattan's annual benefit, May 2012